THE
UNWRITTEN
DIARY
OF ISRAEL
UNGER

To ~~Walter Dee~~ 25/09/2017

With respect

Best wishes

[signature]

LIFE WRITING SERIES

In the **Life Writing Series**, Wilfrid Laurier University Press publishes life writing and new life-writing criticism and theory in order to promote autobiographical accounts, diaries, letters, and testimonials written and/or told by women and men whose political, literary, or philosophical purposes are central to their lives. The Series features accounts written in English, or translated into English from French or the languages of the First Nations, or any of the languages of immigration to Canada.

From its inception, **Life Writing** has aimed to foreground the stories of those who may never have imagined themselves as writers or as people with lives worthy of being (re)told. Its readership has expanded to include scholars, youth, and avid general readers both in Canada and abroad. The Series hopes to continue its work as a leading publisher of life writing of all kinds, as an imprint that aims for both broad representation and scholarly excellence, and as a tool for both historical and autobiographical research.

As its mandate stipulates, the Series privileges those individuals and communities whose stories may not, under normal circumstances, find a welcoming home with a publisher. **Life Writing** also publishes original theoretical investigations about life writing, as long as they are not limited to one author or text.

Series Editor
Marlene Kadar
Humanities Division, York University

Manuscripts to be sent to
Lisa Quinn, Acquisitions Editor
Wilfrid Laurier University Press
75 University Avenue West
Waterloo, Ontario N2L 3C5, Canada

THE UNWRITTEN DIARY OF ISRAEL UNGER

REVISED EDITION

Carolyn Gammon and Israel Unger

WILFRID LAURIER UNIVERSITY PRESS

Wilfrid Laurier University Press acknowledges the support of the Canada Council for the Arts for our publishing program. We acknowledge the financial support of the Government of Canada through the Canada Book Fund for our publishing activities.

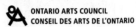

Library and Archives Canada Cataloguing in Publication

Gammon, Carolyn, 1959–, author
    The unwritten diary of Israel Unger / Carolyn Gammon and Israel Unger.—Revised edition.

(Life writing series)
Includes bibliographical references.
Issued in print and electronic formats.
ISBN 978-1-77112-011-1 (pbk.).—ISBN 978-1-77112-013-5 (epub).—
ISBN 978-1-77112-012-8 (pdf)

    1. Unger, Israel, 1938–. 2. Unger, Israel, 1938– —Family. 3. Holocaust, Jewish (1939–1945)—Poland—Tarnów (Województwo Małopolskie)—Personal narratives. 4. Jewish children in the Holocaust—Poland—Tarnów (Województwo Małopolskie)—Biography. 5. Holocaust survivors—Canada—Biography. 6. Deans (Education)—New Brunswick—Saint John—Biography. 7. Tarnów (Województwo Małopolskie, Poland)—Biography. I. Unger, Isaac, 1928–, author II. Title. III. Series: Life writing series

DS134.72.U65A3 2013b   940.5′18092   C2013-905657-2   C2013-905658-0

Cover design by Daiva Villa, Chris Rowat Design. Front-cover photo: Israel Unger (far right) with other Jewish child survivors of the Holocaust at the Holocaust memorial in Tarnow, Poland, 1946. (Photographer unknown. Israel Unger collection.) Text design by Angela Booth Malleau.

This book is printed on FSC recycled paper and is certified Ecologo. It is made from 100% post-consumer fibre, processed chlorine free, and manufactured using biogas energy.

Printed in Canada

Every reasonable effort has been made to acquire permission for copyright material used in this text, and to acknowledge all such indebtedness accurately. Any errors and omissions called to the publisher's attention will be corrected in future printings.

Israel Unger

To David and Hinda Unger
My parents
They did give me life twice

Carolyn Gammon

To my dear friends and mentors
Israel and Marlene Unger

Contents

Foreword

$\mathcal{W}$ *hen* I was in my early teenage years I read Anne Frank's diary. I recall that I was struck by the similarities between Anne's experience and ours. At the time I thought that in comparison to our hiding place and living conditions, Anne's were palatial. I was equally struck by the fact that all nine people in our group survived while in Anne's story only her father, Otto, survived. Shortly after Carolyn and I embarked on our project of writing this book, Carolyn asked what would a good title for the book be? She answered her own question with, "How about The Unwritten Diary?" That instantly seemed to me the most appropriate title.

Within the book we have acknowledged many people who supported and helped us to put together this work. It is a pleasure to acknowledge my co-author's special contributions. Carolyn suggested that we write my story; she was a catalyst and a spark plug. Carolyn was indefatigable and never let anything discourage her or me. Carolyn did most of the research and prodded me with questions and suggestions. I have derived many benefits from this work not the least of which was meeting and making a lifelong friend, Carolyn Gammon.

Israel Unger

Part One

The Only Jews in Poland

Srulik Is Born in Tarnow

My father, Mordechai David Unger, came from a small village near Tarnow, Poland, called Ryglice in what was known as Galicia—a region that encompassed southeastern Poland and western Ukraine. He was born in 1902. He had eight brothers and sisters, but I do not know their names and we do not know exactly what happened to them other than that they were murdered by the Nazis. Unfortunately I did not ask my father about this when he was still alive. I am still trying to find out their names after all these years.

My mother was Hinda Fisch. She was born in 1904 in Bobrowniki Wielkie, a village near Tarnow. Her family was from Dąbrowa Tarnowska, also near Tarnow. Her father was Chaim Fisch and he was apparently a wood merchant. He worked for a nobleman—a *Graf* or Earl. According to my wife, Marlene, who got this from my mother, there were logging drives down a river and the family was involved in this business. His wife was Raizel, my maternal grandmother. She was born Raizel Grossbart—I have that information from my parents' wedding certificate.

My paternal grandfather was Josef Pinkus Unger and my paternal grandmother was Hana Leia Lesser before she became an Unger. My parents totally lost contact with them once the Germans occupied Poland because all communication and movement between Jewish communities was forbidden. They were murdered in the Holocaust.

Unger was a fairly common Jewish name in Poland. There were quite a few Ungers in Ryglice. My father decided to go to Tarnow, about twenty kilometres to the north. As a young man he somehow started a business and became the sole owner of a bakery. He was an up-and-coming businessman and he wanted to get married, so he went to a *schadkhin*, a matchmaker, and the *schadkhin* found him my mother. My father came from a poor family

1

that was rabbinical. My mother was from a family of means and she was well educated for the time. One of the things that she learned was German; her sister learned accounting. It was seen as a good match for both of them. There were some people who didn't want him to marry my mother and they told my father that my mother was a sickly woman and he shouldn't marry her. "That's the woman I am going to marry!" my father said. And he did. They went for a walk a couple of times. I guess my mother thought this was the way it should be done. She was going to marry this man who the *schadkhin* had found and that was fine. It pleases me to note that I never met a couple more loyal and devoted to one another.

One of the first things that my mother did after she was engaged was to begin working on her trousseau. She made a matzo bag so they would have it for the first Passover of their married life. She embroidered the matzo bag and put a little lace frill around it. My mother had been taught like young ladies were taught then, how to do fancy work. That matzo bag was one of my parents' only possessions that survived the war. When we were forced out of our house, whoever got our house packed a few of our belongings in a box. My mother found it after we came out of hiding. My parents were married in Tarnow—in which synagogue I don't know, but definitely orthodox. There were many synagogues in Tarnow at the time and *stiebels* too— little prayer houses. Before the temple in Jerusalem was destroyed there was Temple Judaism. When people came to the Temple there were priests and sacrifices were made. When the Temple was destroyed in the year 70, what were you going to do with Judaism? It then became Rabbinic Judaism, which is what we have today. In eastern Europe at the time, rabbis were not what they are in North America today. The rabbis would basically *paskin shayles*, that is, answer questions about *kashrut*—the dietary laws or minor disputes and so on. The rabbi did not lead the prayer services. Any ten male adults constituted a quorum and could pray. Any one of them could lead the service. You didn't necessarily need a synagogue—a *stiebel* would do. Rabbis did not teach kids; rather there was a *melamed* or teacher. So the rabbi having the role of being head of the

Tarnow Jubilee Synagogue, pre-war. (Tarnow Regional Museum)

synagogue, leading services and teaching kids was something that developed later.

One story my mother told more than once goes like this. Father owned a bakery. He also made wine, but at that time either he did not have a licence or Jews were not allowed to make wine in Poland. He was making wine

Tarnow marketplace pre-war. (Tarnow Regional Museum)

illegally. One day he had a batch of mead on in the back of the bakery. Mead is a wine made from honey and you have to cook it. An inspector came and you could smell the honey all over the place. My mother realized that there could be some serious problems, so she grabbed the laundry and tossed it into the vat of mead. She pretended that they were doing their laundry. It worked!

I was born 30 March 1938. I had a brother Kalman who was four years older. My parents called me Israel but they would have pronounced it Yisruel. As a child they called me Srulik or Sruel—a diminutive of Israel like Willy

Israel and Kalman in Tarnow, circa 1940. (Israel Unger collection)

instead of William. In accordance with Jewish tradition, I was circumcised when I was eight days old. This is recorded on my birth certificate.

On 1 September 1939 the German war machine smashed into Poland. On 8 September 1939, the bombs hit Tarnow and the Nazis marched into the city. On November 9 they destroyed the synagogues. I was a year and a half old.

Wysiedlenia

So what do I remember? Above all, I remember fear. A constant all-pervading fear, for the first years of my life. We knew that the Nazis wanted to murder us. We just wondered when it was going to happen.

Tarnow was a city of about fifty thousand people, half of whom were Jewish and many of whom lived in a part of town called Grabowka. The Jewish community dated back to the 15th century and it was one of the largest in Galicia. There were Jewish doctors and lawyers, musicians, teachers, industrialists, butchers, grocers, peddlers, tailors, shoemakers, jewellers, scribes, bakers, and nurses—all the professions required for the functioning of a community. Some of the city councillors were Jewish and at one time there was a vice-mayor Goldhammer who was Jewish. There were six large synagogues and a few small ones, Jewish schools, and cultural centres.

This means that during the Holocaust, half the city's inhabitants were murdered.

In October 1939, Jews in Tarnow were forced to wear a Star of David armband. Tarnow was the first city in Poland where the Nazis imposed this marking of Jews.

On 9 November 1939, a year after the infamous *Kristallnacht* in Germany, a similar "Crystal Night" happened in Tarnow where most of the synagogues were destroyed in one night. Tarnow was also the city where the very first prisoners to Auschwitz were deported. They were mostly political prisoners—not necessarily Jewish. That was June 1940. In 1941, the German authorities ordered Jews in Tarnow to hand in all their valuables. Thousands of Jews from the surrounding towns and villages were forced into Tarnow. All Jews were forced to live in a certain area of the city.

Jews were rounded up in what the Germans called *Aktions*, but I remember them by the Polish words *wysiedlenie*—a word that technically means "resettling" or "displacing" a population. That was euphemistic because really it meant rounding up Jews and either murdering them on the spot or taking them to the train station for transport to the death camps. In June of 1942 the first *wysiedlenie* took place in Tarnow, during which half of the Jewish

Above: Tarnow town square, 2009. This current photo clearly proves that the historic photo was taken in the Tarnow city square. (Carolyn Gammon photo)

Left: Jews in the city square—the *rynek*—of Tarnow during a *wysiedlenie*, July 1942. (Tarnow Regional Museum)

inhabitants were murdered. Either they were transported to the extermination camp Belzec or shot in the nearby Buczyna forest by Zbylitowska Góra. Many were shot in the streets or in the Jewish cemetery. The massacre lasted for about a week. Survivors and Polish eyewitnesses say the street running down from the main town square was a river of blood.

After the first massacre, the Nazis sealed off the district where Jews had been forced to live making the Tarnow ghetto. Non-Jewish Poles living in that area had to leave. Lwowska Street became the southern border of the ghetto, which was surrounded by a high wooden fence. If you left the ghetto without a permit you were killed. There were not many toilets and there was not much food. My father had to do forced labour in a factory outside the ghetto walls, but at least this meant he could leave the ghetto. In September 1942 several thousand Jews living in the ghetto had to gather in the town square. Those who were considered not "essential" to the Nazi slave labour system were rounded up, "selected," and sent to Belzec extermination camp. More *wysiedlenia* took place throughout the years 1942 and 1943. It was now clear what the Nazis intended for the Jews. It was only a question of when and how.

It is during these *wysiedlenia* that my first childhood memories begin. I was about four years old. I looked out between the shutters of our room. We were in a building, a single room with steel shutters. The building was like a quadrangle and a courtyard was in the centre. We were on the ground floor. I was able to look out through the shutters and see the street. I could see Jews being herded down the street. They were being whipped.

5

There was a little girl whom I played with in the courtyard of our house. I had a very nice coat with a fur collar and I used to show off my coat to that little girl. She disappeared in one of the *wysiedlenie*. It's hazy in my mind whether I actually saw her being taken away or not—sometimes I think I did but I can't really be very definite on that. She lived somewhere in the building that had the courtyard where we played. She would have been the only friend I had at that time.

During another *wysiedlenie* I was being held in my father's arms. I was very afraid. I was asking him to say the *Shema* so that we would go to heaven. That is the

Israel and little girl he played with in the Tarnow ghetto, circa 1942. (Israel Unger collection)

prayer Jews say when they consider that death is imminent. Apparently I expected to die that day. I kept asking my father to say the prayer over and over. The last prayer is *Shema Yisrael*, which is interesting because it is really the most basic and condensed version of the statement of monotheism. The words are *Shema Yisrael Adonai eloheinu Adonai echad*. It basically says, "Hear O Israel The Lord is our God The Lord is One." It continues on from there. It is not saying: Dear Lord save my life. It is talking about the unity of God. I really have no idea as to what my conception of heaven may or may not have been at that time. I think I was asking my father to recite the *Shema Yisrael* simply because I expected to die and somehow heaven was in my mind as a nice place. I wanted to go there rather than some other place. After the war my father told me that on that day he recited that prayer thirty-six times.

Prior to another *wysiedlenie*, the Nazis distributed red cards to some people and black cards to others. They were going to take Jews and deport them depending which colour card they had—*Kennkarte* in German. As a child I remember how important these cards were, whether you had the right or wrong one. I believe the red ones were the vital ones to have. My parents must not have had the red cards for all of us because they decided to hide. They knew that the *Aktion* was likely of limited duration. They decided to split us up so as to increase the chances of at least two of the family surviving. I was with my mother. My father and brother were together elsewhere. My mother and I were in a cellar. I was sort of crouched up against her. There were other Jews there—I think quite a few. I was cautioned not to make any noise, because if we were found we would be murdered. There was water on the walls and ceiling. The ceiling of the cellar was convex, made of brick. I amused myself by imagining faces in the ceiling—I imagined the cracks in the plaster to be all sorts of people or animals. We were in there maybe two or three days.

We had other relatives in the ghetto. My mother had an aunt, *Mume* Zlata; *Mume* is Yiddish for aunt. I remember she was very ill and I was at her bedside and Zlata told someone to get candy for me. My father's parents were not with us in the ghetto. They were in Ryglice and there was no communication with them. There must have been some illegal communication, because news reached Jews in Tarnow that they were sending Jews to Treblinka and killing them there.

My maternal grandfather, Chaim Fisch, was a very orthodox, pious Jew. I was in his upstairs apartment in the ghetto the day the Nazis came to get him. Two Nazis came in and ordered him to go with them. Instead of instantly going with them when commanded, he went and got his prayer bag because it was important to him that he should be able to practise his faith wherever he went. At the head of the stairs one of them pushed or kicked my grandfather and as he was falling, they shot him. Although my family did not speak about the Holocaust later, this was one memory I verified with my mother. She told me that I remembered it correctly. It's a mystery to me why the Nazis let me stay, why they left after they shot my grandfather.

I think that what happened was he was slated to be taken to Belzec or Treblinka or Auschwitz. Auschwitz and Belzec were the two places where the majority of Tarnow Jews were murdered, quite simply because these camps were the closest. I imagine that at some point the Gestapo in Tarnow would have been notified that there was going to be a train on such-and-such a day. There would be twelve cattle cars that could take say three thousand people. The local Gestapo would collect the Jews and assemble them. So my grandfather was one of those who was to go. My conjecture is that he was shot right on the spot because he annoyed the Nazi who came to get him. He was too slow in following their orders. Had he reacted faster, they would have taken him to the assembly point. In my mind's eye I can see him tucking that prayer bag under his left arm. His *tefillin*, his *tallit*, and a *siddur* would have been in there.

My Father's Courage

Once a Nazi was going to shoot my father. It was during one of the *Aktions*. We were in a room and the fellow suddenly came in and straight away pointed his rifle at my father. Kalman ran up and grabbed the rifle and tried to pull it away. The Nazi pulled it back. As that was going on, a person who must have been an officer came in and shouted, "Halt! The *Aktion* is over." They left. When you think of it … one moment it is killing time, the next moment the time for killing is over. My father's life was saved by the few seconds that my brother struggled with that Nazi.

From my earliest memories, my father was missing the index finger on his left hand. He was taken to the Gestapo headquarters and they wanted him to become a *Judenpolizei*. The Germans made the Jewish communities in the ghettos form a type of police force or "Jewish Police." My father refused to join. He was tortured but he still refused. They stuck his finger in the door jamb and slammed the door shut, snapping off his finger. He still refused to join so they kicked him in his side and he fell flat to the ground. Still he refused. Eventually they let him go. The Gestapo headquarters was a long way from the ghetto and he had to make his way back to the ghetto in great pain. Decades later when we were in Montreal he had kidney problems. It turned out he had a shrivelled kidney right at the spot where he had been kicked. He had to have that kidney removed.

I have wondered what I might have done in a similar situation and of course it is impossible to answer because how any person will react in a given situation, particularly in a stressful situation, we cannot know unless we have actually been in that situation. For my father, it was instant improvisation, but he had the courage to refuse the Gestapo.

My father mentioned several times that some people, when they realized that they were destined for death, lost hope. For a few, common morality fell apart in the ghetto. That idea never crossed my parents' minds. They never lost hope. My parents stayed the people they were, even in those conditions. Indeed, they stayed who they were during the ghetto, in the hideout, and after the war.

My father stayed true to our family. We were in a small room in our apartment in the ghetto. Four men came in and in the presence of my mother and my brother and me they said to my father, "The women and children are lost. There is nothing that can be done to help them and if we stay we will all be murdered. We are going to try to escape from the ghetto, join the partisans and fight the Nazis. Will you come with us?" These men were probably part of a Tarnow Jewish resistance movement that had formed during the deportations. My father refused to join the partisans and leave his family. It would have been a perfectly understandable choice on his part if he had joined them. But then I would not be writing this now.

The Germans played games with the Jews before killing them. There was a lineup of Jews. They counted one, two, three, and shot the third person then four, five, six, and shot the sixth person. My Father told the guard next to him, "I have a gold watch in my pocket." "I can't do anything for you," the guard said. "Put me at the end of the line," my father said. The guard did and my father gave him the watch. There was a wall at the end of the line. My father jumped over it and ran. They chased him with dogs and he had the presence of mind to jump into an outhouse, right down the toilet. The dogs went by. How many people would have tried to escape and figured that out? How many people would have thought of jumping into an outhouse? He did not go looking for risks but took risks in desperation and he did not give up. Of all the people in the lineup he was the only one to try to get over the wall.

My father was a short man, shorter than I am. I am five feet six inches tall, so my father was maybe five foot two and yet he was a giant. He was incredible. He saved his family and five other Jews. Only a few hundred were saved out of the twenty-five thousand Jews in Tarnow and my father saved nine of them. But one should not minimize the role of my mother. She was also very small, but she was made of steel. I did not realize until after my parents' deaths that in character they were giants.

Dagnan's Flour Mill

Dagnan's flour mill was on Lwowska Street in Grabowka but on the other side of the street, outside the ghetto wall. It was called Lwowska Street because it leads to the town of Lvov just as Krakovska Street leads to Cracow. My father worked with Dagnan before the Nazi times. There were two Dagnan brothers, Antoni and Augustyn, and it was Augustyn my father worked with. The mill also had a large workshop that made parts and served as a garage and repair shop.

My father and Augustyn Dagnan were partners in business. Dagnan ran the flour mill and my father supplied the Jewish bakeries in Tarnow with flour. Dagnan's flour mill was a landmark. Tarnow was not a big city. It was like Fredericton, New Brunswick, where I live today. A flour mill would have been known like the Chestnut Canoe factory or the Hart Boot and Shoe Company in Fredericton. Under the Nazis a red card to work at a factory such as Dagnan's meant you were okay. I heard my father talk about that several times. It was officially called a *Kennkarte* but in slang such passes were also called *Judenpasse* or Jews' Passes because they extended your life—it meant you had a job and were the last to be deported. The Jewish police had them as did a few Jews who were needed for work outside the ghetto. My father said he gave Mr. Dagnan a lot of money, including gold in order to get Dagnan to hire him officially so he could get a *Judenpass*. He told me that he gave him a lot of gold.

My father went from being partners with Dagnan to working in some capacity in the factory as a slave labourer. Such slave labourers would be

9

taken from the ghetto in the morning under German guard, escorted to the workplace, and then escorted back under guard in the evening. It was in this situation, with the *wysiedlenia* happening regularly, that my father desperately began looking for ways to save his family.

He went up to the attic one day and he saw a false wall being built. He asked to be included in the scheme and he was. The wall was built by Polish workers, brothers called Drozd. They were paid by some of the few remaining Jewish workers at Dagnan's who saw things coming to an end. There were four Jewish men involved in the plan to create a hideout. There was Chaim Bochner, the son of a woman called Mrs. Bochner who ended up in the hideout with us. There

Augustyn Dagnan postwar. (Tarnow Regional Museum)

was the husband of a couple called Aleksandrowicz. There was a father of two girls called Weksler, and then there was my father. They collaborated in having the hideout made. My father told me that he was not one of the originators. When he saw the wall being built, he asked that he and his family

Dagnan flour mill pre-war. (Tarnow Regional Museum)

10

be included. You can appreciate that at the time if a person found a way to save him or herself they could not share it with everybody.

So a fake wall was secretly built in the attic of Dagnan's flour mill. Because the Drozd brothers were known around the factory, I guess it did not stick out that they carried extra bricks up into the attic. Brick by brick they created the illusion that the attic ended when really, behind the false wall, there was an extra space, a hiding space. If you went up to the attic and you didn't know any different, you would think the attic just ended at the false wall. Pieces of machinery and discarded scrap were placed in front of the wall, in particular in front of the hole used to access the hideout so it would not be visible.

It was a very narrow space. It was about ten square metres. I expect they didn't plan for so many people in the beginning. Also they had to make it believable that the attic ended where it should. If they had made it larger anyone from the factory coming up to the attic would have thought, Well, the shop downstairs is so-and-so long, so why is this attic so small? The men put things in there like forks and knives and plates and blankets. The idea was, once the wall was built, the women and children would go into hiding and the men would join them at the last minute. My mother went into hiding before we did.

One night my father took my brother and me to the ghetto wall. It was cold. There was snow on the ground, so it must have been late in the year of 1942 or early 1943. We had to escape over the high ghetto wall. My brother

Arrow pointing to hideout above the workshop in the Dagnan Flour Mill. Photo from 2001. (Tarnow Regional Museum)

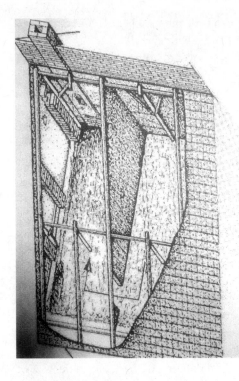

Exact drawing of hideout done in 2001
by Tarnow Regional Museum.

scrambled up to the top of the wall. My father pushed me from below and
with my brother's help from above they got me on top of the wall. We both
fell to the ground and crouched there for a while. We heard shots being
fired. Other Jews were trying to escape. The Nazis were patrolling around
the ghetto perimeter and if they spotted someone trying to escape, they shot
them. Someone met us—a man my father had hired. I believe it was a man
called Skorupa who later brought us food. This man took my brother and me
to the hideout behind the false wall in the Dagnan mill.

The Hideout

My mother was already in the hiding place when we got there. So was
Mrs. Bochner, the two Weksler girls and Mrs. Aleksandrowicz. The men,
including my father, were still doing slave labour for the Nazis, going in
and out of the ghetto with their special passes. They would come to the
attic hideout on alternate nights, taking turns to stay with the women and
children. One night Mr. Aleksandrowicz was to stay and he did, but my father
also stayed. He told me many times after, he had a premonition that he should
stay that night, even though it was not his turn. That night we heard gunfire,
and in fact that is the night the ghetto was liquidated. It was that night that

Mrs. Bochner lost her son and the two girls lost their father and mother. The men had planned to wait until the last minute before going into permanent hiding in the attic. Unfortunately, they waited too long.

The morning after the ghetto was liquidated, my father heard his name being called out in the factory below, "*Panie* Unger, *Panie* Unger!"—Mr. Unger, Mr. Unger! Wisely he did not answer.

It was 3 September 1943 when the Nazis liquidated the Tarnow ghetto. I later learned that they brought Amon Goeth from the Plaszow concentration camp in Cracow to do the job. He was the infamous killer from the movie *Schindler's List*. Everyone from the Tarnow ghetto was murdered on the spot or sent to death camps and murdered there. In the end, there were nine of us hiding in the attic: our family—my brother, mother and father, and me, the Aleksandrowicz husband and wife, Filip and Bertha (called Blima), Mrs. Bochner, and the two Weksler sisters, Anna and Czesia. Anna was ten years older than I was and her sister was seven years older. The father had returned to the ghetto to try to save the mother. The girls lost all their family. Mrs. Bochner who was quite old, in her sixties or seventies, often asked, Why did she make it into hiding and her son, Chaim, did not?

We were about two years in hiding in what really amounted to a crawl space, two metres wide by about five metres long. There was only room enough to stand in about half the space as it was under the slope of the roof. It was very drafty. We were liberated in January of 1945. I was seven when we were liberated.

We tried to sleep during the day and we could move about the attic at night. Underneath were the workshops that muffled the sounds. Still we tried to be quiet all the time. The first thing I remember about living in the hideout was that this young man Skorupa came once a week and brought food. This man's father had been a manager at Dagnan's mill. My mother told Marlene that, before the war, the older Skorupa's father died and my father gave him money to have a burial. The burial was not in Tarnow and so he needed to travel to take care of the funeral and my father paid for it. So my parents clearly knew the Skorupas before we went into hiding. There was the father, who would have been more my father's generation, and four sons. It was one of the son's, Zbyszek Skorupa, who brought us food in the beginning. I just knew him as Skorupa.

Why did Skorupa bring us food? Maybe he was favourably disposed to us. He was certainly at great risk. He was doing a good deed and maybe he wanted to get paid for the good deed. My parents were willing to pay, but there might have been even something deeper about my parents paying in the sense that if you paid him for it, then he is an accomplice. Of course, for the Germans, he's an accomplice even if you don't pay. If you helped a Jew you were dead. But why shouldn't you benefit from it? I don't think it was immoral or unethical. You're sorry to see what is happening to these people; you're going to help them, but you need some help too. So why should it not be symbiotic? I don't have anything against that. I have heard of cases where Jews were helped by Gentiles for money and when the money ran out the Gentiles gave them up to the Germans. That was certainly not the case with Skorupa or with Dagnan. My father told me about giving money to the Dagnans to get a job at the flour mill. I expect that the Dagnans did not ask for money, rather that my father gave it to them as a sort of present in order to help ensure that they gave him a work permit. But if Skorupa brought us, say, thirty *zlotzys* worth of food you had to pay for it, so there had to be money up in the attic. He brought us food for about the first three months of hiding.

One week Skorupa didn't come. We thought that perhaps there was some danger such as a German patrol going by and that he would come the following week. But he never came again. We learnt after the war that he was shot and killed, smuggling Jews across the border from Poland to Hungary. After the war my mother kept in touch with Mrs. Skorupa and sent her food parcels. It could be that my mother felt some sort of guilt or obligation because of Mrs. Skorupa's son getting killed.

At night, we would go out of the hideout to the main part of the attic. My father and Mr. Aleksandrowicz and the older girl Anna went down into the mill where the flour was ground to get flour and barley. We boiled the barley and ate it as soup. We mixed the flour with water and baked it on an electric hot plate. There was a chimney running up through the hideout which produced some heat too. We were very cautious even when we went out into the main part of the attic after the workers had gone home. We were so scared of being discovered. We had an inkling that perhaps some of the workers in the machine shop right below the attic had an idea that my father was in hiding upstairs but not that there were nine of us up there. Maybe they liked my father and so did not report it to the Gestapo. But we thought that if anyone knew, they thought he was the only one in hiding. Just him. My father would find scraps of bread in the garbage can. At times we suspected that it was deliberate because food was so scarce, for non-Jewish Poles too. Maybe if they thought it was my father, they weren't going to inform on him because he had been partners with Dagnan. They might have suspected but did not want to know more. Because if you knew about Jews and didn't report it, then you were liable to be killed yourself. So if you heard a strange noise in the attic—why investigate?

Who knew about the Jews in the attic? I am not sure even to this day. Probably the Dagnans, and the Skorupas, and the Drozds. Why didn't anyone tell on us? Was it humanitarian or were they scared to be caught if we were caught? Were they paid, were they not? Were they "Righteous Gentiles" or simply afraid for themselves? These are questions I cannot answer. Likely about ten non-Jewish people knew about the Jews in hiding and no one told on us. Anne Frank's hideout was perhaps a "palace" compared to ours, but we were much luckier. No one informed on us. We survived and she did not.

There was just enough room behind the false wall for the nine of us all to lie down next to each other side by side. The hiding place was very tight. I slept next to my mother and Mrs. Bochner slept next to me. I would wake up in the morning or in the night sometimes and I would be wet. I didn't know how I got wet so I asked. My mother told me that she had been passing a glass of water to Mrs. Bochner. Mrs. Bochner spilled it on me and that was how I got wet. I recall that I got very angry with Mrs. Bochner for spilling water on me. It wasn't until I was twenty or more that I realized what had been going on. I wet myself and my mother and Mrs. Bochner agreed to concoct this story so that I wouldn't feel bad.

If I associated one colour with life in the attic it would be grey. And the two most common feelings were: boredom and fear. I used to play with my mother's hair and I had a kind of word for what I was doing. I called it *tobu*. It was an inventive thing that I'd do, run my finger in her hair and she just let me do it. My mother's hair was straight and I used to put my finger through it almost like scratching her hair. I did not do it for my gratification. I thought I was doing a good thing for my mother. *Tobu*. I think it was a fantasy word or at least a made up word like if you are holding a child who is crying and you say *sha sha*. It was definitely something positive. I would say *tobu, tobu*, and with one finger stroke my mother's hair.

I have no recollection of crying or making noises and have no recollection of being told not to. That is even before we went into the attic. It was also true in the other hiding places like the cellar where I was alone with my mother. I don't cry over certain things that you might expect people to cry about even today. I did not cry at my father's or mother's funerals. Tears will come to my eyes at emotional things like if I am watching a film and Jews are being marched to a concentration camp. It's not as if tears don't well up in my eyes, but I don't cry for normal things.

My parents were orthodox, observant Jews before the war and stayed religious during the Holocaust and after. My father prayed in the attic and did his best to observe the Jewish holidays and festivals. We spoke Yiddish in the attic. One of the main things that went on in the attic for two years was conversation. I love conversation to this day. The adults knew about the Warsaw ghetto uprising for instance and there was much conversation about that. We knew where the Russian front was. We knew about the D-Day landings. How we got this information, I do not know. It is purely conjecture, but maybe when my father went out to get flour he might have picked up newspapers that were down in the factory. He certainly wouldn't have been listening to a radio.

There was discussion about whether we would make it to liberation and if so, would we be liberated by the Russians or by the Western allies. In fact, one thing I remember is we talked about communism. As a seven-year-old, I thought communism sounded wonderful; people shared everything. But I ask myself, Did we really believe in communism? Or was it because the Soviets were fighting the Nazis? I expect that all the views that we associated with communism were based on the fact that these were the guys who were killing the arrogant murderers. The Red Army represented hope. Even today I could watch film clips of the Red Army taking Berlin twenty-four hours a day. We knew they were coming. The Americans, too, were a huge positive image for us. We did not know whether the Soviets would get to us first or the Americans. After the D-Day landings we thought it could be either.

Or possibly we might be found out. Every minute of the day you worried whether you would be discovered.

The Only Jews in Poland

The adults thought that, probably, we were the only Jews left in Poland. Would we survive until we were liberated?

How did we maintain hygiene up there? I don't know. I'm sure I never had a bath for two years. There were rats. I think they were helping themselves to the stash of a kind of pita-type flatbread that we made. We had a whole barrel of it. That may have been what attracted the rats. My father would go out of the hiding place—not every night. He wanted to be out as little as possible to minimize the chances of being seen. But he would go and bring back flour from the mill and we mixed it with water and then cooked it on the hot plate. My father took more flour than what was needed to build up a reserve. We watched the rats scurrying along the rafters. It was in the main part of the attic where the roof slanted down and the rafters met the wall; there were gaps and daylight coming in. That is where I could see the rats running along. It was part of the entertainment.

The main part of the attic, outside the hiding space, seemed huge. There were rules about when we could or could not go out into this main part. Most of the time, during the day, we stayed in the hiding place. In the evening or at night we crawled in and out through a hole where the roof sloped down. The main attic was half an inverted V. One side you could stand up in. The stairs were at the far end of the main part, but I would not have gone to the stairs. When we crawled back in there was a kind of a wooden thing that was pulled back over the hole. It wasn't just left a hole. There were pieces of machinery and discarded scrap in front of the hole to hide it.

My father went out more than anyone else. It was very dangerous. He had to go across open spaces. He talked about climbing over roofs. He talked of occasionally seeing a sentry. He would go out at night to get the flour and barley. I don't know how much Mr. Aleksandrowicz went out. My father had knowledge of the flour mill because he had worked with Dagnan. I don't think they would have risked both men getting caught and the women and children being on their own. One man going down would be less likely to be seen than two.

My father also retrieved water from the mill. There was water in the shop below the attic. So he carried the water up to us and carried the waste down. One time my father turned the tap on and then he could not turn it off. He was in utter panic. He tried stopping the water with his body, anything. Ultimately he did manage to turn the tap off.

From the hiding place we could not see outside, but from the main part of the attic we could look out through gaps where the rafters met the walls and see what was going on in the courtyard. Occasionally German soldiers came to the flour mill. Whether they were the Nazi elite troops, the SS, or just regular soldiers, I don't know. But they were in the courtyard talking to Polish workers. Our hideout was above a machine shop and the Germans were coming to get repairs done. They would bring in a truck or a car and the Polish workers would have to fix it.

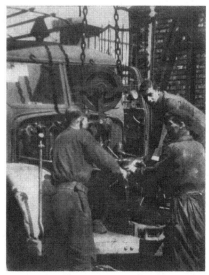

I was very afraid when we saw the Germans. It was terrifying. Seeing Germans meant that possibly someone had informed on us and they had come to get us. Right away we would go back through the hole into the hiding place.

There was cause for fear almost constantly.

Being near Lwowska Street, you might think we could hear sounds

Dagnan factory machine shop workers repairing a German army vehicle, circa 1942. (Tarnow Regional Museum photo)

from the city, but the only memorable impression was seeing German soldiers in the courtyard. I have no visual images of the outside and the outside was scary. If we were seen on the outside we were done for. The outside represented hostility. It represented the Nazis.

Once, close to liberation, we had a bad scare. A worker came up to drink in the attic. He was obviously the type of guy who needed to drink in the middle of the day. We heard someone up in the main part of the attic. My father decided that the best thing to do was just go out and see the man rather than have him discover us. So my father came out of the hole and kind of confronted the man. For us it was a huge fear, a double fear that he would tell on us and get paid by the Nazis for turning us in. Or, what if he got drunk some time and let it slip that he knew where there were some Jews hiding. My father tried to pay him off with some jewellery so he wouldn't inform on us, but the fellow ran away. My father ran after him, begging him not to tell and trying to put money in his pocket. The man was scared because he was a drinker and he was scared of being discovered and my father was scared that we had been discovered. It was an absurd situation—a real Alphonse and Gaston in a morbid way. At the end of this episode, my father just put the payment in the guy's pocket. There were two facets to that: one, a payoff, but also a way to make the man complicit and therefore afraid to report us.

I don't remember dreaming in the attic. I dreamt more afterwards.

One recurring dream, which continues even to the present day but in decreasing frequency, was that I was being chased and I want to run but I cannot lift my legs. I want to move but I cannot move, as if I were in quicksand. I may be acting as an amateur psychologist, but clearly this is a response to fear—about being frightened and not being able to get away—the situation in the attic.

There was another complication too. My father had a huge boil on the side of his neck near the jaw, the left side I think—it was the size of a Ping-Pong ball. He managed to cure that by putting a piece of bacon rind—fat and all—on the boil. Normally my father would not go ten feet near bacon! How we got the bacon, I don't know. In due course the boil pierced and drained. Using things to draw out bad stuff was fairly common. For instance, if a person had a bad cold, they would put *bainkes* on his or her back. *Bainkes* were sort of small glass cups with methanol which was lit and then, when the flame had gone out, you would quickly place it on the person's back. The vacuum would suck part of the body into the cup. This was supposed to draw out the "bad"—whatever was making the person sick, but I think most of the time it just burned the person's back.

There must have been some preparation before going into the hideout because we had some utensils and there were photos. We had a box of photos and one of the games I played was to take a needle and punch out the eyes of the people in the pictures. My mother let me do it. I don't know what it means, but it scares me actually. It was somehow an entertainment to pass the time. I would show it to my mother as if I was proud that I was improving the picture. When I reflect on it, it disturbs me. Was this some sort of sign of cruelty? Very odd. But my mother let me do it and she wasn't a child psychologist. There were no toys in the attic. Playing with the pictures was a substitute for toys.

Israel's aunt Baila and grandmother Raizel Grossbart Fisch in the Carpathian Mountains pre-war. (Israel Unger collection)

I don't remember much interaction with any of the others. I don't remember being taught anything in the attic or whether the two sisters interacted with me. I definitely don't remember being carried by them or being fussed over by them.

I have very few memories of my brother in the shelter. Kalman was nine when we went into hiding. He would have been five and a half at the outbreak

Photo of uncle, grandmother, and aunt, with needle pinpricks. (Israel Unger collection)

of the war, so he wouldn't have gone to school. My brother and I didn't play games that I recall. He developed terrible stomach pains at one point. It might have been appendicitis, because after the war he had the same pains. That was in Paris and my parents took him to the hospital on a Saturday and Kalman underwent an emergency appendectomy. When he had those pains in the hideout, the adults discussed it. What would they do with the body when he died? How do you dispose of a body when you are hidden up in an attic? He survived. He lived.

About food. Every now and then my father would go down in the factory and scrounge around in the garbage cans and find a crust of bread. My mother would take that and she would soak it in water and then she would put it on the hot plate and we would eat that. That was like manna from heaven. I remember in particular we had bowls and spoons. When we had barley soup—and this must have been towards the end—my mother would give me a bowl of it and I would have a spoonful or maybe two spoonfuls then I would stop. I would place the spoon straight up in the soup and measure how much soup there was left. Then I would have another spoonful and again I would measure how much I had eaten. I was very hungry but I couldn't stand this barley soup. I knew I had to eat it, so I would eat and measure how much I still had to eat. I was glad to see it go. The food was so bland, so unappetizing, that I forced myself to eat it. I was hungry, but I had to force myself to eat. I am very bowlegged and I think that was diet related. My mother was having a hard time getting me to eat. I just couldn't eat anymore. We were all getting weaker and weaker.

We weren't the only Jews in hiding in Tarnow. There were others, and as time went on hiding places were discovered and I think we might even have known about that. There was talk in the attic about how, if we survived, we would be a curiosity. We would be like a museum piece. We thought that they would take us to the United States and display us as the only Jews left alive in Poland.

Kissing a Soviet Soldier's Boots

There was a time towards the very end when there was an air raid at night and we all went downstairs into the machine shop. The idea was to get to safety in the bottom of the building. We may have gone down even further into a cellar of the machine shop. I don't remember much. It was so much more roomy but it did not feel safe. Safety was in the hiding place.

One day we thought we heard the Front. Before liberation, it is my understanding that the Soviet army had come quite close to Tarnow and then stopped, re-supplied, and re-equipped before starting their final offensive.

They stayed there for what seemed to us an eternity. We hoped every day that they would come but they didn't. Every day, every hour to survive was such a desperate thing.

Then one day they came. We did not hear a big cannonade. We heard small-arms fire and the next thing we saw were Soviet troops moving about the streets of Tarnow. I don't think there was a fight within Tarnow; there was no shootout. There was a deliberate withdrawal by the Germans west of Tarnow and the Soviets moved in. It was definitely infantry and they were in white camouflage because it was January. They were walking very cautiously. Then I recall seeing some of them come in to the flour mill.

I saw three Soviet soldiers. I think they were taking inventory of the equipment that was in the factory. I cannot express how truly overjoyed we were, an indescribable feeling of relief mixed with happiness on seeing the Soviet soldiers. I rushed out to greet them and fell down the stairs of the attic. I don't know if it was because I had forgotten how to walk on stairs or because I was so weak. I found myself right next to the three soldiers. I put my arms around the legs of the one nearest to me and kissed his boots!

My mother told Marlene many years later that she thinks that if we had not been liberated, I might not have lived another month.

We were liberated on 17 January 1945. Our joy did not last very long, because the German army had only retreated beyond the river in Tarnow and from there they started shelling the Soviets. Now we had been exposed. Everybody had seen us. Lots of people had seen us! The adults started worrying that the Germans were coming back and we had been revealed. My father went out and somehow he found a Soviet officer and he went up to him and he said, "If you retreat, please take us with you. We've been seen." Apparently the Soviet officer said to my father, "Don't worry, we are never going back." My father used to tell this story to show the mentality of the Soviet army. The officer happened to be Jewish and would have spoken Yiddish. My father said he was a *pulkownik*—a colonel.

The Soviets had come very early in the morning. Night came and I don't know where I was, but I was lying on my back and I could see the shells going up overhead. It was very exciting because first the shelling went from west to east, from the German lines to the Russian lines, and then the shelling started to go the other way. It went massively from the Russians to the Germans! Then the German shelling died out and you knew the Russians were banging the hell out of the Germans. It felt so good to see our tormentors getting shelled!

Until this day I have a warm spot for the Red Army. It was undoubtedly due to being liberated by the Soviet soldiers, but there was another element. The Nazis had slandered us from the rise of the Nazi party onward. They were so arrogant and considered themselves to be the master race. They wanted not only to murder us but also to humiliate us. The Red Army humbled our oppressors. Even today if I see newsreel footage and I see how cocky and proud the Nazis were with their uniforms and their jackboots and their *Heil Hitlers* it produces certain emotions in me. Then when I see the Soviet army counterattacking and I see the rocket launchers, the *katyushas*—it makes me feel great.

Matzos from America

After we came out of hiding, we lived on *ulica Zydowska*—Jew's Street—right in the middle of town off the *rynek*, the main town square. Our apartment looked out on four pillars that were the remains of the *bima* of Tarnow's oldest synagogue—the only such Jewish remains in the city. The *bima* is the raised platform in a synagogue from which the Torah is read. I knew what those ruins were and what had happened. Just a *bima* standing there means a missing synagogue. I don't think that we ever actually walked on that plot of land where the *bima* was. There were plants or weeds growing out of the top of the *bima*. The wind must have carried some seeds up there. It was incongruous to me to see grass growing out of what had been a *bima*. It had been destroyed in 1939, so this was six years later. It was an awful and constant reminder. You looked out the apartment window and you saw it. I don't know how many times I looked at it.

I know too that the little burial hall in the Jewish cemetery had holes in its roof. There was a space for mass graves. The Germans had forced Jews to dig mass graves and then the bodies had just been tossed in. Over the site of the mass graves a broken pillar from another destroyed synagogue had been placed as a memorial. As children we were taken there one day. I believe it might have been an excursion we took with children from the postwar Jewish centre. I don't recall the day specifically, but I know now that the

Ruins of the Jubilee Synagogue, Tarnow. This is the *bima* with plants growing out the top seen from Israel's postwar apartment. (This photo appears in the Tarnow Yizkor book.)

Israel (far right) and Charlie (right of female adult) with surviving Jewish children of Tarnow at Holocaust memorial in Tarnow cemetery, 1946. (Israel Unger collection)

memorial was erected on 11 June 1946, which was the fourth anniversary of the first liquidation of the Jews of Tarnow. The photo had to have been taken on or after this date. It shows the few surviving Jewish children of Tarnow at that monument. My brother and I are in that photo.

Very early on in Poland after the war, when Passover came in early April 1945 we needed matzos. There was no way of having them made locally. We received Manischewitz matzos from the United States. They were square matzos in a box and that was like something from Mars for us. We had never seen anything like that before. It was a marvel that you could get machine-made matzos in a box.

The first taste of matzos I remember in my life were these Manischewitz matzos from America.

Then my father started baking again. He was alone and had a small bakery—maybe the one he had before the war. He made matzos for the Jews left in Tarnow and for us. They were handmade and more or less round. There was a cousin of my mother's in Haifa who also sent us food immediately after liberation.

We still had the matzo bag that my mother had embroidered during her engagement, and we had a few monogrammed sheets with "U" for Unger. These are the few things that were in the box returned to us by a neighbour.

I recall that I enjoyed certain foods after we got out of hiding. I enjoyed a mushroom soup that my mother cooked that was unlike any mushroom soup that I have had since though I keep trying mushroom soups in restaurants around the world hoping to find something similar to what my mother cooked. Also, I remember bread with butter when we were out of the attic. It may have been when I started going to school that I had bread with butter. My brother must have had a friend who was even more destitute than we were because he gave some of his bread to a poor kid. He told my mother that she need not put so much butter on part of the bread and she asked why, and

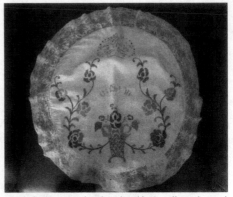

Matzo bag sewn and embroidered by Israel's mother and recovered after the war. (Carolyn Gammon photo)

he told her that he was sharing it with another non-Jewish boy. Food was scarce but my mother still kept giving him the bread and I believe she did not put less butter on the half intended for the other boy. Was he friends with that boy? Were there friendships between Jews and non-Jews after the war? I don't know.

After the war we also ate bread with milk scum. We boiled milk and when it cooled a scum formed on top that we spread on bread like marmalade. If we had chicken we used every bit of it, including the fat that would be rendered, then solidified, and we used that as a spread on bread too. It was salted and very tasty. When the fat was rendered there was something left over called *grieven,* which is Yiddish for scraps, and it was the scraps of chicken fat and skin fried with onions and they were absolutely delicious. They still are absolutely delicious.

I recall seeing Soviet troops heading back home to the Soviet Union and coming through Tarnow. They came in various ways, sometimes in trucks, sometimes on horseback, and often driving German prisoners. They were taking prisoners of war back with them to the Soviet Union. There would be a column of Germans walking down the road and there would be four Soviet soldiers on horses, two in front and two in back.

I very much wanted to be a soldier. There were no toys, but I had a piece of wood that I pretended was a rifle. I would hang out where the trucks passed. Their radiators would sometimes run out of water, so I would offer to fetch the water for the soldiers. But the jugs were too heavy for me to carry, so the soldier would come with me and help to carry the can. In reality they carried the whole thing. I thought I was doing them a service, but they were just being kind. They would even give me some sort of present, some trifle or another, for offering to help with the water in spite of the fact that they had very little to give away. One of the things I wanted to have badly and never did get was a hat with a red star on it—those hats that have the earflaps tied up on top. I was very impressed with the red star. They probably only had the one hat per soldier.

The Russians were kind, and years later I heard another story about this. When I was sitting *shiva* for my brother in Montreal, Marlene met a Jewish woman from Tarnow who said that the Russians gave her so much food that she could make soup for a year! This woman had returned to Tarnow with the Russian army. I recall too a story about a Russian soldier who went into a movie theatre in Tarnow and shot up the screen. Why, I don't know. Perhaps he thought it was real?

At some point there was a Nazi who was on trial in Tarnow and he was being taken to prison. A detachment of Polish soldiers were taking him down the street, a group of soldiers in front and a group in back. In the middle was this German officer in uniform. That brought gladness to my heart! Even at that young age I loved seeing that. A Russian soldier just came out of nowhere, walked right through the Polish soldiers and up to the German officer and slapped him in the face. The German fell to the ground and the Russian just kept on going. I thought that was wonderful.

There is a line in William Shirer's book *The Rise and Fall of the Third Reich*, which I must have read in about 1965. It is in "the fall." I read only that section. Reading "the rise" was just too difficult for me. In "the fall" there is the part where Hitler gave some sort of order as to what the German army was to do and Shirer states that at this point it was not Hitler and the German army who were determining the course of events, it was the Soviet Red Army. That still makes me feel good. Perhaps there is something wrong with my character, but when I see clips of the Second World War and I see Hitler and his generals and German troops strutting proudly with their uniforms and their hats and their leather boots, I think to myself contemptuously, This is the *"Herren* Race" and then when I see the Soviets counterattacking with their *katyushas* firing, it makes me feel good.

We felt positive towards the Russian soldiers as liberators. There was one person I met who instinctively understood this. Decades later when I was a professor at the University of New Brunswick, I had lunch several times with a Canadian general, General Geddry. He was stationed at Camp Gagetown, near Fredericton. At the time I was very much involved in the peace movement. In fact I was one of the founders and president of the Canadian Science for Peace for New Brunswick. We came from different points of view. I felt it was important to learn the views of a high-ranking member of the military. Somewhere along the line I said to him that I had a warm spot for the Soviet

Red Army and instantly he said, "Are you a Holocaust survivor?" Or perhaps he said, "Were you liberated by them?" This was the first lunch I ever had with him. He was a Canadian general commanding Canada's largest military base at the height of the Cold War and I wanted to develop a relationship with him, but I wanted him to know where I was coming from.

In Tarnow after the war, there was not immediate total collectivization. The communist government started a store and their goods were cheaper than anywhere else. I used to go and buy matches there because they were something like a *zloty* and then I would try to resell them at a profit yet cheaper than what they cost in any other store.

There was a Jewish community centre re-established in Tarnow soon after the war on Goldhammer Street three. A man called Abraham Ladner had a prayer house at number one Goldhammer Street. I guess that must be where my parents prayed. One day I was in front of the community centre with some other Jewish kids, maybe three or four of us, and there was a Polish officer on a horse. I don't know what we did, perhaps we startled the horse, but we did something to annoy him. He chased us and we ran into the Jewish community centre and hid under a table. He came in and asked people where we were. They said they had not seen us. I don't think they were lying; they hadn't seen us. I guess we fled there because it represented safety.

I don't know if Auschwitz was a word I knew back then. I definitely knew about concentration camps. We knew the German word for camp: *Lager*.

Israel's mother Hinda (left) with her brother David and sister Baila, pre-war. (Israel Unger collection)

My parents tried to find out if any of their relatives were left alive. They made contact with the cousin in Haifa who sent us food. They met one man who survived the camps and came back to Tarnow. He had known my uncle David on my mother's side. He was in the same camp as David. For some reason Buchenwald comes to mind, but I can't be sure. They were liberated by Americans and according to the man who talked to my parents, after the liberation David ate too much and died. His system just couldn't take the food. It happened to many prisoners. He made it through, but died a few days later.

Part Two

Sans Pays

The Kielce Pogrom and a Gash on the Head

We lived about a year and a half in Tarnow after the liberation. I know now that the Kielce pogrom was July 1946. Kielce is not far from Tarnow. On 4 July 1946, a mob of locals, Polish government officials, and military attacked and killed forty-two Jewish survivors who had returned to Kielce. It was only one of many deadly assaults on Jews in Poland after the war. It is estimated that fifteen hundred survivors returning to Poland or coming out of hiding were killed *after* the Holocaust. Every one of these deaths shocked Jews around the world but particularly Jews in Poland. I have no doubt my parents would have heard about Kielce and the other killings.

Many Polish Jews who had somehow survived the Holocaust tried to leave at that point. But as a child I did not put the Kielce pogrom together with our departure. There were also a couple of personal incidents that convinced my parents that we had to leave.

First I was beaten up after school. I went to school for the first time in my life in the fall of 1945 at age seven. I walked to school; it wasn't far. I must have learned the Polish alphabet at least because I knew there were letters that do not exist in English, like the "Ł" with a slash through it which is pronounced like the English "W." But I don't know when actually I learned to read and write. First thing every morning at school the priest would come in and teach catechism to the students and I would leave the room and come back when the priest left. It did not take long for the other students to realize that I was "different." There was one other older boy who was Jewish, but he was not in my classroom.

My teacher might have been a woman, because when I was beaten up it was a female teacher who came to speak with my parents. One day on my way home from school, I was attacked by a group of students. They knocked me down and banged my head against the curb. They didn't continue to beat up on me. It was brief but it produced a gash on my forehead. My parents made more out of it than I did. It did not even hurt very much and I didn't have to go for medical help; I was treated at home. My parents decided that I would not return to school. After I was attacked, a teacher came to our apartment and talked with my parents. Why exactly she came I do not know, but I have put the two things together in my head. I suspect that it was not a normal thing for a teacher to come to a pupil's home. I used to have a scar on the left side at the temple. It became faint with time.

Then another incident occurred. There was a small Jewish children's camp that my brother went to, like kids go to summer camp now. That would have been in the summer of 1946. There might have been a half dozen kids at the camp. My brother was supposed to be there for a week, but he came back after just three days in the middle of the night.

He was brought home by the camp director. There were two attacks on the camp. At the time there were Polish partisans who were trying to free the country from the Russians. The Russians were a formidable foe—Jewish kids were a far easier target. The camp was in a country house, and the first night the kids were there a grenade was thrown at the house. There was a detachment of Russian soldiers nearby and among them there were at least two who were Jewish. So they went over and stayed with the kids.

Two nights later there was apparently a full-scale firefight. Polish partisans attacked that house. The Jewish Russian soldiers beat them back. At that point the man who was in charge of the camp decided they could not keep the kids there safely and brought them back to Tarnow. So now I had been beaten up by school kids and my brother had been attacked at the camp. And there was the Kielce pogrom.

Out of the 3.5 million Jews in Poland, three hundred thousand had survived somehow. Within a few years after the end of the war, that was down to thirty-five thousand. In one way or another, people left. It was not just my parents.

If you could conjure up my parents and ask them why they left, they would probably give a very general answer and say anti-Semitism was intense in Poland after the war. They might then, if you prodded them, tell you the individual things that led up to their decision to leave. Another motivator was that it was obvious that you would not be able to get established in business again under communism. My parents were positive towards Zionist socialism but definitely not to communism. My father was a businessman. He started right away to try to set up his business again. He tried to set up a bakery. With communism, private enterprise was finished. My parents wanted to go to the United States. We were on the Polish quota for the United States. The Americans did not differentiate on the basis of religion, only on the country of birth. Since we were born in Poland we were on the Polish quota. Based on the 1924 Immigration Act, foreigners were allowed in according to a percent of how many were already in the United States in the year 1890. In 1924 the quota was set at two percent. Say there were a quarter million Poles in the United States in 1890, then the quota was two percent of that or, five thousand Poles a year. The quotas were not re-adjusted for the Holocaust. Even after the war, it depended when you applied. I think it was in 1956, five years after arriving in Canada, that we received notice in Montreal that we were now eligible to emigrate to the United States.

My parents had clearly decided to leave Poland, but it was not easy to leave. It was impossible to leave legally. There must have been a Soviet-influenced government policy that kept people from leaving, perhaps the same type of policy that prevented East Germans from moving to the West. Jews were also not allowed to leave the USSR. There would be no way that my parents would have separated the family if there had been a legal way for us to leave together.

My father found out that there was a group of Jewish orphan children in Cracow who were leaving Poland legally. He went to Cracow and managed to get my bother and me included in that group.

I recall the day that my father came back from Cracow, I was playing by myself in the street, on *ulica Zydowska*, when I saw him. He was coming down the street from the town square. It is a short street and I ran to greet him. He picked me up and I smelled alcohol on his breath. It was the first and only time in my life that I smelled alcohol on my father's breath. This was not like my father. Undoubtedly he had just arranged for my brother and me to leave. I think that the alcohol was his way of coping with the fact that he was going to say goodbye to his kids.

My brother and I were to be sent out of Poland as "orphans."

Becoming "Orphans"

Shortly thereafter my father took Kalman and me to Cracow. Before leaving, my mother said goodbye to us. She sewed an American ten-dollar bill into the brim of my hat and my brother's. It was that kind of hat I'm wearing in the one childhood picture of me from Tarnow. We left in the fall of 1946. We were wearing coats, but there was no snow.

The three of us travelled to Cracow, about eighty kilometres to the west by train. In those postwar days train travel in Poland was by boxcar, a cattle car with a big sliding door. We sat on straw in one corner of the boxcar. There were other people in the wagon, but we sat in a corner all by ourselves. We were very scared. Trains were being stopped and searched and we worried if Jews were found on board we would be killed. Periodically the train would stop. Someone would flag it down because they wanted to get on. We did not know why it was being stopped—for passengers? Or partisans? There was no conductor who said, "Now we are arriving in Bochnia, the stop here will be ten minutes." The train just stopped, the door would slide open and somebody would get on. We feared that it was Polish partisans who might have stopped the train looking for Jews or Soviets. Not all, but some of the partisans were very nationalistic and anti-Semitic. So every time the train stopped, we were very frightened.

Kalman, Israel, and their mother, Hinda Fisch Unger, in Tarnow, 1946. Their mother sewed $10 for the trip into the brims of the hats. (Israel Unger collection)

When we arrived in Cracow, my father took us to a big house where all the other Jewish orphans were staying. It was an assembly point. My father went to the head of the group, a man by the name of Rabbi Schonfeld, who with a group of rabbis, had organized the whole thing. Rabbi Schonfeld had agreed to take us even though we were not orphans. I do not know if my father knew where we were going at that point. He knew that we would be heading out to Prague—but after that? The organizers did him a huge favour in taking us because they only had permission to take orphans from Poland. We said goodbye. I had no idea whether we would ever see my father or mother again.

I was very lonely. I think this is when I began to substitute my brother for my parents. I depended on him. I looked up to him. He was now my father figure and my mother figure. I had this notion that my brother was the big guy, the hero. I had an extraordinary regard for him. He was going to look after me and I would do anything to earn his affection. That lasted for a long time. That lasted way beyond our time in Europe.

It was not always reciprocated and it was not always a good relationship.

We were not in Cracow very long. A couple of days later we went to the train station by truck. It was evening. When we arrived at the train station the whole orphanage was there. We were all leaving together. This was it. We were leaving Poland.

Kalman and I each had a rucksack that contained all our possessions. We waited at the track. A train pulled in but they did not open any of the cars. Then somebody said that they were opening the cars at the head of the train. We ran to the front. My rucksack was almost as big as I was and when I ran it bounced up and down and bumped on the ground. It was one of those rucksacks with metal ribs you occasionally see even today in Europe. When we got to the front of the train the doors were not open and we were told they were going to open the doors at the back, so we ran in that direction. I remember having a really hard time with that rucksack bumping along the platform as I ran.

Eventually we got on the train. It was a regular passenger train with windows. There were about four hundred kids on that train in that group of orphans. We *were* the train. Everyone was speaking Yiddish. It was very crowded, and since I was small I was put on the overhead baggage rack. I slept there. I did not know where we were headed. The train ride seemed very long.

The entire group received cans of milk from the United States. In the centre of the can there was a tube that was about 1.5 centimetres in diameter filled with waxy petroleum that could be lit to heat the milk. The first place we stopped was just outside of Prague, about ten kilometres from the city. I now know from research that there were two such camps for Jewish orphan children fleeing Poland after the Kielce pogrom. They were in Dablice and Hloubetin. I no longer know which camp we were in, but to us it seemed, ironically, like a former concentration camp. It was surrounded by barbed wire and we were not allowed out.

My brother asked me to give him the ten dollars my mother had sewn into the brim of my hat. I gave it to him willingly. I very much looked up to Kalman and considered him my only friend and would do almost anything he asked. My brother and several other boys dug under the barbed wire and made their way to Prague. I was not a part of that—I stayed in the camp. I was separated from my brother but only for half a day or so. I anxiously waited for him to come back. I knew he was gone and that he would come back, but I was fearful about it. He had gone with the other boys to deal on the black market. He traded the twenty American dollars for American cigarettes and then proceeded to barter those for food to supplement our very meager rations. He sold the cigarettes in various places as we went along. Ten dollars was only ten dollars, but if you had a carton of cigarettes you could trade them individually and American cigarettes were currency.

When we left Prague, the train ride went on forever. As we passed through Germany I saw burned-out tanks. We did not stop until we got to France. We arrived in a small place called Aix-les-Bains. It is in southeastern France, just south of Geneva, Switzerland. We were taken to a big house that was a former hotel called Hôtel Beau Site. It wasn't what one would think of as a hotel today, but it was much better than the trains we had slept on or the camp near Prague.

We went in and there was a dining room with long tables with plates of bread and butter. They were piled high—not baguettes but large loaves of bread thickly sliced and plenty of butter on each slice. You could have as much as you wanted! That was the first time since I left my parents home that I could have as much bread and butter as I wanted. It was absolutely delicious.

Aix-les-Bains

The good times did not last long. The next day, and from then on, we each received two slices of bread and butter in the morning. At lunchtime there was one slice of bread. I started a ritual of hiding one slice of bread between the bedsprings of my bed in case they would not give us any the next day. I ate one and hid one. So each day I had one slice of fresh bread and one from the day before.

Food was very scarce. For lunch we had a bowl of soup which was reddish in colour and had a piece of onion in it. It was basically a couple of pieces of onion floating around in water and the water had some red "grease-eyes." Supper was a slice of bread. We were hungry most of the time. One night, there was a kind of spontaneous uprising. Kids from all over the building ran to the kitchen and raided it. I took part. We broke open the locked door and scrambled for the food. We were always hungry.

The hunger in Aix-les-Bains was different from what I had known in the attic. In the attic it was hunger and blah. Two years of barley soup and a kind of pita and a hunger for something different. In Aix-les-Bains it was not real hunger, just not getting enough.

In France I looked up to my brother for absolutely everything. He was the only person I knew personally. He was it for me. And in some ways he did protect me. When we were in Aix-les-Bains, all the boys had their hair shaved, even my brother had his head shaved, but not me! I did not want to have it shaved and somehow my brother managed to see to it that it did not happen to me. Actually it would have been smarter if I had let them shave my hair off, because I had lice and they really hurt. Sometimes I was so tormented by the pain from the lice that I ran up to the room and, with a fine-tooth comb, scraped my scalp to try and get rid of the lice, to relieve the itch.

One of the counsellors at Aix-les-Bains was Benzion Singer, an older man, maybe in his mid-forties. We regarded him as a nice fellow, a benevolent presence. I think he ended up with most of the kids from the orphanage in Israel.

In the orphanage, the boys and girls were separated. There were no girls in our building. My brother slept in a room with many other boys whereas

I slept in a room with Benzion Singer. I am not sure why I was not in the dorms. Perhaps they were overcrowded and I was one of the youngest so they put me in with a counsellor. But I saw my brother every day.

One salient memory is that at some point we were issued new clothing. That felt wonderful. Then photos were taken of us, and as soon as that was done the new clothing was taken away. I felt cheated. There is one official photo of me from Aix-les-Bains and I believe those are the clothes I have on in that photo.

Aix-les-Bains is in the French Alps. But I think we might have had a hike into the mountains just once. Ninety-nine percent of

Benzion Singer, counsellor at Aix-les-Bains. (Israel Unger collection)

the time we were in the hotel vicinity. We occupied the whole hotel.

We played some vicious games. There was an iron pole, a light pole, I believe, and there was a short in the electricity running through it. If you touched it you would feel an electric current going through you. If you grabbed another kid, he got the current instead of you. We would form a chain and electrify the last one. In another game, we divided the number of players in two, about fifty kids on each side. We had something like a sock

Boys at Aix-les-Bain orphanage, circa 1947. (Yeshiva University Archives)

35

Dormitory, Aix-les-Bains. The child sitting to the far left might be Israel—perhaps visiting Charlie in the boys' dorm. (Yeshiva University Archives)

with some rocks in it. You would throw it at the other team. If you hit a kid and he did not catch it, he was out. Then that team would throw it at you. So the trick was to hit a kid, but if you were on the receiving end you had to catch the sock with rocks.

On Fridays we received a clean shirt. We gave up the old one and it would get laundered. We were given clean underwear once a week.

Somewhere along the line there must have been prayers or classes, because I learned to read Hebrew but not very well. It was not systematic. There was no distinction made between kids my age and kids who were older. It was not like starting with the alphabet and the vowels. You started reading and there were prayers. I can read Hebrew but I never properly learned it. I never learned it the way you would learn starting from scratch.

To the best of my knowledge during most of our time in Aix-les-Bains there was no word from our parents. Then my brother turned thirteen. This was the occasion of my father's first visit—for my brother's *bar mitzvah*. It must have been January 1947. We had been there some months, maybe half a year. One day, I kind of looked up and there he was, my father. I certainly recognized him and in my mind's eye I can see him still. He was wearing a fedora.

The *bar mitzvah* was a very simple affair. My brother was called up to read from the Torah and put on *teffilin* for the first time—the small boxes containing scrolls of parchment with verses from the Torah. Religious Jews strap these to the arm and head during morning prayer. My father stayed for a day and then left again. I cannot recall, but I am sure he would have told us that he was coming back. He was not gone very long.

In April 1947 he came back and took us with him to Paris. I never had any contact again with the kids we left behind.

My parents smuggled their way out of Poland. I don't know exactly how they were able to leave. They found their way to Germany and were in a displaced persons (DP) camp there. I believe this is when they learned that my brother and I were in a camp in France. They had been waiting to go to Israel and would have done so if they had not found out that we were in France.

When my father split the family I think he was trying to diminish the risk—something like he had done when we were hiding from the *wysiedlenia*.

My parents had decided they had to leave Poland. There was anti-Semitism; there was communism. The older one, Kalman, was attacked in a children's summer camp. The little one, Srulik, had gotten his head bashed coming from school. My father found a legal way out for the kids, and now instead of four people crossing the border illegally only two had to go. Clearly it was less risky trying to smuggle your way out of the country as two adults rather than two adults and two kids. It must have been fairly common for Jews in Poland to smuggle their way out and head west after the war. The first country west, of course, was Germany. Most of them ended up in DP camps in Germany and most then made their way to Israel. How did my father know to find us in Aix-les-Bains? Apparently it was a destination for many of the Jewish kids coming out of Poland. Jewish orphans were placed in homes all over France. There were four places where children were housed in Aix-les-Bains alone. Hôtel Beau Site was just one of them.

My mother had a surviving aunt in Paris, so we went there first. When I got to Paris I had been away from my parents for about a year. My mother was strange to me and I was strange with her. When she realized that I had head lice she wanted to get rid of them, but at first I resisted letting her do that. I did not react to her like my mother. I knew she was my mother, but it wasn't the way it had been before. There was a distance. I don't think it persisted very long.

I know exactly how she took care of the head lice. She did not cut my hair off. She washed my head in vinegar. I had to put my head into a basin and she combed my hair with a very fine-tooth comb. It did not take long before I was cured.

Sans Pays in Paris

France at that time was not very welcoming to immigrants. But, then again, no country wanted us. In France we had documents that simply stated our status as *sans pays*, "without a country," stateless. That was our official designation.

My mother's aunt would have been a Grossbart. I think her name was Malka and she was married to Kalman Hammer. They were reasonably well off. Kalman had a butcher shop in the Jewish part of Paris, the Marais, near the rue de Rivoli. They had three children: two boys, Henri and Zola, and a girl, Rachel, who was already married. We did not live with them—we saw them every couple of weeks. We lived in a small apartment near the *métro* station Stalingrad. Undoubtedly it had a different name before the war. In Paris the vast majority of the *métro* is underground, but in certain places it is above ground like at Stalingrad. We could look out our window and see the *métro* going by. We lived in a single room and conditions were really tough, tough for everybody but even more so for us. We had no kitchen or toilet facilities.

I was hungry up until I was reunited with my parents in France.

There was rationing, but children had extra rations that allowed us to have milk. Milk was one of the biggies. Later we experienced rationing in England too, but one of the differences was that in France regular bread made from wheat flour was available, whereas in England it was made with

Kalman Hammer and his wife Malka (Grossbart)—Israel's maternal great aunt, in Paris, late 1940s. (Israel Unger collection)

corn. In France my father would send me to the store with a bottle and they would fill it with beer.

One day my father brought home four oranges. I so enjoyed my orange that my parents gave me theirs and went without. Later, when I was in England and ate lunch at school, one day they gave us orange wedges. One wedge per student. Then just about every table got a second wedge, but the table I was at did not.

Kalman Hammer was considered wealthy for the day. How they survived the Holocaust, I don't know. The two boys worked with their father in the butcher shop. My mother worked for her aunt Malka as a maid in her house. They were so wealthy they had a regular flush in their apartment. My mother had a fishnet bag that she would take with her and occasionally her aunt would slip a piece of meat wrapped in paper into that bag. My mother had a kind of a ribbed metal plate like a washboard and she would put the beef on that metal plate and cook it on the top of the stove. To me it was the most delicious thing you could imagine. That was the first time I had grilled meat in my life. But when Malka gave my mother the meat, she would tell my mother not to say anything about it. The aunt was afraid that her husband would find out. He was awfully stingy. Zola, the oldest boy, was very nice and very kind. If I went to see my mother at work, Zola sometimes gave me one hundred francs. At the time that was equivalent to twenty-five cents, but the purchasing power was like a few dollars today. Henri never bothered with us at all. We did not live near them and I did not have much reason to visit. My father had a difficult time finding a job. My parents really could not support us.

My mother did not keep in touch with Malka much after we came to Canada. Zola came to see us once on a business trip. He was nice—always nice, mild, and decent. Of that family he was by far the nicest person. When he came to see us in Montreal he gave me some money then too. He was a warm person. I have been to the place in Paris since, but there is no longer a butcher shop there.

I turned ten in Paris. After having lived in Tarnow and Aix-les-Bains it was absolutely huge to me—and very interesting. The thing that amazed me the most were the escalators! It was the first time I had ever seen them. They were in the *métro* and I thought it was a huge thing to run up the down escalator. I think I actually thought that the *métro* trains ran by themselves. I didn't know that there were drivers. I remember how the doors opened: you flipped a little lever and pushed and they would open.

My time in Paris prior to going to England was short, just a few months. One thing I remember distinctly from that time though is re-meeting one of the rabbis from Aix-les-Bains. One day my father took my brother and me to a hotel in Paris. We went up to the room where Rabbi Schonfeld was staying. His accommodations were the absolute lap of luxury! At least so it seemed to us at the time. He was no longer affiliated with the orphanage by then. The project had kind of wrapped up by that time.

My father did not have a job. He had a surviving brother, Abraham Unger, who had moved to London, England, before the war so my parents decided to send my brother and me to England until they could get themselves established. My parents were not allowed to immigrate to England but my brother and I were. We, my father, brother, and I, had to go to the British Embassy in Paris. There were young secretaries at the reception of the embassy. In Poland there is a tradition that men, particularly older men, will kiss the hand of a woman. You still see it today. When we were applying for permission to go to England, my father wanted me to kiss the hand of the secretary because, in his mind, this would show that we were polite and it would enhance our chance of obtaining papers for England. I resented that, being forced to kiss the hand of that secretary in the embassy. It was ridiculous because, among other things, she was the receptionist. But I did it. I do not recall ever defying my father or mother openly. If I were going to do something that they disapproved of I would do it secretly.

My brother and I travelled alone to England. This time I knew I would see my parents again. We sailed across from Calais and I remember seeing the White Cliffs of Dover. We were met by my aunt. Her name was Esther. She was Abraham's second wife. He left Poland—I don't know when— but his first wife and children were left behind and they perished in the Holocaust. Abraham and Esther lived at thirty-two Higham Station Avenue, in Chingford, north London. My aunt and uncle owned a house and my uncle had a clothing factory in Whitechapel.

Charlie and Sydney in London

When we got to England my aunt very promptly asked me what my name was. I told her Israel—or I would have said "Yisruel." My brother might have said, "He is called Srulik." Anyway, she decided that was not an appropriate English name so she said henceforth I would be called Sydney. I guess I thought that was the translation of Yisruel, and so I accepted it. I went around England as Sydney. My aunt and uncle also decided that Kalman would be called Charles. They decided that we needed English names and Israel just wouldn't do. Charlie and I stopped speaking Yiddish to one another very quickly and learned English. Like many of my friends who were survivors, we felt that Yiddish was a ghetto language. We were ashamed to speak it. We considered Hebrew to be the language of the modern, proud generations of

Jews. As an adult I realized that there was a huge, rich culture of Yiddish and there was also much to be proud of. I spoke Yiddish for many years afterwards with my parents.

In England I was very lonely. My aunt and uncle were in their mid-fifties, had no children, and were not particularly interested in having my brother and me come and live with them. They agreed only because my parents begged them to take us.

Rationing was in force in England. In the back of my uncle and aunt's house was a small yard, and they had chickens that laid eggs. With the rationing you could make substitutions, so they substituted eggs for cheese. In the living room there was a cupboard and it was locked and that is where they kept the cheese. It was almost a ritual. Every month they would lock a chunk of cheese in the cupboard. At the end of the month the cheese would be stale and they would throw it out and put a fresh chunk in the cupboard. I never got to eat any of that cheese. My brother may have raided the cupboard. There were also sardines in the cupboard in cans, Brisling sardines, from Norway. They were very small and very delicious. We seldom got any.

I had no toys. My aunt and uncle did not offer to buy me any and I did not ask or expect them to give me any. In those days in London when you took the bus you bought a ticket for the distance that you travelled, so you could get a one-penny ticket or two- or three-penny ticket—they were colour-coded. I used to collect those tickets and sort them by denomination. Those tickets became my toys.

Charlie and I went to different schools. School was also difficult even though I learned English very fast. Every morning there was an assembly and we all had to sit on the floor in a big hall. The headmaster would give a lecture about righteousness and Christianity and then we had to pray. The headmaster lead the prayer and we all had to bow our heads and repeat the prayer after him. For me praying to Jesus was idol worship, a grave sin, so under my breath I would mumble curses in Yiddish or Polish so as not to commit idol worship.

During class, I had to urinate frequently and I dreaded asking the teachers to be excused, I did not want the other kids to look at me and I did not want the teachers to think that I was making it up just to get out of class. One time I put up my hand and said, "Sir, may I be excused?" That was the protocol. The teacher would not allow me to leave and shortly thereafter I wet myself. When the teacher saw a trickle of liquid under my chair he allowed me to leave.

I was caned severely once. When we went out to the playground for recess we had to line up two by two to re-enter the school. One time the teacher said that the next boy who stepped out of line would be caned.

Someone jostled me and I was pushed out of line—not maliciously, just like kids do—so I was caned on both hands. The procedure was that you had to go to the headmaster's office and pick up the register for caning and the cane. The register recorded that you were being caned and what the offence was. Then you had to take these to the teacher. You stood in front of the class with your hands outstretched, palms up, and got whacked several times across the palms. I was caned so severely that my hands swelled up.

My brother found out that I had been caned and he told my aunt and uncle—not out of sympathy but sort of squealing on me that I had done something bad and had been caned. My aunt and uncle looked at my hands and saw that they were swollen. They were annoyed with the school, so they went and protested to the headmaster that I had been caned to the point that my hands were swollen. The headmaster called me in and looked at my hands and he said, "That's just dirt on your hands. That's nothing."

The worst incident of all during my time in England was when I was caught stealing candy at the corner store at the end of our street. That's where we bought our pop. They used to mix soda and beer and call it a shandy. My aunt would send me, or sometimes my brother, to get the pop. There was candy, something like Pez candy, on the countertop and all the kids on the street talked about the fact that when the clerk went to get something at the back of the store, they would help themselves to the candy, so I decided to do the same thing. One day I went in and asked for some soda and when the storekeeper went in back, I picked up a candy. There was a man who had come in after me. Somehow I got the giggles because I had taken the candy. The storekeeper came out with the pop and asked, "Why are you giggling?" and I just kept on giggling. "He is laughing because he just stole some candy," the man behind me said. I gave the candy back. I was mortified that I had been caught. I was so embarrassed and ashamed and convinced that it was such a grievous act that I would not go back to that store—ever. I was a thief and I had been caught.

Now I had a very serious problem because my aunt did not know about this and I did not want her to know. So every time she sent me for pop I had to get my brother to go for me. He would do it, but now I was even more in his debt because this was a huge favour he was doing me. And that had some consequences. My brother could always get me to do anything he wanted because I looked up to him and wanted his affection. Now he could expose me. He never actually threatened to tell, but I felt this extra burden. It was in my mind. Somebody knows something about me that I don't want anybody else to know.

My aunt and uncle would hang their coats on a rack as you entered the house and sometimes there was money in their pockets, loose change,

Charlie used to help himself to some of it. One day they came into our room and said they were going to search us because they were missing money. My brother jumped right up and helped them search. In so doing he hid the money! He was so proud of that. He had it in a little handkerchief all tied up. Of course I never told on him. I never even considered that I had anything on him.

When we were in England I would have done anything to buy his affection. Sometimes he was nice to me, other times he wasn't. Some of the time I was a nuisance to him. He was the person who I felt closest to. I did not feel close to my uncle and aunt ever. I wanted to be close to my brother. I wanted his affection desperately. In France, in the orphanage, he became my father and mother replacement. He was the one that I looked to for everything. In England it was even worse. That persisted for a long time.

Charlie was quite the entrepreneur and he often got me in on his schemes. One such scheme involved my lunch money. Lunch for a whole week at school was two shillings; at recess you received a free pint of milk. My aunt and uncle would give me two shillings. My brother asked me to give him my lunch money because he said we were going to run away from England. We were going to become stowaways on a ship heading for America. Neither of us was happy with life in the United Kingdom. He went down to the docks to look over the ships and he even met some American sailors on the merchant ships. Charlie was going to save up the lunch money for both of us so we would have some when we got to the United States. So I gave him my lunch money—he did not have to try very hard to convince me to do so. I did most anything he wanted. But that meant I had to lie to the teacher and to my aunt and uncle. Every Sunday night I told my aunt that I was going to have lunch at school and she gave me two shillings and every Monday morning I would tell the teacher that I was not having lunch and gave the money to Charlie. During the lunch break I walked the streets instead. I'm not sure what he really did with the money—went out with friends, smoked, stuff like that. My brother was very tough. For my brother, to do something semi-legal was a joy. Then the lunch money scheme was discovered. Eventually my aunt came looking for me one lunch hour and found out that I had been lying. So I was punished by both the school and my aunt and uncle. I did not say what I had done with my two shillings.

My aunt and uncle insisted that Charlie and I do everything together. But Charlie was four years older—I was ten and he was fourteen. He was interested in things that I was not yet ready for, like smoking and girls. Young teenagers who are beginning to experiment with things don't have much time for ten-year-old kids.

Every Saturday evening my aunt and uncle gave us sixpence each for the cinema on the condition that my brother would take me along. He was old enough to get in without an adult. There would be a lot of kids hanging around the movie theatre and if they saw a single man going in they would ask, "Sir, will you buy me a ticket?" Sometimes my brother would take me, but sometimes he wanted to be with his friends and he did not want a ten-year-old hanging around. The way he solved that problem was that he gave me a few blows and told me to go home. In movie theatres at that time, every second seat had an ashtray on the back of the seat in front of you. That's what my brother was doing when he went to the movies and he did not want me around when he was smoking. He didn't take my sixpence, though, so then I might hang around and see if I could get someone to buy me a ticket. I remember watching Hopalong Cassidy and Laurel and Hardy. American cowboy movies were thrilling to me. Sometimes on my way home from school I would pretend I was a cowboy and hop along like on a horse all the way home.

I must have made some friends in England because once I was invited to a birthday party. My brother was supposed to take me there but he forgot or had better things to do, so I missed the party. I went to the street where I thought the party might be and listened outside houses to see if I could hear party noises, but I couldn't find it. The next day the boy who had invited me to the party brought me a carton of cookies—it looked like a milk carton. I was super-delighted with the cookies. At recess we had a pint of milk, so I had a cookie or two with my milk. Then I went home and my brother came along with a friend of his. His friend was called Spiv, which is not a name, really, but meant something like a slick operator. I showed them my carton of cookies. My brother wanted some and I offered them both a cookie. My brother wanted more, so he grabbed the carton and hit me. I fell down in the front yard. He took the carton, helped himself and Spiv, and then threw it back to me.

I don't know if the problems with my brother were as big as they seemed at the time or if it was just the whole circumstance in England. There was a big difference in our ages, and because of my aunt and uncle he was stuck with me at times. I believe that the Holocaust affected Charlie far, far worse than it affected me, simply because he was four years older and had to be much more aware of what was going on than I was. I was fortunate in that I was very young during the Holocaust and therefore probably did not fully understand what was happening and so was not affected as badly as an older person. If one had to go through the Holocaust then it was lucky to be saved rather than trying to save oneself.

The second year we were in England Charlie stopped going to school and started working in my uncle's clothing factory in Whitechapel. At that time in England it was decided at a very early age, like twelve or fourteen, whether you would go on with your education or not. If you were not continuing with school, you went to work. Anyway, I would arrive back from school first and my aunt, uncle, and brother would only get home several hours later. So I was home all by myself and in the winter, when it became dark early, I would sit in the little room by the kitchen and listen to the radio and there used to be scary programs. If I needed to go upstairs to the bathroom I became very frightened. I would try to hold it as long as possible. There were electric lights, but even to get to the light switch was scary. I imagined ghosts. Ultimately, when I could not stand it any longer, I would run upstairs as fast as I could, take a quick pee and run back downstairs ... and get frightened all over again.

There were some pleasant things in London too. I went to a synagogue near our home for Jewish studies after school and I enjoyed translating the weekly portion of the Torah from Hebrew to English. I did quite well in the sense that the teacher would read a sentence and ask what it meant and I was able to figure it out. Israel was founded as a state on 14 May 1948. I was ten years old at the time. I don't recall it being celebrated in my uncle and aunt's home. I do recall being very thrilled. The idea of Israel had always been exciting for me—I believe we even talked about it in the hideout.

My aunt and uncle were not very observant. I don't remember much about going to services on Shabbat when we lived with them.

I think my aunt and uncle expected my brother and me to entertain ourselves. There were stock-car races near where we lived and we went to those a few times, just the two of us. Stock cars were regular cars souped up for racing—they drove around an oval racetrack. We didn't bet on the cars; we just went to watch.

Things American were very popular and in school they started to teach us to play baseball. I was quite good at it, though I didn't have a glove. Once, I went to France to visit my parents and when I got back, teams had been chosen. I was left out because I had been away. That was the end of my baseball career. In the streets we played cricket just as kids play baseball in Canada or in the United States. It was an imitation game because we did not have all the real bats and wickets. I certainly enjoyed it when we could go to Paris to visit my parents. They never came to England while we were there. They did not have the financial resources and would not have been able to get visas.

On one of these trips to Paris we learned that my father had been arrested. He had gone off to Belgium to see if his brother-in-law Yakov could help us in any way. Yakov Fisch was my mother's brother, her only sibling to survive. He survived by fleeing to Switzerland. At the time the Swiss had a law that

45

stated that if they caught you within twelve kilometres of the Swiss border they sent you back, but if you were further in than that they allowed you to stay.

Yakov lived in Antwerp. But my father did not have the proper papers for Belgium. When he got to the train station in Antwerp, Yakov was not there to meet him, so he took a taxi and the taxi driver, recognizing that my father was a foreigner, took him to the police station, where he was arrested and jailed for smuggling himself into Belgium. My father was in jail in Belgium for about a month. He was suspected of being a member of the *Lehi*, or the Stern Gang. The *Lehi* (which stands for *Lohamei Herut Israel*, or Fighters for the Freedom of Israel) were a group agitating to

Israel's uncle, Yakov Fisch, and his wife, Rachel, at the coast of Belgium, pre-war. (Israel Unger collection)

get the British out of Palestine so as to allow unrestricted immigration of Jews to Palestine. It was founded by a man named Stern in the British Mandate for Palestine, so the authorities called the group, derogatorily, the Stern Gang. By this time the *Lehi* was no longer operating, but obviously they were still looking for its members abroad. So my father was interrogated several times, including by the British. He was amazed that the British interrogator, who was Gentile, spoke Yiddish! When they were satisfied that he was not a member of the Stern Gang he was released and deported back to France.

At school, I enjoyed doing math, particularly converting pence into shillings and pounds. There were problems like: a boy has eight hundred and fifty-six pence, how many, pounds, shillings, and pence does that make? So you had to divide by twelve to get the number of shillings and the remainder was the number of pence, and then divide the number of shillings by twenty to get the number of pounds and the remainder was the number of shillings. The answer would then be three pounds, eleven shillings, and four pence. I was good at it.

And there was Jockey. My aunt had a little black mongrel dog I liked enormously. It was the first and only time I had a pet as a child. He was possibly my best friend in England. I played with him a lot. He was small, about the size of a large cat.

One time I had tonsillitis and ended up in a hospital for about a week. I didn't have my tonsils out—I believe I was treated with penicillin. It was my first ever stay in a hospital. I was even more lonely than usual, and when I got back home the thing that delighted me the most was Jockey. We were in England for about a year when Jockey was run over by a bicycle. My aunt, brother and I took him to a vet. Jockey could no longer walk at that point. The vet took him to an inner room and told us that Jockey could not be saved and would have to be put to sleep. We kind of looked through a door and Jockey was on a table and looked at us with a plaintive, sad look. We had to leave. I can still picture the look in Jockey's eyes when we left. It was as if he was saying, "Don't leave me." As if he knew what was going to happen. We left and I was heartbroken. I still feel sick about having to give that dog in to be put down and that last look. Today there is a proper way to do such things; you give them the first little shot and you can stroke them. On top of every thing else I was bitterly lonely. I missed Jockey a great deal. Marlene has told me that when we got together, after I told her I was born in Poland, the next thing I told her about was Jockey.

To me, my aunt and uncle's house was enormous because I was coming from that one room in Paris. There was an upstairs and a downstairs. There were two bedrooms upstairs and a bathroom. My brother and I shared a double bed in one bedroom and my aunt and uncle had the other one. Downstairs there was a dining room and a small kitchen and a small room off the kitchen where you ate if you were not entertaining. In 1967 I went back to London. My aunt and uncle were dead by then. I went back to thirty-two Higham Station Avenue and saw that in reality it was a very tiny house on a tiny piece of land.

My uncle and aunt had a gramophone. It was a record player that you wound up by hand. They would buy a record and play it and that was entertainment. Danny Kaye, the Jewish American comedian and singer, was one of the records they played. Occasionally they had guests for dinner and sometimes they were invited to other people's homes. When they entertained they served fish—a big flat round fish about the size of a plate—a flounder, I believe. When they were invited out they took us with them.

I started to develop an interest in girls when I was eleven or so. In school we had mixed classes. There was one girl who used to talk to me and once she told me that someone was following her. She sort of wanted me to act as a detective. That was my first contact with a girl—as a detective!

My uncle and aunt opened a bank account for my brother and me and they gave us a half a crown every week. We were not allowed to do anything with that money other than to deposit it. At that time in England small accounts were handled by the post office, so every week we had to deposit that money. Going to a movie cost six pence, so half a crown would have been thirty pence—the equivalent of about ten dollars today. I'm not sure what happened to my savings after we went back to France. I imagine that either my aunt and uncle or Charlie withdrew it. Or, who knows, possibly it is still there today.

I don't think my aunt and uncle were unkind, it is just that they did not understand kids. I had the feeling they did not want me. I was foisted upon them. Here was a woman who had never had children herself. She would have been in her mid- to late forties or older and my uncle would have been about fifty-two at the time. There were eight siblings in my father's family and Abraham was born in the 1897. Take a couple in their fifties with no children and spring a couple of young kids on them who they didn't particularly want but took in because the brother was in distress. My uncle had the clothing factory and they were very busy with that. They were not uncaring people, they just didn't know about the needs of a ten-year-old.

Actually my aunt was Abraham's third wife, not his second—we found that out by chance. One day my brother and I were home alone and there was a knock on the door and we answered it. There was a woman standing there. "I'm your aunt," she said. "You have to be mistaken. We have an aunt. You have the wrong house." She told us she was my uncle's first wife in England. It was a shock to us. We were just flummoxed. It would have been as if someone today would tell you your mother is not your mother. That is how strange the concept of divorce was to us. We did not know whether we should tell my uncle about this or not. Ultimately we told him there was a woman here who said she was his wife.

I am not sure why he divorced his first wife in England. He had this small shop in Whitechapel—a shop meant a small factory. He employed about sixteen people to make men's clothes. I think Esther had a bit of money and she helped him start his shop. Maybe that is why he switched wives. Esther worked at the shop.

My father used to tell an amusing story about Abraham from the time when he lived in Poland. At that time, apparently, when you went from Poland to Hungary you could use Polish money there. At the border officials stamped the actual bills and there was a charge for stamping them. My uncle Abraham went into the business of stamping people's money and charging less than the Polish authorities. It was definitely illegal. The Polish authorities found out about that and were after him and that's what caused him to go to England. He got out of Poland and therefore he lived. That illegal activity saved his life.

Back to Paris: Quartier Père Lachaise

In 1949, after about a year and a half in London, my father had found work and my parents' financial position had improved, so they brought me back to Paris. They could afford to have one child back with them, so naturally they took the younger one. Charlie stayed on in London for about another year. I was glad to leave England.

By the time I was back with my parents, they were unfamiliar to me. I had forgotten Yiddish and I could not communicate with them. My brother's birthday had been in early January and I arrived back in France shortly after this. I tried to tell my mother that he had just had his birthday and I could not make her understand. That changed rapidly. Over the years, I learned languages and forgot them and learned them again. Back in Paris everything seemed more normal. I was no longer Sydney, I was Israel again, pronounced the French way.

We lived at forty rue des Amandiers—where the famous cemetery is, in the *vingtième arrondissement*—the twentieth district, a working-class district. The *métro* station was also called Père Lachaise. It was a real step up compared to how we had lived before in Paris. But actually it was also very tiny. Years later I took Marlene's parents to Paris and showed them the house. Marlene's mother cried when she saw the poor circumstances in which we had lived.

There were two tiny rooms. One was a bedroom, the other was a living room and there was a sliver of a kitchen, almost like a hallway. If one person was standing in the kitchen, another could not get by. There was a sink and we would use it for washing ourselves as well as the cleaning dishes. There was no private bathroom—the toilet was down the hall and common for all tenants. There was no flush toilet but a hole in the floor and a couple of footmarks in front of the hole. You brought your own paper, which was newspaper. My mother would pre-rip the paper on Fridays so on Shabbat she would not have to tear it. That continued throughout her life, though in Canada she used regular toilet paper. For Shabbat she would use the variety that came in sheets like tissues. For bathing, my parents sent me to a communal bathhouse once a week on Friday. My mother gave me the money and fresh laundry and I went to the public bathhouse for a shower. At the time lots of people did not have a shower or tub at home.

My mother cooked excellent meals in this tiny kitchen. I was glad to be back with my parents. It felt more relaxed, more normal. It had not been a happy situation in England, and above all else I was relieved to get out of the business of having Charlie buy the soda at the grocery store for me.

It did not seem to bother Charlie to be left behind. He was learning a trade. My father's ambition for Charlie was that he should learn a trade and become a clothing designer. He started as a presser in my uncle's shop. Pressing at that time was done by taking a heavy iron, heating it in an oven, and then you had to wrap the wooden handle with cloth to use it. The notion was that you had to learn everything about tailoring as a start for designing. He enrolled in evening classes at a design school as well and went for about a year.

My father now worked at a furrier in Paris, cutting paw. When fur arrives at the furrier it is in irregular shapes. It then has to be trimmed so the pieces can be sewn to make a coat or a wrap. Cutting paw was cutting fur so that it can be sewn together. That skill came in useful, as he ended up doing that same job in Montreal too as a second job.

I went to a Jewish school, École Yabne, near by the *métro* station Censier Daubenton. I made friends. Life was looking up. There was a boy I particularly chummed around with called Natan Grinbaum. He was a tall, handsome fellow and he was wealthy or what I considered wealthy at the time. He was undoubtedly a child of survivors but probably from Western Europe. We were in the same class at school. I looked to be around people who were important and I think this was true for this kid. He stood out. He was the big, handsome guy in school so I hoped maybe some of that would rub off on me. There was another reason why I chummed with him. In Paris at the time in city squares they had a kind of mini-carnival and one of the rides was electric bumper cars. You paid fifty francs and you could ride for a few minutes and bump into other people's bumper cars. I used to walk by those things and look at them forever. I never had the money to actually have a ride. If I went with Natan, then occasionally he would pay for a bumper car and I would ride with him. Natan still lives in Paris, or he did a few years ago, because when I visited my cousin in Antwerp they talked about Natan.

There was another boy named Jacques, a tall blond girl named Hessa, and a set of twins who came to the school from England as well. I would try to show off in front of girls. In the schoolyard I would run around showing how macho I was. I was a member of a Zionist organization. There were girls there too. At an early age I started appreciating girls. I recall that a couple of times I walked with girls from the school, not holding hands but just walking with them. I didn't get to hold hands till Montreal.

I visited the Père Lachaise graveyard on a few occasions. The grave that I remember in particular was that of Chopin. It is really very modest. I was impressed with Chopin, not because of his Polish roots but because of his

Israel as a boy of eleven or twelve in Paris, 1949 or 1950. (Israel Unger collection)

great achievements in music. Another tomb that impressed me was of a husband and wife; she was Jewish, he was a Gentile. The inscription spoke of their everlasting love. Decades later when I visited Paris with my daughters, Père Lachaise cemetery was one of the places I took them to see. So it must have made an impression on me.

In 1950 Charlie returned to France. He was now sixteen and I was twelve. By that time he could take a bolt of cloth and turn it in to a coat! He did this work when he went to Canada as well. Starting with a pattern, he would mark it out on the cloth, cut the cloth, sew it, and press the finished garment. He made a gabardine coat for me.

Because my uncle in England was not observant, no one had pushed my brother towards religion for those two years. At that age you are beginning to sample the world and what it has to offer: cigarettes, movies, and perhaps girls. He had done all that in England. I still very much looked up to him.

I have a very positive story about my brother. One day as we were walking home from the *métro* station, a group of four young men jostled us as we walked by. My brother immediately confronted them, raised his fists, and said in English: "Do you want to fight!" They all declined and said, "Ce n'était pas moi, c'était lui"—it wasn't me who did it, he did it! I was so proud of Charlie. He was a huge hero in my eyes.

On a negative side, for some reason I got into a squabble with a kid of my age in the courtyard of the building we lived in. He called me a "sale juif," a dirty Jew, so I called him a "sale français," a dirty Frenchman. When my father found out about this episode he insisted that I go and apologize to the parents of that boy for fear that they would make trouble for us. We were still *sans pays* or "stateless" in France. My father was afraid of repercussions. Fortunately we did not know where that boy lived, so I did not have to go through with the apology.

If you were stateless in France, periodically you had to renew your permission to stay in the country. First they gave you six weeks, then three months, then six months, then a year. We had actually made it to the point where my parents had a three-year permission to stay—not on your way to citizenship but at least permission to stay. The other thing that you had to get was permission to work. Obviously one without the other was useless. To get permission to work you had to have your potential employer provide a written statement saying that they could not employ a Frenchman in your place. Employers would provide that if you agreed to work for lower wages than a Frenchman. These permits were issued in the central police station in Paris. This was a very important thing and every time my parents needed to get their permits renewed it was a crisis. My father would go to the synagogue beforehand and recite special prayers so that he would get the permits. He wanted God to be at his side. That is why my father was in such a panic when I had the fight with that boy. He was horrified that the incident had taken place. Imagine the extension of that thinking. What if a Frenchman complains about me? They might kick us out of the country!

I may confuse what happened during my first time in Paris and my second time. I recall seeing the Eiffel Tower and the Champs-Élysées. One time my father took my brother and me to the zoo. One time only. There was a colony of monkeys—that was my favourite.

In France I read the newspapers and could tell my parents what was going on. We did not have a radio but there was *Le Monde* or *Le Figaro* or *France Soir*. There were five editions from morning to evening, and when the Korean War broke out in 1950 we would buy every edition. We were worried about the world situation. We knew what the world situation could do to us. My parents were afraid the Korean War was a prelude to another world war in the same way the Spanish Civil War had been a prelude to the Second World War. My brother was now sixteen and the French were fighting in Algeria and in Vietnam and he was getting close to draft age. My parents did not want Charlie to be drafted. They were not only motivated to get away from France—they were motivated to get away from Europe.

My father had foresight and knew when to take risks. He left Ryglice and his family to go to Tarnow. Then he went into business and somehow managed to get the money to start a bakery, go into business with Dagnan, acquire real estate, go into winemaking, and so forth. Then when we were forced to live in the Tarnow ghetto he took that huge risk of refusing to join the Jewish police when the Gestapo tried to force him to do so with violence. In terms of saving his own life, it was more of a risk to stay with his wife and kids than to try to escape the ghetto and join the partisans. It was certainly a risk going into hiding rather than staying put and hoping for the best. Then, the whole time in hiding, sneaking out to get food and water was very risky. After the war he sent his children off with a group of Jewish orphans and smuggled himself and my mother out of Poland. He took a risk again smuggling himself to Belgium to seek help from my uncle in Antwerp. Obviously some of these risks my father was compelled to take, but others were calculated risks that worked out. And now he was going to take another risk to immigrate to Canada, not knowing the language or culture and not having any marketable skills.

My parents' preferred destination was the United States, but we were on the Polish quota and at that time they were accepting people who had applied from Poland in the 1930s. The idea of going to Canada came fairly late. My mother found out she had a cousin in Montreal, a man by the name of Leon Margulies, and he agreed to sponsor us. I think we only had to wait about six months after applying, to immigrate to Canada. Everyone had to pass a medical exam and we were worried that my mother would not pass. She had a calcium deficiency after the war and had been given some injections for it. The exam involved giving a blood sample. After applying for the visas things went quickly.

Visions of Canada: Mounties, Snow, and Sheepskin

I had been having a normal life in France. I was with my parents, I was going to École Yabne. I had made friends and I was becoming interested in girls. We were still very poor, but conditions were improving. Then one time at the Zionist organization they were talking about the phenomenon of Jews immigrating to Canada. I thought about it and I thought: We are the ones being talked about. There were many like us.

I had mythic, romantic visions of Canada. It was a big country. It was a tough country. It was the land of snow and cold. At the time there was a coat in France that they called a *Canadienne*. It was leather with sheepskin on the inside like the Second World War pilots used to wear. I had one of those coats and I had heroic images of Canada in my mind—the immensity of the land. I thought it was going to be modern, huge, tough like the Canadian soldiers, the Mounties. I viewed Canada very positively. I was very excited.

My parents of course were anxious about the new country. What were we going to do? How were we going to live? What jobs would they get? Our papers came through early in 1951.

Our relatives from Belgium came to Paris to see us off. There was my uncle Yakov from Antwerp. He came with my cousin Renée and one of his sons, Hirsh. The other boy was called Kalman, like my brother. The youngest, Hirsh, is virtually identical to me in age. They spent a few days in Paris with us. Charlie was sixteen and Renée was about the same age. This was the first time I met my cousins. I felt a lot of affection for them, as did Charlie. I would not see them again for many years, but when I did make contact again I found Renée to be the extraordinarily nice person I remembered. She married an extraordinarily nice man—a Holocaust survivor who made his way to Antwerp after the war. He became one of the most successful diamond dealers there and a pillar of the Belgian Jewish community. I also have had contact with Hirsch and Kalman over the years.

My father was leaving behind his only surviving sibling in London. Abraham left Poland before the war and they never saw each other after that. My father never got to England. Travel was expensive and with visas and whatnot, it was not easy. There was quite an age difference between them. Abraham was a bit of a black sheep because of the money stamping scheme and having the Polish authorities after him. My mother too was leaving her only remaining brother, Yakov, in Antwerp. They had not communicated much in Europe. We did not have a phone. They did write to one another. It seems to me that leaving her brother behind in Europe would not have been dominant on her mind. Given the awful things that my parents experienced in their lives, leaving a relative behind would not have been a huge thing. Still, Yakov was her closest living relative and she did not know, or perhaps even expect, to ever see him again.

We sailed from Le Havre, France, for Halifax, Nova Scotia, shortly before my thirteenth birthday, when I would have my *bar mitzvah,* so I had a *bar mitzvah* suit packed. I believe we had our bedding. We each had a Swiss watch, a Tissot or a Doxa, and we had some French perfume, Chanel No. 5. That was a way to take valuables with you—they were for resale. Though I did get to keep my watch—a Tissot. I believe my parents had their original wedding rings. They had a valuable diamond ring that they may have acquired from Yakov as part of their savings. Years later, that ring was stolen from my father on a bus in Montreal. My mother's main worry was that my father would make himself sick grieving over the loss of that ring. My parents also had a genuine fifty-piece silver cutlery set—fifty pieces! I'm not sure where they got it—they had certainly not brought it with them from Poland. We only had a few personal possessions from Poland: the matzo bag embroidered by my mother, some monogrammed sheets, and the photos we had with us in hiding.

The boat was the *S.S.* (for steamship) *Goya*, a former German cargo ship, captured during the war and allocated to the Norwegians. There were huge cabins that could hold up to fifty people sleeping in bunk beds. There was a cabin for men and one for women. My father, brother, and I slept in one cabin. I was on a top bunk. My mother slept in another and we would see her during the day. There was a dining hall on the ship but it smelled awful, like cooking grease and diesel oil. We did not eat any of the food on the boat because it was not kosher. My parents had brought along some salami, a great big long beef salami. And we had bread and tea—that was it.

The trip was about eight days and somewhere in the middle there was a bad storm. I was seasick for a day or so. Everyone was, most people even worse than I. The boat would be on the crest of a wave and looking down it seemed like you were on top of a mountain of water, then the boat would be on the bottom of the wave and looking up, all you could see was a huge wall of water all around. It looked as if it were going to crash in on us.

Charlie worked in the kitchen on the boat and when he wasn't doing that we did some exploring. It was a boat full of immigrants, not a tourist boat. There were some other Jews on board. My father tried to get together a *minyan*—the ten adult males you need for a prayer service. He must have approached men who spoke Yiddish. One man told him, "Sorry, I just recently converted to Christianity." I don't know if he got his *minyan* or not.

Part Three

Canadian Through and Through

An Airplane, a Stevedore, and His Plymouth: Arriving at Pier 21

I was so excited to spot land. As we approached Halifax the boat slowed down, the waves got smaller. We were arriving at the now famous Pier 21— the Ellis Island of Canada. One of the first things Canadian that I saw was a Canadian airplane that flew over the ship, circled it, and headed back to land. It was not a commercial aircraft, so we assumed it was an air force plane checking us out. We figured they had to go and have a look at any ship coming in. When we landed there were some workers on the dock. I shouted down from the boat to them. One longshoreman talked to me. There were several cars nearby and I learned that one of those cars belonged to a longshoreman. It was a black Plymouth and this stevedore said it was his. New cars were rare in Europe at the time so I thought: What a country where stevedores own cars!

The airplane, the stevedore with his Plymouth ... I didn't notice anything else. The only thing that mattered was getting ashore and being in Canada. We arrived about midday on a Friday. The immigration process at Pier 21 in Halifax must have gone fast, as I would remember something special about it if it had taken a long time or if there were problems. It was a simple and swift process. My parents had zero English and their French would have been very weak. I had forgotten my English but not totally, so Charlie and I translated for our parents.

I have never really tried to learn languages. I speak Yiddish. I have a little German, though if I tried to communicate in German people would probably recognize that most of my German is Yiddish. My Polish is meager. I had no interest in maintaining it. I can get by in Hebrew. I speak French and English, but that was not always so. When I returned to France from London as a child I could speak English but not French. Then I learned French and lost

57

my English. When I arrived in Canada I had to relearn English. As an adult I made an effort to relearn French.

So there we stood, translating for our parents and filling out the immigration forms. For this book project, I requested a copy of my arrival document from Pier 21. It says I was born in Poland and that we sailed from Le Havre, France, on the *Goya*, 8 February 1951. We landed in Halifax on 16 February 1951. It states that I was twelve, my brother sixteen, father forty-four, and mother forty-three. Actually they were forty-nine and forty-eight, so I can only speculate that they lied about their ages in order to increase their chances of being accepted as immigrants. This might have happened already when filling out forms in France. The document also says that our destination was to a "Father Cousin" Mr. Leon Margulies, 1117 St. Catherine Street, Montreal. He was actually my mother's cousin, so maybe there was a hitch in the translation.

The Ungers' immigration document, saying they sailed with the *Goya* in 1951. (Israel Unger collection)

It was Friday afternoon when we finished with the immigration process. Our destination was Montreal, but we had to stop in Halifax because it was Shabbat and my parents would not travel on Shabbat. Members of the Jewish community in Halifax helped us find a hotel to stay in overnight. It was not far from the railroad station. The hotel was not plush—not the Lord Nelson. It was a small thing, one room, but for us it was excellent. It may have been on Quinpool Road, because the first time I went back to Halifax that street was the only one that was familiar to me. Near the hotel I saw something I had never seen before—parking meters. I'm not sure that I knew what they were, but they were part of this huge adventure. A Plymouth and a parking meter are two images from the time of my arrival. In the late forties and very early fifties cars in the United States and Canada underwent a huge styling change. The Plymouth was of the new style. You did not see that in France. I was interested in cars in France as well, American cars were the rage. Natan, the boy I hung around with in Paris, told me that the ultimate in cars was a Cadillac. One day in France I saw a Cadillac; I read the name on the car. I told Natan that I had seen a Cadillac and he asked what year? I didn't know that there was such a thing as model years.

It was Saturday evening when we boarded a train for Montreal. It was after dark. I fell asleep on a bench and sometime during the night I was woken up by three men who had just boarded and needed to sit down. They were polite and we tried to communicate, but at that time my English was poor. As a kind of memento, I gave each of them a two-franc coin. At that time the exchange rate was about four hundred francs to a dollar. They each gave me a quarter. When I got to Montreal I realized how much they had given me! A Coke at the time was five cents and in some stores you could get it for three cents. A fudgesicle was five cents and a hot dog was five cents. That was a great exchange!

We were on a CN (Canadian National) train and it went through New Brunswick. According to Marlene, we passed between Chipman and Minto, a place called The Ridge, which is eight kilometres from Minto. Marlene, who is from Minto, has said many times since that had she known, she would have gone to the train crossing and shouted to me: "Israel you are coming back in eight years and we are going to be married!"

Home à la Mordecai Richler

We arrived in Montreal and were met at the train station by my mother's cousin, Leon Margulies. He had arranged for us to live in a shared apartment and he took us straight there. Although we only saw him infrequently after that, he was always ready to help if called upon. He had found us a place to live, subletting from a couple in an apartment on Jeanne-Mance Street. A relative of this couple arrived in Montreal a few months later, and they needed the room. So, soon after, we moved to another apartment, on Hutchinson Street, close to St-Viateur on the 5300 block, and sublet two rooms from another couple, the Landers. Nusha and Aaron Lander were also recent immigrants. They were also survivors, both from Lodz. Mr. Lander had run away to the Soviet Union and enlisted in the army. Mrs. Lander had lived on false Christian papers. They met when he returned with the Soviet army. He said that when he returned to his hometown and house, his parents, everyone was gone, murdered by the Nazis.

We lived in the Jewish part of Montreal: Park Avenue and Bernard Street, St-Viateur, Fairmont, Esplanade, St. Urbain, Waverly, Laurier, and St. Joseph. These were the streets we lived and worked on and where I went to school. It is officially the northwestern section of The Plateau in Montreal, but we simply knew it as the new Jewish immigrant neighbourhood. There was a wealthier Jewish neighbourhood to the west, in Outremont, where Jews who were born in Canada or had come to the country before the war lived. Then there were the poorer Jews who lived between Park Avenue and St. Lawrence and were mostly postwar immigrants. We were part of the immigrant group.

I think that immigrants tend to move to areas where other immigrants live because they share a similar experience and speak a common language. Because life was not easy, the main thing for us was to concentrate on the present and the future. That is why we never dealt with the past.

One of my first impressions of Montreal that was different from Paris, was that there were staircases outside the house that led to people's apartments. The first house where we lived had three floors and there was a winding outdoor wrought-iron staircase. That was common in that section of Montreal. What was also different was milk being delivered to your door. You left the empty bottles out and a guy with a horse and wagon delivered fresh milk in glass bottles.

When I arrived in Canada I was still wearing those type of European boy's pants which were buckled at the calf. They were called knickerbockers and were like golf pants. One of the first things I did was to unfasten the part on the leg of my pants that went around the calf. I wanted to try to make them look like regular pants. I did not want to be recognized as an immigrant, but I did not have the funds to buy long trousers. Many in the neighbourhood were immigrants as well. My father tried to get any work he could to supplement his income. He never really got into business again as in Poland. He was nearly fifty when we came to Canada, but the important difference was that in Poland he knew the language, he knew the customs, and he was familiar with the culture. What he wanted to do in Canada was start a winery. They actually talked about that, but it was illegal. It was illegal in Poland as well, but that had not stopped him.

My father and mother were very poor when we came to Canada. That is why for the first few years we could not afford to have our own apartment. The apartment was on the ground floor of a three-storey apartment house. We rented two bedrooms and shared the kitchen and bathroom with the Landers. We ate supper at 5:30 p.m. and they ate at 6:30 p.m.

In Canada, in the beginning, it wasn't easy. My parents worried about whether they would find work and what kind. My father had a letter from a man he worked for in Paris to that fellow's relative in Montreal saying that David Unger was a good worker and you should hire him. He found work in a clothing factory sweeping floors. He earned twenty-two dollars a week. That was very little even in 1951. He swept the floor in the cutting room and then baled the remnants, which were sold to be reprocessed into new cloth.

The factory moved from St. Catherine Street and Bleury Street to the east end of Montreal. The commute to the new location was about one and a half hours. This presented a huge problem for my father, because in the wintertime he could not get home before dark on Friday and thus would violate the Sabbath. He asked his foreman to let him leave work at 3 p.m. on Fridays, offering to make up the hours on another day. He was refused. He tried to see the owner of the factory but was not allowed to. He found out which synagogue the factory owner attended, and one Saturday morning he walked across town to see the owner. It must have taken him at least two hours to walk there. I know he left at 6 a.m. to go there. He did manage to see the owner and said, "My name is David Unger. I work at your factory. I am an observant Jew. I am not asking you for charity; I just want to be able to keep my faith. I need to leave early on Fridays in the winter time and I will be pleased to make up the time evenings or Sundays." He was fired.

I see this story as proof of my father's courage, his indomitable spirit, and unshakable faith. Interestingly, my father then got a job in a wholesale dry goods store at a higher salary. All his religious problems were solved, because the owner of the dry goods store was an observant orthodox Jew who closed the store for all Jewish holidays and early on Fridays in the wintertime. Shortly after my father started to work there, he was promoted to salesperson and his salary was raised again.

My mother worked as an operator—that meant sewing in a clothing factory and she earned twenty-four dollars a week. English-speaking people in the factory called her Helen, not Hinda. At work she was afraid to leave her workplace to go to the toilet, because the foreman was checking how much time workers spent in the bathroom.

My brother managed to find work too. He did not go to school again. His education had ended in England at age fourteen and he worked from then on in. He worked in a clothing factory as a pieceworker and earned more than both my parents, about thirty-five dollars a week. A fridge in those days cost one hundred fifty dollars—seven weeks' wages for my father. Yet when my father went to the synagogue on Friday evening he took a few coins with him and put them in charity boxes.

Today in Fredericton, we have a few Jewish families from the former Soviet Union who have come to the city. The Jewish community has tried to assist them to find jobs, find apartments, enable them to send their children to a Jewish summer camp. This is what communities should do. This did not happen to us. At age thirteen I started to work, evenings and weekends and in the summer. This did not bother me. But one of the things that did disturb me, and still does, is that for the most part there was little sympathy for survivors of the Holocaust from the Jewish community in Canada that had settled here before the war.

There is a book by Franklin Bialystok, *Delayed Impact: The Holocaust and the Canadian Jewish Community*, in which he discusses the reaction of Canadian Jews to European Jews right after the Holocaust. He concludes that Canadian Jews were not able to comprehend the immensity of the atrocities of the Holocaust and so a gulf developed between the groups. That gulf did not begin to disappear until the mid-sixties. Canadian Jews were called "gehler"—yellow ones—and we new ones were known as the "greeners"— green ones. We did not mix socially. We attended different synagogues. There certainly was no effort to provide any financial assistance to the new immigrants. In some instances parents of settled Jews frowned on their sons and daughters marrying a greener.

I started going to Baron Byng High School, the one that Mordecai Richler had attended a few years earlier, although I did not know it at the time. I recall I found it very big but I don't recall much more, because after about two weeks my father took me out of that school and enrolled me in a *yeshiva*, a Jewish religious school that also had secular subjects. I had no choice about this. I would have preferred to stay at Baron Byng, but I just accepted my father's decision.

I then went to the Merkaz Hatorah Yeshiva on Saint Joseph Boulevard and Esplanade. It had been founded in 1942, when Canadian Jews were able to help save a group of European *yeshiva* students. When they arrived in Montreal they founded this *yeshiva*. When I was there its head scholar was Rabbi Pinchas Hirschsprung, a Polish Jew who had escaped the Holocaust via Cuba and Shanghai. He ended up becoming the chief rabbi of Montreal. The *yeshiva* was for boys only, of course. There were greater expectations in the *yeshiva*. You had to get there at 8 a.m. for morning prayers, then there was breakfast, then religious studies. In the afternoon we had secular studies according to the regular English curriculum. In grade nine school ended at 4:30 p.m., and in grades ten and eleven it ended at 6 p.m. so you could satisfy the regular high school curriculum. In Montreal at that time Jewish schools came under the control of the Protestant school board.

The *yeshiva* started at grade nine. I was supposed to be in grade eight. So in Baron Byng I was in grade eight for two weeks and at the *yeshiva* I was in grade nine. That is why I ended up starting university at age sixteen. On Friday we had only morning classes and it was the secular part. Then on Sunday we were expected to come for half a day for religious studies to make up for the half day we had missed on Friday.

I had geometry for the first time in my life. They were doing theorems; there were fourteen theorems. At the first exam my English was not sufficiently good to understand the questions, so I memorized the fourteen theorems and wrote them all out on the exam. I wrote too that I was not sure what the questions were but hoped the answers were somewhere in those fourteen theorems. I passed the exam. I remember discovering algebra and I loved it. I loved chemistry too. That I was good at these subjects did not occur to me as anything special.

Friday afternoon we were given passes to the YMHA (Young Men's Hebrew Association) to do sports. It was located at Mount Royal and Park. Secular and religious Jews went there. I taught myself how to swim, although we had done some swimming at the school in England. When I was fourteen I had my first full winter in Canada. To ice-skate, I thought that all one had to do was to put on a pair of skates and go! I had no idea you had to learn to do it. I bought a second-hand pair of skates and soon found out that there was a lot more to it. I saw six-year-olds who could skate better than I could. I taught myself on an outdoor rink in Outremont.

One day when we were living on Hutchinson at the Landers there was a fire in the top-floor apartment—we were on the bottom floor. The Montreal fire department came and they were very efficient putting out the fire. While one bunch was fighting the fire, another bunch came and put thick rubber mats over all the furniture in our apartment to limit water damage. This happened on a Saturday night. The whole thing was over by about midnight. My father had a part-time job after the Sabbath ended. He came home from work after the fire was already out. Water was dripping down and my brother had a great idea. He decided we should gain something from this episode for the trouble we had been put through. So he took a bunch of his clothes and trampled over them and poured water on them. The Landers and my parents followed suit. We were finished by about 3 a.m. My father then half seriously said, "Look how good God is. When he gives you a fire he does it on the weekend so you have time to make the water damage." My brother operated on the theory that the insurance company would pay for all new clothes but what they did was pay for dry cleaning. It could have been written by Richler.

Life in Canada started to resemble normality. My parents did not know and could not be expected to know what a teenage boy needed. They did not know about sports, they could not advise me about what to do in school, and I did not have a room to study in. My parents did not believe that enjoyment was something that one should try to find. They were so serious they did not laugh. My brother would occasionally talk about enjoying himself to my parents but that was a foreign concept to them. If my father heard somebody say that they wanted to enjoy themselves, he would make a sarcastic remark. "He needs to *enjoy* himself." They frowned at the notion of enjoying oneself whether it was in sports or in other activities. As far as I know my parents went to a movie just once in Montreal. I think it was true for other parents who were survivors. Most of the time at home we only talked about serious things. My parents did not enjoy humour. I love humour. Later in life humour was almost indispensable when I lectured. I used to prepare cartoons to break up my lectures. I had collections of cartoons. I believed in it and I loved doing it. The only time I would never ever use humour is in talking about the Holocaust.

I don't think that either of my parents were happy, probably because of what they went through in the Holocaust. My parents did have times of contentment and satisfaction. They enjoyed the Sabbath and Jewish festivals and holidays. They were pleased to see their children make their way in life.

When I speak publicly about my experiences of the Holocaust, I end with the liberation by the Russians. Listeners may think: Liberation, rah rah! But life was enormously difficult after that too for a long while. People who are not survivors don't understand that.

Ich hab dir gegebn lebn zwei mol—"I gave you life twice"

Somehow even at the age of thirteen I could not be religious. I wanted to feel it, to sense it, to be part of it. I would go the synagogue and pray and try to feel it. I did a lot of pretending. But it just wasn't there. It was the greatest difference and the greatest barrier between my parents and me that they were religious and from a very young age I was not. I wanted to be, but I just could not believe. I did respect my parents and I did my best to try to make them happy, but I lived in a different world from theirs. Today I think I should have tried harder and wish I would have understood them better.

I would leave the *yeshiva* and take my *yarmulke* off when I was a couple of blocks away so no one could see me. Every Saturday morning my parents insisted that I go to a synagogue, but I used to meet up with similar-minded friends and instead of going to synagogue we would play cards. We played hearts and then we graduated to poker. This would have some interesting consequences. I would be having such a good time playing cards that we would play too long and I would get home late. My parents would think I had been praying a lot that day and my father would then ask, "Where did you go to that they had such a long service?" I might have answered, "At the yeshiva." And then I would feel guilty. I did not go through the kind of reasoning that I would go through today. I am a secular Jew today.

My father was orthodox, very observant, a firm believer, as was my mother. My father wanted me to be religious and when he started to realize that I was not, he would say, "Most parents give their children life once, I gave you life twice." In Yiddish he said something like this: *Ich hab dir gegebn lebn zwei mol.* I absolutely despised that comment. I thought: But that is what fathers do, they save their children. I was not grateful to my parents for saving my life. I should have been, but I wasn't. I was alive.

I know that there are Holocaust survivors who say, "Why was I spared? Why did I survive?" That question never came to my mind. It has never ever come to my mind that there was some higher purpose in me surviving. Today I know that I survived because of my parents, but I took that as a given and I did not want to hear it from my father. That was probably the worst thing he could say to me. He was saying: Where is your gratitude? I resented that statement. It was meant to make me feel guilty and bring me in line.

Charlie was not religious either. I think it was out of convenience. It just was not very convenient to obey the Sabbath. This might not be doing Charlie justice but I would say to myself that I had come to be irreligious out of conviction and he had come to it out of convenience. He found it convenient to smoke on Saturday, to work on Saturday, to drive a car on Saturday, and to go to a Chinese restaurant and eat non-kosher food.

When I first ate non-kosher food I deliberately went to a non-kosher restaurant and made myself order the food. I did not do it because I thought this other food was tasty. I had been conditioned to eat kosher, but I did not believe the religious strictures underlying this. So I had to bring into concert my head and my conditioning. It was a deliberate act. I was about seventeen.

I think the pressure to be religious was greater on me than on Charlie, because he was already a lot older. It was my father who did it, not my mother. My mother expected my father to be the disciplinarian.

My conjecture is that because of that particular statement—*Ich hab dir gegebn lebn zwei mol*—I did not come to appreciate my parents in the way I do now. I did not appreciate then how heroic they were during the Holocaust. When my father made that statement I thought to myself, You did not do anything more that any father would have done. It was perfectly natural. I don't want to hear this. Perhaps if my father had not made such statements I would have been more interested about asking him about the Holocaust. I can't say I would have for sure, but that was an extreme turn-off for me.

Most of the kids I associated with in Montreal had more or less the same experience as I did. Most were also survivors. We looked at our parents as being old-fashioned. We did not look at them as heroes. In fact, I looked at them almost like I accuse the Montreal community of looking at them. We even mimicked their accents.

There was a boy I knew whose name was Shimshon, Samson. His parents would have been even beyond my parents in this regard. Samson had a pair of skates that he had to keep at a friend's house. He could not take them home, because skating was not something his parents approved of. I had a pair of skates that I could keep at home. There was no way on earth that I would ask my parents to buy me skates. I bought them second-hand with money that I earned in my various jobs, but I could keep them at home. My parents were not unique and the kids were not unique.

My parents never offered to speak about the Holocaust to us. That said, sometimes when my parents had visitors, other survivors, they would recount some of their experiences and I would have heard these stories.

Saturdays were very special for my parents. The Sabbath would start Friday evening. My father would come home from work, have a bath, and put on his Sabbath suit. My mother would light the candles—I can just picture the way she did it. After she lit the candles my father would go to the synagogue. We lived in a very Jewish area and my father could go to the same type of synagogue he would have gone to in Tarnow. He would always take a few coins with him and put them in the alms boxes, *pishkes*, which were near the door. After the prayers he would come home and the lights would be off. The only light would be from the Sabbath candles. My father would sing songs in Hebrew, religious songs for the holy Sabbath. He would make *kiddush*, reciting blessings over the wine, and pass the wineglass to my mother and then to Charlie and me. Then my mother would serve the first course, usually fish or chopped chicken liver or chopped egg. After the first course my father would sing a few more songs, then he would say, "*Nu* Hindzu, serve the soup." My mother would say, "Sing a few more songs, then I will." It was a ritual. So he would sing a few more songs and she would serve the soup. Chicken soup, then the fried chicken or boiled chicken that had been used to make the soup.

There was no dessert. My father would wash his hands, ritually, and recite the benediction after the meal. Then they would go to bed. In the winter, before going to bed he would read from the *Pirkai Avot*, or "Ethics of Our Fathers." It is a compilation of historical rabbinical teachings.

Saturday morning he would have tea with a piece of cake, pound cake or cheesecake, or cookies that my mother had baked. My mother was a great cook. Then my father would go to the synagogue. He did not go and seek out the big synagogue on Fairmount Avenue, he went to his local *stiebel*, a small prayer house, the size of a big room, on the corner of Jeanne-Mance and St-Viateur Streets. He would come home for lunch and essentially the Friday evening routine was repeated. Then they would have a rest and when they got up they would go for a walk. Occasionally, rarely, but occasionally I would go for a walk with them. One time during the winter we were walking along and a snowplow came by. My father looked at it and shook his head and said, "In Poland it would have taken a hundred men with shovels to do that." He marvelled at the technology. I have often thought to myself that had my father seen an ATM he would have said, "Look at that! Look at what a great country Canada is. Machines give you money." When the Sabbath was over it was the same thing, there was the *havdala* ceremony, a ritual of saying goodbye to the Sabbath. I remember these rituals in France and in Canada but not in Poland.

Shortly after arriving in Montreal, I had my thirteenth birthday on March 30 and my *bar mitzvah*—the ceremony signifying the beginning of religious and personal responsibility. It was a very small affair. It was held at the *yeshiva*. When we left France they had bought me a suit with long pant legs—not knickerbockers—for me to wear at my *bar mitzvah*. They acquired a speech for me from my cousin Hirsh in Belgium because the tradition was that the *bar mitzvah* boy gave a speech on his *parsha*.

The *parsha* is the portion of the Torah that is read on the day that I was born. The Hebrew testament is divided into weekly portions and so over the year the whole Torah is read through. I was born on a leap year on the Hebrew lunar calendar and thirteen years later it was a leap year again. So my *parsha* was based on my birthdate and it was called *Tazria* and is *Leviticus* 12:1–13:59. The first line of that *parsha* is *Isha ki tazria v'yaldah*. It is about a woman who has given birth and the purity laws surrounding that. I had to learn my *parsha*. I had a speech that was not exactly on my *parsha* because my cousin Hirsh is about six months older than I am. He had his *bar mitzvah* before me and I had his speech. It was in Yiddish. It was a scholarly discourse. For instance, in the *parsha* where Abraham circumcised himself for the first time his name is spelled Abraham not Abram. Why is this? There are scads of commentaries on this. There is Rashi, the medieval French rabbi who is

67

Hinda and David Unger in Montreal, circa 1960 (Israel Unger collection)

considered the father of all commentators on the Talmud—so Rashi would have a commentary on this. Every Rabbi who has studied the Torah thinks to himself, I have an interpretation. The interpretation on that one would be that prior to circumcision he was only Abram, but after he had made the covenant with God through circumcision of himself and all males in his family he was now a Jew and father of a nation so he became Abraham. Abram means father and Abraham means "father of a multitude." So you give a discourse on your *parsha*. Today usually the kid stands up and says I want to thank my mother and my father and he speaks about his siblings and so on. Of course it's written for them by somebody else, then or today. A few people were invited to my *bar mitzvah* and they would have given me some gifts, but it was nothing major. My parents were not in a position to make a big deal out of it.

The Yeshiva and Bnei Akiva

The first few years we were in Canada, my father earned about twenty-five dollars a week. He worked at a men's clothing manufacturer sweeping the floors in the cutting room. He always looked for ways of supplementing his income. One of the extra jobs was on Saturday nights after the Sabbath was over he worked for a furrier cutting paw—the same job he had done in France.

He also got jobs leading the High Holiday services for Rosh Hashanah and Yom Kippur in small towns in Quebec and Ontario. That paid something like seventy dollars—a huge amount compared to his weekly wage at the time. So my dad looked for such jobs and I would go with him. He had me blow the *shofar* for him. The *shofar* is a long ram's horn blown on Rosh Hashanah, the New Year's services. It makes a trumpet-like sound. It appears often in the Hebrew Bible, but its most famous appearance is when the *shofar* was blown to bring down the walls of Jericho. It is not that easy to blow the *shofar*. The strange thing is that while I am reasonably good at it I have no idea how I do it. No one ever showed me and I would not be able to teach anybody. It comes to me. I first blew *shofar* for my father when I was about fifteen or sixteen. In 2009 I did it again for the first time since, because there was no rabbi in Fredericton that year and the cantor did not know how. I have a Yemini *shofar*, a great big thing. It is really loud. I was asked again the next year despite the fact that there was a rabbi who knows how to blow the *shofar*. So I must not have lost my touch.

Israel Unger blowing the *shofar* at the Sgoolai Israel Synagogue, Fredericton, 2012. (Marlene Unger photo)

At the *yeshiva* we were all boys, some rich kids and some poor kids. Generally the rich kids were the sons of settled Jews—that is, Jews who were living in Canada prior to the war and the poor kids were the sons of recent immigrants. Some of the well-off kids were there because they didn't do well in the secular schools.

Our social life revolved around the religious Zionist club *Bnei Akiva*, which means sons of Akiva. Akiva was a well-known rabbi in Roman times who came to Torah study late in life. He wanted to marry and his wife-to-be said, "Go study Torah." He went and came back and heard his future wife saying to a neighbour, "If he wanted to study another seven years I would gladly have him do it." So off he went and studied again! The Jews revolted against the Romans. Akiva was captured. The Romans skinned him and flailed him to death. He said he was sorry that he had only one life to give. He was glad to die for God. The motto of the Zionist group was *Torah veAvoda*: Torah and work. Be religious, study Torah, be a worker.

I went to *Bnei Akiva* throughout my high school days. The club was in a little basement apartment in a nondescript building on Park Avenue near St-Viateur. Mostly it was kids my age and older, up to about age twenty. It was the older ones who led it. We met on Friday or Saturday evenings and occasionally there were events on Sunday. We sang Hebrew songs about Israel or about the *Palmach*—the striking force of the Jewish underground army during the British Mandate in Palestine and later in the Israeli War of Independence. There were talks about life in Israel. I certainly believed in their principles. I was a Zionist then and today. I've been a Zionist for as long as I can remember, even in the hideout in Tarnow, though I don't think I knew the word Zionism then. But I was aware of a place where Jews were equal to all others and wanted to build a nation. To me Zionism meant that Jews could be like everyone else, that they could be farmers, soldiers, carpenters, and most of all that they need not be beholden to any one, that they need not feel that they were at someone's mercy.

That there were girls at the Zionist youth group was of course a big bonus. The girls went to their schools, religious and secular, and we boys went to the *yeshiva* or secular schools, but we all belonged to this religious Zionist organization. So joining *Bnei Akiva* fulfilled two passions: Zionism and meeting girls! The only female we ever saw at the *yeshiva* was our French teacher. Naturally we were very interested in girls but could not really say so, certainly not to our parents or teachers, so *Bnei Akiva* was an outlet for that interest. Friday evening after services and dinner we would head to the Zionist club and so did the girls. After songs and talks, we walked the girls home. That was a real big deal to walk them home. Some of them lived a long way away. In the wintertime I marched across half the city—and the average temperature in winter in Montreal is about minus ten degrees. I did not go with one particular girl. Anyone who would have looked at me I would be pleased to walk home. I was chivalrous. Marlene still accuses me of being chivalrous when I won't let her do something. She gets mad at me. She will say, "Stop being so chivalrous!"

Also around this time some of the girls started having birthday parties, sweet-sixteen parties in private homes—with the parents present of course. The whole group celebrated. There was some dancing, with the girls teaching the boys how to dance. I never really learned; I just kind of moved around. There was cake and soft drinks but no games such as spin the bottle, though we knew that these party games existed. I had my first kiss sitting on a couch with a girl at one of those parties. Really there was no pairing up, though later several of the group married and immigrated to Israel.

Sometimes on Saturday evening we would go to the movies as a group, but that did not happen until age sixteen. In Montreal there had been a fire in a movie theatre with a lot of children killed back in 1927. It was called the Laurier Palace Theatre fire. The children did not die from the fire so much as from the mayhem and lack of proper exits. So there was a law enacted saying no one under sixteen could go to a movie theatre. After the movie our group would go to a kosher restaurant like Levitts for a hot dog and Coke or, for the well-to-do, a smoked-meat sandwich and a soft drink. A hot dog was an extravagance for me.

I started smoking early, as did Charlie. I started because I thought it was manly to do so. But it was expensive and I had to keep it hidden from my parents. There was a store on the corner of Jeanne-Mance and St-Viateur that sold cigarettes at two for five cents. A package was about forty cents at the time. Of course, they were not allowed to sell to minors, but they did and I felt that they were doing me a favour. When I was sixteen and enrolled at university, I once went for a physical exam to a doctor to get pills to stay awake while studying. My mother, who was with me, said to the physician, "Doctor tell him not to smoke so much." That is when I realized my parents knew that I smoked. I smoked for twenty-two years until I realized how harmful it was.

There were two kinds of students at the *yeshiva*: genuinely religious students and a few that were there because no one else would take them. One of the religious ones was a fellow by the name Kossower and one of the other variety was Morris. (I don't recall their first names.) Morris was about fifteen or sixteen at the time, and like every other teenager his hormones were flowing. One day he announced that he and a friend had lined up a couple of girls and they were going to "do it" the next night. In preparation for the event he had acquired some condoms, which he locked in his geometry set in his desk. Kossower thought that Morris was going to commit a grave sin, so when Morris left he broke into Morris's desk, removed the condoms, took them home, and showed them to his parents. The next day Mrs. Kossower stormed into the *yeshiva* and flung the condoms on the chief rabbi's desk and shouted, "This is what you do at the *yeshiva*! Look what the boys are up to!" The rabbi had no way out other then to expel Morris. Morris did not take kindly to this. Not only was he expelled, but he lost his condoms and more importantly his chance to have sex. Morris, at some point in the morning, chased one of the rabbis with a knife and eventually showed his displeasure by taking Kossower's bicycle apart to the point where the latter took it home in a shopping bag. Mr. Kossower had the bicycle put together again at a cost of eighteen dollars and change. This was a huge amount at the time. According to what I heard, Mr. Kossower sent the bill to Morris's father and it was returned to Mr. Kossower a couple of weeks later. It seems that Mr. Morris had wiped his rear with it, folded it neatly, and sent it back.

While I was at the *yeshiva* it was expected, though not mandatory, that we attend Saturday and holiday prayers there. One particular festival *Simchat Torah*, literally "rejoicing over the Torah," is interesting because the rejoicing is partly fuelled by liquor. The rabbis always laid in a supply of beer for the occasion and locked it in the kitchen. A friend and I knew that there was booze in the kitchen and wanted some. The kitchen door was locked but we were determined so we took the door off its hinges and got the stash of beer and hid it under the porch. It was very cold that night, the beer froze and all the bottles exploded. My friend and I decided that we best go to synagogue services anyway so as to show that we were not the ones responsible. Our tactic did not work. Somehow the rabbis found out who the culprits were and when we showed up for services they chased us out, kicking at us as we ran.

Canadian Through and Through

When we finally came to Canada we were treated equally under the law. I had the same rights and privileges and responsibilities as any other Canadian. That was the first time in my life that happened. There was anti-Semitism but officially we were equal to all other Canadians. From the beginning I wanted to be a Canadian, I wanted to become a citizen. It was very important to me. We had to wait five years before we could apply.

I desperately wanted to be Canadian. I was ashamed of being born in Poland. I still have difficulty with that today. Poland was something I did not want to be associated with. I have no feelings for Poland. It is too much of a Jewish graveyard. I envied people who were born in Canada, and even today when I am outside of the country I have a difficult time saying that I was born in Poland. I like for people that I meet to think of me as a Canadian, period.

That said, I believe that Polish Jews were Poles. Once there was a German woman from Chicago who was doing a Ph.D. and wanted to interview me. She was working on the theme of relationships between people in the ghetto. I told her I could not tell her much about that because I was so young at the time. During the interview she used the words "Jews" and "Poles" separately. I corrected her and said, "I was a Pole, I was born a Pole, and I'm Jewish, and there were people who were Poles and Christians." She instantly understood what I was getting at. From there on in she never did that again and she was very careful. She would talk about Jewish Poles. It's a mentality. There were of course Jewish Poles and Christian Poles and maybe atheist Poles, but what I am talking about is the perception that somehow Jews in Poland were not Polish, were not native to Poland—did not have the same claim to being Polish as non-Jews, even though Jews had been there over one thousand years and certainly as long as the non-Jewish Poles. Some people still do not consider that Jews were part and parcel of Poland. Unfortunately, this was true in Germany prior to the Holocaust as well, that many Germans did not think of Jews as Germans. Undoubtedly this was true of many countries in Europe at the time and today as well.

This brings me back to what Zionism meant and continues to mean to me. I was once asked what Israel meant to me in a class at St. Thomas University in Fredericton. I replied it means that I can walk with my head held high. When Israel obtained statehood it meant Jews no longer had to depend on the sufferance of whoever was in control of whatever country they found themselves in. The vast majority of Canadians have roots that they can relate to and be proud of: English, French, Haitian. But what are my roots? What is my heritage? Certainly not Poland. When you are in Fredericton and someone asks you what you are, they are asking: Is your ancestry Scottish or German or Polish? But if they ask me then the question they are asking is, Are you Jewish? I don't want to be Polish. I'm a Canadian through and through. The existence of Israel makes me a better Canadian. Israel meant that I had roots like other Canadians, even though I was not born here. And therefore I am equal to other Canadians.

Canada enabled me to achieve whatever I did achieve. To me the greatest thing about Canada is that we give young people opportunities. We have universities from one end of the country to the other that are very access- ible. We have many examples of people who have achieved extraordinary success who were the sons and daughters of fishermen, farmers, woodsmen. The country gave me opportunities. There were tough times. I had to work hard. I did experience anti-Semitism at university and I did have to struggle more than non-Jews to finance my undergraduate studies, but I could do it. Most importantly, a university education was available—that is one of the great features of Canada. The other is that if you did have something to contribute to the country, doors were open to government, to academia, to business. I am not saying that these things do not exist in other nations, but they certainly exist in Canada.

The Octet Rule

When I was in the *yeshiva* in Montreal there was a co-student from Belgium, Max Pearl, who was orphaned in the Holocaust. He was two years older than I was. How Max came to Canada, I do not know. He lived with Rabbi Baron, the chief rabbi at the *yeshiva*. Max was very bright and different, but I cannot really say how he was different. I was very impressed by Max and he is the fellow who got me started reading. I considered anything Max did was sophisticated and grown up, so I emulated him. After I left the *yeshiva* I lost touch with Max, although I did learn that he eventually ended up at the Laval medical school and specialized in psychiatry. One day while I was visiting my parents back in Montreal I ran into Rabbi Baron and we chatted briefly. He knew that Max was in Montreal and he asked me, "Why doesn't Max come to see me?" I shrugged my shoulders. But I wasn't surprised. I guessed that there was a clash with Max living in Quebec City, attending Laval University, and perhaps having francophone girlfriends. I knew that Max was not religious and felt guilty about that and hence did not want to see the rabbi. I found out about Max's death in a strange way. Several years later Marlene and I went to the French islands off of Newfoundland, Saint-Pierre and Miquelon, and met a young couple from Quebec who were both MDs and had been to medical school with Max. They told us that Max had been elected class president—quite an achievement for a Jew in Quebec City in the early sixties. They told us too that Max had committed suicide as a young man. I was shocked. I had no idea that he was predisposed to such deep depression. Possibly it came from having lost his whole family in the Holocaust and he could not find any comfort in religion, even though he lived with the head rabbi of the *yeshiva*. I would not have called him a friend at the *yeshiva* but a fellow I held in very high esteem. In retrospect I don't think he was particularly close to anyone.

One problem at the Landers was that I didn't have a place to study. I shared a room with Charlie and I had no desk to study on. I had no one to teach me how to study. Again, I was self-taught. So I studied at the *yeshiva*. In my last year of high school we left the Landers and moved to Jeanne-Mance Street, actually back to the apartment we had originally stayed in when we first arrived in the city. That couple left and we moved into an apartment by ourselves for the first time since arriving in Canada. My parents remained friends with the Landers for the rest of their lives. In fact, they later bought a house together. The Landers were not observant and my parents were, which shows it was possible to be tolerant and respect one another despite these differences. Our new apartment was at 5977 Jeanne-Mance Street, between Bernard Avenue and Van Horne Avenue. We lived on the third floor. There I had my own room for the first time.

I did not start reading seriously until I was in Canada and then it was under Max's influence. Both my parents read Yiddish newspapers. My father was a terrific reader. The first things I read were newspapers. I was very impressionable. Max said he read mysteries by Erle Stanley Gardner (author of the Perry Mason series), so I started reading those. Then in university I thought that you could not consider yourself educated if you had not read Dostoevsky's *Crime and Punishment* and *The Brothers Karamazov*, or *The Story of Philosophy* by Will Durant, *The Communist Manifesto* by Marx and Engels, Karl Marx's *Das Kapital*, the abridged version. I wanted to be a civilized, educated person so I read these works, among others. There was a period I went through when I was very interested in the Second World War and read a lot of history books on the subject.

In the Jewish part of the curriculum at the *yeshiva* we studied the Torah usually by reading the portion of the week and going through the various commentaries on that portion. The secular part of the curriculum was set by the Protestant School Board of Montreal. The topic I enjoyed the most was chemistry. It was taught by Archie Handel. He was the principal of secular education. He was Jewish but not religious. What caught my interest was the Octet Rule. Atoms try to have eight electrons in their outer shell, hence the name "octet." Take NaCl, sodium chloride. Sodium has two electrons in its first shell, eight in the next, but only one electron its outer shell. It wants to get rid of that one electron to have eight it its outer shell, so to say. Then you have chlorine, which has two electrons in its first shell, eight in the next and seven in its outer shell. So chlorine wants to pick up an electron so it will have eight in its outer shell. They are a perfect match! Sodium gives up the electron which chlorine is desperately looking for. That way they both have fulfilled the Octet Rule. Sodium is a metal and extremely reactive. It will burst into flame if you put a piece of it in water. You have to store it under oil. Chlorine is a deadly gas on its own. But when sodium and chlorine react they form a compound that is essential for life: ordinary table salt. The Octet Rule was so logical and so interesting. It explained everything—it was phenomenal.

An additional attraction to me about chemistry and science in general, besides the fact that I was good at it, was that regardless of religion, colour, or any of the other biases, science is science. The laws of science are the same regardless of who is exploring them. I decided at that point that I wanted to be a professor and to do research. My concept of research at that stage was very shallow and did not resemble actual research. My view of university life was that it was a "city on a hill," with professors sitting in leather chairs discussing weighty ideas strictly on their intellectual merit. Life in university turned out to be very different from what I had imagined. University faculty are subject to the same foibles as the rest of society. They have the same prejudices and biases, the same desires, the same egos, and they make the same mistakes. Still, I would not hesitate to do it all over again!

Archie was a great human though not a spellbinding teacher. He actually had me explain to the other students why chemicals reacted. I really enjoyed that. Trigonometry also went click. I could do the problems. I did them the long way using the definitions of sine and cosine. I enjoyed the non-math and science subjects, too. In English, we did some Shakespeare—*Hamlet* I recall in particular. Archie was not much older than I. I maintained a friendship with him long after I left Montreal.

Collecting Butcher Bills

I was very hard up for money from day zero in Canada. I had room and board and clothing—the necessities were covered. Everything else I paid for. I had jobs on weekends, evenings, and during the summer from age thirteen on. My entire school time, high school and later in university, I worked. I did not receive and did not expect an allowance. I knew other boys at the *yeshiva* whose parents came to Canada before the Holocaust and they got an allowance. It never dawned on me to ask for one.

I had a variety of interesting jobs. I used to go to the Montreal Star building for the newspaper as soon as it came out so I could get a jump on reading the want ads, thereby improving my chances of finding a job. One of my first jobs was in a dressmaking factory. I was to run errands, sweep the floor, and so on for fifty cents per hour. I kept tabs of the hours I worked and the first time I was paid the envelope had twenty dollars minus some deductions. But I had worked more than forty hours. I screwed up my courage and asked the boss how come I had only been paid twenty dollars. "That is your pay—twenty dollars a week." "I was under the impression," I said, "that I was supposed to get fifty cents per hour." "No. Twenty dollars per week." Since I had no alternative I continued working at that shop. One day I took some skirts to a pleating factory and the owner asked me if I had any friends that needed a job. I replied that I might be looking for a job. The owner asked why I would look for a job when I already had one. So I informed him that I was expected to work overtime and not get paid for it. "Well, I am not as rich as the man you are working for. I can only pay forty cents per hour, but you will have lots of overtime and I will pay you for it." So I took the job, decreased my salary from twenty dollars to sixteen dollars per week, but put in enough hours to make over twenty dollars per week. It was a brutal job. Pleating in those days was done by putting a piece of cloth between two sheets of heavy cardboard that had the desired pleat, then rolling it and steaming it in an oven for half an hour. Montreal summers are hot and humid anyway, so working with steam made it that much worse.

Perhaps the most interesting job was collecting butcher bills. In those days there were many small butcher shops. Housewives would order meat several times a week and the butcher kept a tab. Saturday evening after the Sabbath was over, boys like me would go and pick up the butcher bills and then on Sunday go collecting. The butcher paid us 1.5 percent or if you were lucky 2 percent of what we collected. Typically the bills ranged between three dollars and six dollars. Some were higher, a lot higher. The first time I went collecting I was particularly thrilled with the big bills including one for over one hundred dollars. I thought I was going to be rich! When I got to the apartment building that had the one-hundred-dollar bill I ran up the stairs to the fourth floor, rang the bell, and a man answered. I announced, "Butcher boy collecting." The man shouted in the direction of their kitchen. "Sarah, it's the butcher boy. Do you want to give him any thing this week?" I think they ended paying three dollars. That is how I discovered that people had big bills because they did not pay them. Typically I worked from about 8 a.m. to 3 p.m. on a Sunday. I would collect between one hundred fifty dollars and two hundred dollars and so I earned between three dollars and four dollars. My father did this job sometimes too. He was the only fifty-year-old "butcher boy." I collected the butcher bills in three ways: on foot close to home; on bicycle (loaned to me by my brother); or with the butcher in his half-ton truck. He did the driving; I would collect. At first I did it by foot in the Outrement area, but as the Jewish community spread, I had to spread out too.

I envied the boys at the *yeshiva* who had bikes. One reason I learned to bike was to deliver orders for drugstores and grocery stores. I worked just one day in a grocery store where I was expected to sweep the floor, bring produce up from the cellar, and deliver groceries by bicycle. I quit that job because they offered me only eight dollars a week. When I asked the owner why I was to be paid so little, he said, "I am teaching you a trade."

At another grocery store I had to bring watermelons from downstairs to upstairs, crates of oranges—heavy work. They had these big delivery bicycles with huge baskets. I'm a relatively small guy and there was this great big basket in front loaded with groceries. I was on that damn bicycle and went out delivering and I had to make a left turn off Park Avenue onto Fairmount Avenue. My wheel got stuck in the streetcar track and I crashed and the groceries flew all over the place.

The Maislin Brothers were a Jewish trucking company. Somehow my father got to know the Maislins. I think it was that their father died and they had my father say *kaddish* for them—a prayer recited in honour of the dead. For that service, my father persuaded them to hire me as a trucker's assistant. They had a fleet of trucks that went from Montreal to New York to Philadelphia—with the high-class drivers. Then there were the low-class drivers who drove around within Montreal. So if you were shipping beef hearts to New York you would phone Maislin and a driver would come and collect them in a smaller truck. We would receive them in the depot and fill the big truck for the long distance deliveries. I was the driver's assistant; it was heavy work and it was dirty work. It was hot and we would be in the back alleys doing this heavy work. One time we had to take large barrels and roll them from the depot, into the elevator, out of the elevator and into the truck. The driver who was with me, he would just put his right foot up against the barrel, grab the other end and swing it over so the barrel was on its edge and it would roll. The first time I tried to do that, I put my foot up against the barrel like I saw the driver do it and I pulled it towards me. The barrel stayed exactly where it was and I went over the barrel. I don't know how many times the barrel got me instead of me getting the barrel.

I also worked at Friedman Company, a men's clothing factory that produced high-end clothes. The first job at that company was in the stockroom. We received and recorded bolts of cloth and then sent them out for pre-shrinking. When they returned, we stocked them in bins and delivered them to the cutters. This was hard work, because the bolts of cloth were very heavy and in the summer time the place was a steam bath. There were no windows in the stockroom. Then I was switched to a better job in the shipping room. It involved preparing cardboard boxes, packing clothes in them, and labelling the boxes. There was a real advantage to this job because the factory was close to where I did my undergraduate work. When the academic year started I could work for an hour or two between classes.

I had a job at the Montreal Stock Exchange. That was the most boring job I ever had. I was given a uniform to wear and given a sector of the floor to cover. I would take the receipts for any transaction that occurred in my sector and deliver them to the buyers' and sellers' cubicles and to the tickertape machine. We were busy from about 10 a.m. to 11 a.m. and again from about 3 p.m. to 4 p.m. The rest of the time I pretty well stared at the clock—even though I did my best not to. I sold magazine subscriptions and received a commission. This was okay other than it was a violation of municipal law.

I worked in a metal fabricating plant as an assistant. It was noisy and dirty but paid well. I worked in a lacemaking factory changing the bobbins on the lace machines. There I worked the night shift, which I quite enjoyed. I was responsible for some twenty-six machines and was the only one present during that shift.

At the end of grade eleven we wrote Protestant school board exams, called the matriculations, or matrics for short. There was no grade twelve in Quebec at that time. It was a slog. There were ten subjects. I passed every one of them but just barely. I think this was due to the many disruptions in my life: first no school, then starting school in Poland after the war in Polish, then again no school when we were "orphans," then English in England, then French in France, then in the middle of a year English again in Canada, and then skipping a year. I spent high school, undergraduate school, and probably a good deal of graduate school with a huge fear of failure. So I was overjoyed to pass the matrics!

I was sixteen, it was 1954 and now came the question of which university to go to. If you passed the matrics, McGill University would accept you. There was also the smaller Sir George Williams University—today Concordia University—which did not have the reputation or the cachet of McGill. At the time of applying we had not yet moved and so I didn't have a room or even a desk at home for studying. I felt intimidated by McGill, so I didn't even apply there. I chose Sir George Williams University. McGill was just too awesome for me. My parents were not in a position to give me advice. I made all my own decisions.

Kafkaesque Encounters

My classes were held in a former YMCA on Mountain Street and an auditorium near by. The Norris Building of Sir George Williams University on Drummond Street was just under construction my first year and we did not get to use it until my second year. The chemistry department then was on the fourth floor, as well as the labs. I had to travel by streetcar from home, three tickets for twenty-five cents for students. Finances continued to be a serious problem for me. I earned enough during summer work to pay my tuition fees and buy books. Other expenses, like the streetcar fare or anything for personal spending, I had to earn during the academic year. At first I had enough because I had a part-time job at the Friedman Company for ten dollars per week but then they moved from downtown to the suburbs so that ended my part-time job. When I worked part-time I paid unemployment insurance. I objected to this but I had no choice. When I lost my job, I applied for unemployment benefits. I did all the paperwork and stated the reason I lost my job was because the factory moved. Well, why didn't I take the bus to the new location? I was asked. I replied that I had to attend lectures. The unemployment officer said that if I were going to school I was not eligible for unemployment. I said, "Well, I paid unemployment when I was going to school. Why did I pay it, if I was ineligible?" This went on for several weeks with various higher-ups until finally they sent my case to Ottawa. A ruling was made that I was to receive nine dollars a week unemployment benefits. I had been paid ten dollars for twenty hours' work and now I was to receive nine dollars for not working! This was wonderful news!

There was a catch, however. I had to report to the unemployment office every Friday at 10 a.m. The office was far away and I had a lecture in advanced calculus at 10 a.m. So I compromised. One week I would miss my lecture and be on time at the unemployment office. The next week I would attend the lecture and be late at the unemployment office. On the days that I was late at the unemployment office the procedure was very tiresome. Because I was late I had to go to a different wicket where the first question they asked was, "Why are you late?" I would answer, "I had to attend a lecture." The officer would then say, "If you are going to school you are ineligible for unemployment. Go upstairs." Upstairs they asked a bunch of questions as if I were trying to get a job. Finally, the man would sign my book, but then I had to go downstairs to the late wicket and be issued a cheque, then go to yet another line to ultimately get my nine dollars. Every second week I would have to go through this whole maze again. On the university end, since the advanced calculus class was small, the professor noticed that I missed class every second Friday and asked me why. I explained it to him and he was very understanding.

I dreaded my Friday-morning encounters with the unemployment people. In retrospect such Kafkaesque encounters with bureaucrats are funny or even absurd, but at the time they are hell. For instance, in the Second World War identity papers were very important. If a German soldier was asked for his papers towards the end of the war and they were not in order he could be shot by a *Schnellrichter*, a summary executioner. The day after the surrender there was no German army and no one needed those papers anymore. Similarly the Gestapo was a feared institution and a day after the end of war they were in hiding or attempting to disavow that they had ever been members of that organization.

Another idea I had as to how to earn my way through school was that I tried to enlist in the Canadian Officer Training Corps (COTC). When I first enrolled in university, I thought COTC was the answer to all my financial problems. They paid for your tuition, your books, there was a small allowance during the academic year, and you had a guaranteed job during the summer at fifty-five dollars per week—the best I ever had was twenty-four dollars a week. I went through the application and then an interview. When they asked me my age I said, "Sixteen." "Sorry, you are too young." The next fall I tried again. This time I got by the age thing but then they asked, "Are you a Canadian citizen?" I said, "No." "Are you a British subject?" "No." "Are you a member of a NATO country?" "No." "Where were you born?" "Poland." "We can't take you. That is a communist country." That year I received my Canadian citizenship, so the next fall I tried again. This time I got through all the questions but then they asked, "What year are you going into?" I said, "Third." "We can't take you because you will be available for only one summer."

In first year university I did well in calculus and very much enjoyed the subject. My professor, Edna Vowles, once told me that I was a good mathematician because I was a lazy mathematician. I tried to find shortcuts. I believe I had the highest mark in calculus in my class, so when a tutoring job for calculus came up I thought that would be good for me. At that time Sir George Williams University had an employment office staffed by two older men. Job opportunities were posted outside their office and if you felt you wanted to apply for a particular position, you would take that notice and ask one of them to send you out for an interview. I tried several times, but they never sent me out for an interview. Then one day in second year there was this notice put up by a first-year female student who wanted help with calculus. Thinking this was ideal job for me, I went into the office and asked to be put in contact with the student. The man I was speaking with started to fill out a form and was clearly uncomfortable. Then he asked the other fellow, "Bill, do you think we should send Israel out for this job?" He sort of spat out my name. Bill, who had been fidgeting in his chair, replied, "No. I don't think we should send him out. He is not mature enough." "What does maturity have to do with it? Why don't you phone Professor Vowles and ask her if I have the ability to tutor first-year calculus?" They refused. The employment officers would not speak to her and they would not let the young woman make the decision as to whether I had anything to offer. They refused to allow me to speak to her. It seems to me there was something besides their concern about my maturity that was at play.

Anti-Semitism in my view, unlike pregnancy, is not either you are or are not. It is a bell curve with a small percentage of people being at zero, a few having a bit of antipathy and holding some stereotypes, and some being virulent haters. A study carried out by a McGill University sociologist a few years ago found that anti-Semitism in Canada was substantial across the country. I am well aware that frequently Jews point at anti-Semitism when faced with criticism or failure. I hope that I am not prone to that. I wanted to believe that anti-Semitism had disappeared at the end of the Second World

War. Later in my life at the University of New Brunswick, there was a young, very bright Jewish professor who I used to lunch with and he would talk about anti-Semitism in Canada. I used to think that he was being obsessive. One day he recounted an event that happened to him on airplane from Calgary to Toronto. He was sitting next to a man and they struck up a conversation that soon led to housing costs in Toronto. Bernie said, "I don't have the money to buy such a house." "You would have the money if you were a member of the tribe," the guy next to him said. I asked Bernie, "How come all these anti-Semitic comments happen to you? I never hear any of them." "When you introduce yourself to people, Israel, they instantly know you are Jewish and so they don't reveal their feelings about Jews."

Anti-Semitism has been prevalent throughout history and goes back two thousand years. If Hitler and the Nazis had arisen in a country other than Germany, the Holocaust could have happened there. The Nazis had collaborators in every European country. One of the great tragedies during the Holocaust was the silence of all other nations, including Canada and the United States, as witnessed by the Evian Conference in July of 1938. In a resort town called Évian-les-Bains in France, the American president Franklin D. Roosevelt convened a conference to discuss the growing number of Jewish refugees fleeing Nazi persecution. Thirty-one countries were represented. Virtually no country responded to the plight of European Jews. The conference was later called "Hitler's 'green light' for genocide." Canada sent a delegate, Hume Wrong, who did nothing to help. In fact, Canada had a very anti-Semitic immigration policy detailed in the book *None Is Too Many: Canada and the Jews of Europe 1933–1948*, by Irving Abella and Harold Troper. "None is too many," was a statement made by a Canadian immigration official at the time when asked how many Jewish refugees should be allowed to come to Canada. All this to say that anti-Semitism may have been involved in the incident at the employment office, in that they did not allow me to at least try for that tutoring job.

In third year things got much better. I applied and got a job working in the stockroom of the chemistry department. I was so proud to finally have a chemistry lab job. It involved passing out equipment and chemicals to students and instructors and preparing solutions. It was a part-time day job. In fourth year I graduated to lab instructor, which was better paid and, I felt, much more important. It fed my ego. I did demonstrations in the evenings for students taking their courses at night school. Labs ended around 10 p.m. and then I went and drank beer with the instructors at a nearby tavern.

I was nineteen and felt grown up and mature. One evening a McGill University professor of physics was at our table, I was really feeling sophisticated, drinking beer with a prof—from McGill to boot. At some point the conversation turned to McGill's quota for accepting Jews into medical school—5 per year in a class of 108 students. The professor very seriously said, "What can you do? Jews are smart and work hard. If you just let them in based on marks, half the class would be Jews." I am ashamed every time I think of that episode that we actually sat there and dis-

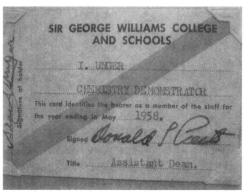

Israel's identification card as a chemistry demonstrator at Sir George Williams University, 1958. (Israel Unger collection)

cussed what he said instead of just telling him that he was a bigot. Presumably that man would prefer to be treated by a not-so-bright non-Jewish doctor rather than a smart, hard-working Jew.

I tried to get jobs in the chemical industry but never succeeded. This was disappointing, particularly since many other students including ones who I studied with, and even tutored, did get such work. One day I applied to a company called Canadian Industries Limited (C.I.L.), a large chemical company based in the United Kingdom, with a subsidiary in Canada. I did not get the job. I asked the person who interviewed me if he could tell me why I was having such difficult time getting work in the chemical industry. "You are Jewish and our experience is that Jews are very bright, they work very hard, but then they go out and start their own companies and compete with us. So we don't hire Jews." Here I was nineteen years old, looking for summer work, and C.I.L. was afraid I might go into competition with them! Two years after that, C.I.L. offered me a graduate fellowship and after some reflection I accepted. When I received the fellowship the person who came from C.I.L to present the award said, "Look, there are no strings attached, but we would be pleased when you receive your Ph.D. if you would come to our plant in Sarnia and look us over." I did, but I did not go to work for them.

About the time I started going to university I started dating. The dates were always on Saturday evening and usually involved a movie and then a snack in a restaurant and taking the girl home. If you were lucky and bold you might get a goodnight kiss on the third date or thereabouts. When I had a date lined up, Saturday night seemed ages and ages away. I did not have many girlfriends, but do recall one that makes me blush even today. For the story I'll call her Abbey. She asked me to escort her to a wedding. I was thrilled to accept. Abbey lived a long way away, but the wedding was in my neighbourhood of Montreal. It took me about an hour and three bus changes to get to her home to pick her up, then back to my area, then after the wedding to escort her back home. Her parents owned a small grocery store and lived above it. When we got to her home we were on the stairs and started smooching. I was really into that until at some point Abbey said, "We must stop." "Why?" I asked. "My father is not going to let me go out with you. Your father works in a factory." I then tried to persuade her that she should not judge me adversely because my father worked in a factory. She didn't even know that my father swept the floor in the factory. It makes me blush to think I tried to reason with her.

What I find interesting about the Abbey episode is not only that her parents judged character and worth based on occupation, but they concluded that I was going to be a factory worker because my father was one. Perhaps they considered financial ability the only important criterion for a suitor for their daughter. Even more interesting is that Abbey accepted their decision but decided to keep me around until the wedding was over to be certain that she had an escort! My parents expected me to date Jewish girls. It did not occur to them that I would consider anyone else.

In third-year university I met and kept company with a very warm, intelligent, and interesting co-student, Suzanne Destroismaisons. Not only did I fall for Suzanne but also for her mother and father. They were absolutely wonderful people and I had a lot of affection for both of them. Many of our dates we spent at her family home in Saint-Lambert. Suzanne's father was a French Huguenot but totally anglicized. He had started his career at CN railway as a member of a surveying crew, on the "chain gang," as they called it, because his job was to hold one end of a sixty-six-foot length of chain. He was ambitious and hard-working. He studied at night and became an engineer. He worked his way up until he was next in line at CN to be district engineer, but he did not get that promotion because of his French name. So he quit CN and went to work for the federal government in an equivalent position. Later CN had a change of view and asked Suzanne's father to come back as district engineer and he did. Most of our dates consisted of playing bridge with Suzanne's parents—they taught me to play bridge. A couple times we went to a restaurant called the Pam Pam on Drummond Street across the street from Sir George Williams University. It was a small basement restaurant, Hungarian, with delicious goulash. I also took her to a New Year's Eve party one time.

I also had a few male friends. One was Hank Sinofsky, who was a year ahead of me. He was about to leave Canada to do graduate work in the United States, so the two of us went downtown together. We had a few beers in the area. Around midnight we were walking along and singing and, despite the fact that it is a pretty loud place that time of night, we were arrested for disturbing the peace! Being in jail for a night in a drunk tank was not a lot of fun, so I resolved to refrain from singing in public ever again.

I graduated from Sir George Williams University in 1958. I attended the ceremony, which was in a church on St. Catherine Street near Eaton's—on a Friday evening. It was no big deal because, in part, I was not aware that people made it a big deal. I did not think much of it at the time. None of my family

Israel, graduation photo from Sir George Williams University, 1958. (Israel Unger collection)

attended. When I graduated I chose to go to the University of New Brunswick for graduate school. Suzanne and I expected to continue our relationship.

My Brother Charlie

When we got to Canada, Charlie and I led very different lives. We had very different personalities. I do not mean to imply that he was bad and I am good, just that we were very different people. He was a risk taker. He was daring. I was scared of getting caught, of being shamed—what would people think of me? Charlie liked to defy the authorities. He had a totally different focus in life too. He wanted to achieve in business.

Charlie did not have the chance to go to school for any length of time. He was eleven when we got out of the attic, so he went to school in Poland for no more than a year and about the same amount of time in London. His education ended in England at age fourteen, when he started working in our uncle's clothing shop. He worked from there on in. He was seventeen when we came to Canada and he went to work at the Friedman Co. clothing manufacturer. Charlie worked as an operator in that factory for about three or four years.

Charlie liked to play cards and pinball machines. He had no other hobbies. He did not do sports. I think he started going with girls or at least trying to when he was fourteen. I was not jealous of Charlie but I did want to do grown-up things like going out with girls. I was however jealous of other older males who had girlfriends and I could not wait to be their age so I could have girlfriends. Charlie never talked to me about the "birds and the bees." I think Charlie was handsome, though I consider the vast majority of men and women to be handsome and don't know how one can make fine distinctions about one person being more handsome than another. I don't know who his heroes were, but he was still one of mine.

At least on one occasion my father saw us get into a physical fight. We were about the same size—I was growing bigger, he had already stopped growing, so I was beginning to hold my own. I don't know what we were fighting about, but my father was extremely upset. He tried to separate us and in so doing he fell to the floor screaming in pain. That stopped the fight. It may have been an act, though he did have angina.

From the time I was sixteen to about twenty Charlie and I were reasonable friends. Charlie had a car in partnership with another fellow, a little black Vanguard. The transmission went on the car and it cost fifty dollars to fix it. He did not ask but I gave him the money. That was about two and a half weeks' work for me. I did it out of a feeling of compassion for him and perhaps too I was still trying to buy his affection.

Early on in Canada Charlie got a job as a storekeeper on the DEW line. The Distant Early Warning line was a series of American radar stations for defence in Alaska and in the Canadian Arctic during the Cold War to warn of possible Soviet airplane attacks. He worked on the DEW line for about a year and earned one hundred dollars per week, which was big money in those

days. He came home once during that year and brought me many packages of American cigarettes. We chummed around together and I really enjoyed that. We actually went out on double dates a couple of times. I felt very sophisticated. That was probably our closest time together.

When he came back to Montreal permanently he met his first wife, Lily Mizrahi. It was instant love. Lily came from a large Jewish Egyptian family. The only ones not married were Lily and her older sister Mimi. Lily was twenty-four then, a year older than Charlie, and she

Charlie, circa 1956. (Israel Unger collection)

really wanted to get married. So they were married about six months later. I was nineteen at the time.

Charlie started to work for his father-in-law, who was in wholesale hardware. That did not last long, as Lily's father went bankrupt. Charlie told me this exact story. They were selling files by the dozen. Charlie goes to Pascal's in Montreal, a retail hardware store, and wants to sell them files at two dollars for a dozen files, the price his father-in-law has set. But another wholesaler is selling the same brand for one dollar and fifty cents a dozen. "We have to lower our price," Charlie tells his father-in-law. "Let's sell at a dollar and fifty cents and we'll still make fifty cents." His father-in-law refuses and says, "Listen, the guy that is selling them at one dollar and fifty cents—he's going to run out of stock, then we will raise the price to two dollars and fifty cents." Surprise, surprise, they went bankrupt.

Charlie and Lily had their first child about a year after marrying. That was a happy year for them. I think that was the best year of his life. We were good friends then. I went to their apartment sometimes and had dinner with them. Then after the first year, their marriage became quite stormy. It was characterized by periodic fights.

Lily thought of herself as sophisticated and intellectual, a bourgeois woman. Charlie was anything but. She wanted a husband who was refined,

Charlie, his wife, Lily, and their daughters Rosie and Joycie. (Israel Unger collection)

who read books and poetry. Charlie was an aggressive businessman who made good money. They had a beautiful home and he was a good provider. He was "the father." He liked making the decisions. They had three children and raised them Jewish. Lily expected Charlie to change, even after twenty years!

After the bankruptcy, Charlie took a job in a wholesale dry goods store. I went to see him at his work one time. When I got to the store I asked to see Charles Unger and they sent me down to the cellar through a trap door in the floor. There was a single light bulb hanging from the ceiling and there was water dripping from the walls. Charlie was the only person down there and he was sorting clothes. I felt very sorry for him. But Charlie did so well in that store that within a short while he was brought up from the cellar and went on to become a salesman and a buyer and did well. He asked to become a partner and the owners agreed, but they offered him only a small percentage so he decided to start his own store.

Charlie had gotten to know a peddler, that is, a man who bought dry goods from the wholesaler and then took them in a suitcase to small stores. They went into partnership together and opened a small store. It did well and so they moved to a larger store and moved again into an even larger store. Charlie was doing well financially and by now he and Lily had three children, all girls. The fights continued, however.

Charlie and Lily were married in 1957. My mother offered them the silverware set we had brought with us from France. Lily declined because it was too difficult to clean. Eventually my mother gave it to the son of the relative in Haifa who had sent us food immediately after liberation. He was a captain on an Israeli ship. I thought the silverware was beautiful and I wished we could have kept it.

A year later, I left Montreal. From then on, Charlie and I drifted apart, although we remained on good terms.

Part Four

The Bubble Counter

Leaving Home: Montreal to Fredericton

It was 1958. I was twenty years old and had just graduated from Sir George Williams University. I left to do graduate work at the University of New Brunswick (UNB) in Fredericton and became independent. Fredericton was reasonably close to Montreal and it had a good reputation for chemistry. I was very excited. It was the first time in my life that I voluntarily left home. My initial impression of Fredericton was that it was a village. Prior to living in Fredericton I had lived in Paris, London, and Montreal. But actually when I think about it, Fredericton is about the same size as Tarnow. UNB on the other hand was a delight, a real campus! UNB is the oldest university in North America, founded in 1785, and over the years a series of Georgian-style red-brick buildings have created a campus up the hill in Fredericton. The student cafeteria food was awful; even the bread was awful—sliced white bread wrapped in cellophane. My parents sent me food parcels: cookies, pie, hamburgers. I did not find Fredericton a friendly place, although I made friends among other graduate students.

I contacted the Jewish community through the synagogue. The rabbi found me my first boarding house with Mr. and Mrs. Graser. Their son was Weldon Graser, who was a sportscaster at the time and then went to UNB law school. He went on to have a brilliant career as a lawyer in Fredericton and eventually ended up a judge in Saint John. I attended High Holiday services at the Sgoolai Israel Synagogue. I had an odd experience with anti-Semitism early on in Fredericton. After living with the Grasers I rented a room from a non-Jewish woman. After a few months, the landlady tried to compliment me by saying, "I told my friends that you were a really nice person and they could also rent to Jews." Other than that, I don't recall experiencing much overt anti-Semitism in Fredericton.

I financed my time at UNB with teaching assistantships—as a lab demonstrator and then a C.I.L. fellowship. I was given my own lab in a new building

Israel (right) as graduate student at UNB, 1959. (Israel Unger collection)

that I shared with just one other graduate student. I was given a problem to work on. My excitement soon died, however, and I became depressed.

About three months into my time in Fredericton, Suzanne decided she did not want to continue our relationship. We had gone together two years. She broke up with me by letter. I was absolutely devastated and took a long while to get over it. Suzanne later married a Protestant minister, which surprised me. I wonder if going out with me had something to do with that. The second reason that first year away from home was difficult was because my research was going absolutely nowhere. My research director was a very nice person but not great at directing research.

I fell in with a hard-drinking bunch from the boarding house that did some crazy things. We would go out to the woods at night and one time I was with a group who blew up a small dam with stolen industrial dynamite. I was not involved in the dynamite episode, but I was there. I spent my spare time in the lab or going for a few beers with fellow grad students at the 252 Club. You had to have some association with the Royal Canadian Air Force to be a member, but members could bring guests and I knew people who could sign me in.

I learned to drive when I was a graduate student. That was considered quite late. My parents thought that a car was a huge luxury and I did not have

the financial resources in Montreal to
own a car. I had a couple of lessons
from other graduate students but, like
many things, I more or less learned
on my own. At first I walked around
Fredericton, but then I bought a used
car, a 1949 Studebaker, for fifty dollars
and drove everywhere.

That first year in Fredericton I
did not do much other than my grad
work and some socializing. I went
skating at the Lady Beaverbrook Rink.

Israel in 1958 in Fredericton with his first car, a
1949 Studebaker. (Israel Unger collection)

I was homesick. I did not really get over the breakup with Suzanne until I
started going out with Marlene. If it had not been for Marlene, I might have
quit graduate school.

The Bubble Counter

I met Marlene when I blocked her car with mine in the chemistry building
parking lot. Larry Hawton, a fellow grad student, said that a woman had
come in looking for whoever had blocked her car. I was annoyed that I had
to go out and move my car. I think I may even have given the owner of the
car—Marlene—a dirty look! But of course I moved my car. Then I noticed her
because there was a public phone outside my lab and I saw Marlene coming
to use it. I think she may have been using the one near my lab on purpose.

Not long after, my car was having trouble on University Avenue and
Marlene drove by honking and waving—as if to say, "Serves you right" for
blocking her car on campus. That same evening I had asked a friend to help
me fix my car and, as fate would have it, that friend was driven over by ...
Marlene! We started dating almost immediately after that.

Marlene was just my age. She was born in 1938 in Minto, New
Brunswick—a village 45 kilometres west of Fredericton. She was also studying at UNB. When I met Marlene things started to straighten out. She really
boosted my morale. I spent time with her rather than with the drinking
crew. Our dates were mostly UNB-oriented. We belonged to the UNB bridge
club and even earned a master point. We belonged to the film society that
brought American and foreign movies into Fredericton. Once a month when
I was paid for being a lab instructor, we went to the Sun Grill for spare ribs.
When we were going out I so enjoyed going for drives. I am into cars. I used
to have a particular cozy feeling from a car. It was almost like a closed protective shell—even more so if it was raining out. But much of our social life

revolved around the chemistry lab and Marlene spent many hours with me and Larry—who, some time later, was the best man at our wedding.

After dating for several months I went to Marlene one day and said I did not want to date any longer. I was disappointed because she had not introduced me to her parents. She called her parents in Minto immediately and said we were coming. That's when I met Alfred and Wally Parker. After that we went to Minto every Friday night. Minto is a small place of about two thousand people, in rural New Brunswick, about an hour's drive from Fredericton. I remember asking Marlene if she were related to the whole town. Her father was one of twelve and her mother was one of eight and most of the family had stayed close to home. It was new for me to be part of such a large extended family. Marlene maintains that her mother loved me because she saw me as a starving boy and she happily fed me. Her father liked me because I was getting an education. I respected and liked Marlene's parents from the get-go.

The first time Marlene met my parents was on the occasion when my father was hospitalized with heart problems. I wanted to see him and Marlene offered to drive me. I wanted to be prim and proper and said to Marlene, "If your parents agree, tell them we will take along chaperones." Marlene went home and asked her mother if she could drive me to Montreal. Her mother gave her fifty dollars and said, "I will ask your father." Wally then went to Alfred and said, "Marlene wants to take Izzy to Montreal to see his father." "How much money did you give her?" Alfred wanted to know. Wally replied, "Fifty dollars." "Don't be so mean," Alfred said. "Give her another fifty dollars."

We took Marlene's roommate and her boyfriend along as chaperones, even though Marlene's parents had not said a word about that. We stayed with my mother and went to see my father in the Montreal General Hospital. The hospital did not have a kosher kitchen, so my mother would cook food at home and take it to my father; in fact she was almost full-time there. My father was recovering and seemed okay at that point. The "chaperones" spent the two days in Montreal in an assortment of bars. Finally we had to fish them out of a nightclub at 2 a.m. Sunday. We headed back to Fredericton—a fourteen-hour drive in those days. They slept all the way back. Marlene and I were dead tired by the time we reached home.

I brought the fear of exams with me from Montreal. There was a fear of embarrassment in it. At UNB I had to take a course in physics, which was always my most difficult subject. It turned out that I was writing my exam at the same time and in the same location as Marlene was writing an exam. I had told Marlene that if I failed I was going to leave and go back to Montreal. She spent the whole time looking at me and worrying about how I was doing and not worrying about her own exam. I did pass it.

I went out with Marlene for about a year and did not mention that I was a Holocaust survivor. I did not say I was born in Montreal, but I think I led Marlene to believe that. I didn't lie but I did not tell the truth. I didn't want people to know I was from Poland. I told Marlene when it was clear that we would be together for a long time. It was a night when we went to see the play *Anne Frank's Diary* at UNB. It was put on by the Drama Society—it must have been 1960. When we came out, Marlene tells me, I was very upset and emotional. She was too.

"Her hiding place was a palace," I said. "What are you talking about!?" Marlene was annoyed at my statement so I told her that I was not born in Montreal but had lived through the Holocaust myself. I told her about our hiding place, that it was just a crawl space for nine people. I often think of this, that Anne Frank's hiding place was palatial compared to ours. But I survived and she didn't.

In the spring of 1960 my research director decided to return to Holland, his home country. I had been working on the oxidation and photo-oxidation of ascorbic acid and now here I was with no results after nearly two years. I had come close to quitting, and without Marlene's support I might not have lasted. I had to do something, so I devised my own problem and ran three experiments simultaneously for forty-eight hours at a time taking measurements every fifteen minutes. At that point Marlene started doing my laundry because I was so busy in the lab. She would bring me sandwiches and drinks at work and gave me moral support. Then she began to stay later and help me in the lab.

I needed to measure the flow of gas into my reaction vessels but I did not have a flow meter. Purchasing one was out of the question, because it was too expensive and too time-consuming. I built a flow meter of sorts by filling a one-litre volumetric flask with water and then bubbling the gas through the flask, thereby emptying it out. I counted the bubbles and that way I knew that so many bubbles meant a flow rate of such-and-such. Marlene was the bubble counter while I was on the

Israel as a UNB Master of Science grad, 1960, with Marlene and her father, Alfred Parker, on the UNB campus. (Israel Unger collection)

other side of the bench doing other things. Those were our dates. Why she married me is still a mystery.

Photochemistry in Texas

I was proud to get a Master of Science and I appreciated the UNB ceremony much more than the one at Sir George Williams University in Montreal. Marlene and her parents attended the ceremony. No one came from Montreal, because they were not in a position to come and I did not ask. I do believe that they were pleased.

The professor who replaced my first director was a breath of fresh air. He was young, very intelligent, and his area of research was photochemistry, which was much more interesting than what I had been involved in for my master's degree. So I started my Ph.D. and Marlene graduated and became a high school teacher. She taught first in Chipman, New Brunswick, and lived at home in Minto. Once a week or so she would come to Fredericton and spend the evening with me. On weekends I went to Minto and stayed at Marlene's parents' home.

When my Ph.D. was within sight I applied for a post-doctoral fellowship with a very well-known and highly regarded professor at the University of Rochester, W. Albert Noyes. To my delight he accepted me and said that he would pay me six thousand and three hundred dollars per year. I was thrilled both to have been accepted and by the money, which was at the top end of what post-docs were getting. A couple of months later my new director wrote again and said that he was moving to the University of Texas. He asked me to join him there and said that my new salary would be six thousand and eight hundred dollars. Needless to say it took me about one tenth of a second to say that I would be delighted to join him in Austin. After I went through my thesis defence and completed all the requirements for my Ph.D., I stayed in Fredericton for an extra month to train the graduate who had just arrived and was going to take over my equipment. I thought that was the best way I could say thank you to my Ph.D. director.

I arrived in Austin in September 1963 and loved it instantly. I had my own apartment, was earning a good salary, and had a fabulous director with a worldwide reputation whose knowledge was equalled by his personality. I had no responsibilities, no exams to write, no lectures to prepare, no labs to demonstrate. Finally I could just do research. My project was to study the photochemistry of fluorobenzene.

Photochemistry is the action of visible and ultraviolet light on molecules. It is associated with colour, what we see and why—with lasers and with very fast processes. Photochemists can measure processes that take one billionth of a second. It tells why the ozone layer is depleting, why pesticides stay in the environment for a long period of time, how photosynthesis comes about, and how solar panels work. My Ph.D. work had been on the photolysis—photochemical breakup—and photosensitized decomposition of chloroform. For my post-doc work my director suggested a topic and I suggested a different one.

Israel's post-doc identification for the University of Texas. (Israel Unger collection)

He told me to go ahead and work on the one I had suggested, which was the photochemistry of fluorobenzene. I eventually published the work.

I made several friends in Austin and one close friend. I played poker with a group more for social reasons than anything else but stopped because I lost twenty dollars in one session. That bothered me a great deal. I realized I was not a good loser, so I stopped playing.

Professor Noyes was invited to attend a by-invitation-only conference in Santa Barbara, California. He was not able to go and asked me if I wanted to. I was thrilled to accept. Noyes wrote and said a young, interesting post-doc would be attending in his place. My expenses were paid. The conference was superb. There were some thirty top photochemists present. Edward Teller, an early member of the Manhattan Project, attended, although he was a physicist. Noyes recommended I take an extra couple of days to visit San Francisco, too, which I did, but all I could think of was how much more fun it would be if Marlene were with me. In fact, the only negative thing about Texas was that I missed Marlene terribly.

One day during President Kennedy's visit to Texas, while I was eating lunch with friends at the university, a woman ran by hysterically shouting that Kennedy had been shot. We were all shocked and speechless. Then one of our group said, "Let's go to the common room, there is a TV there." We did and perhaps fifteen minutes later we heard on TV that Kennedy was dead. It was as if each of us, including me, had lost a very close relative. No one said anything. The university emptied out. I went home. I had been thrilled when Kennedy was elected and I was devastated when he was assassinated.

From the Friday of Kennedy's assassination until Monday I just stayed in my apartment. Sunday morning I was watching TV and talking to Marlene. We called each other once a week. In those days long-distance phone calls were expensive. Suddenly, while talking to Marlene, I saw Jack Ruby shoot

Lee Harvey Oswald and so I told Marlene. That news took a few minutes to get to Canada, so Marlene was one of the first informed.

Under the Chuppah in Minto, New Brunswick

In the late winter of 1964, I bought a diamond engagement ring and headed to New Brunswick. The flight had a stopover without changing planes in New Orleans and you could get off the plane. So I left my coat on the plane and I went to look over the New Orleans airport. There was a game room, so I played a pinball machine to while away the time. As a matter of habit I did not play pinball machines and had no experience with them, but I won several free games so I continued playing, figuring that there would be an announcement when my flight was due to depart. I did not hear any, so after playing all my free games I went and checked the notice board and to my horror I saw that my plane was due to leave in five minutes. I ran full out. Security at that time was non-existent. I got to the gate and there were three Delta Airlines DC-8s parked in a row. I was not sure which airplane I was on. I chose the centre one. The ground crew had already removed the staircase from the economy class of the aircraft but not from first class. I ran up the stairs and to the back of the airplane. Can you imagine how relieved I was when I saw my coat there which had the diamond engagement ring for Marlene in the pocket? How on earth would I ever have explained to her that I had lost the ring because I was playing pinball in New Orleans!?

I did not propose to Marlene. We just knew we were going to get married. Marlene converted to Judaism before we were married. It was for practical reasons. She studied for it and converted even though neither of us had strong religious feelings. It was important for my parents. Marlene's conversion solved the religion problem. It was to be a secular wedding, though by law a minister had to be present. We had been to see the Baptist minister, Reverend Harold Morgan. He was very sensitive to the fact that I was Jewish—there was to be no religion in the ceremony. We couldn't deal with the Fredericton rabbi at the time. We knew that we would be having a Jewish wedding in Texas.

My parents did not attend the wedding, as my father was already ill at that point. He had had a kidney removed; he had angina and heart problems. Plane travel was not common then and train travel from Montreal to Fredericton was a nightmare, so they did not attend. Marlene and I went to Montreal a couple of days after our wedding.

We were married on 6 July 1964 in Minto, New Brunswick. Just before the start of the ceremony Marlene's cousin was adjusting my tie in the kitchen of her parents' home and Wally was helping Alfred with his tie. Alfred, who

Israel and Marlene under the *chuppah* in Minto, New Brunswick, with Marlene's parents, Wally and Alfred Parker, 1964. (Israel Unger collection)

was a man of few words, said, "I told you, Wally, that you should have let me put the run to him when he first came here. It's too late now."

The ceremony took place on Alfred's and Wally's front lawn. The arbour was the *chuppah*. Marlene's father built it and a local florist trimmed it. I expect that it was the first time in Minto that there was a wedding that did not take place in a church. My best man was the fellow who shared the lab with me at UNB, Larry Hawton, and Marlene's best woman was a long-time friend from Minto, Teddy Buxton. There was an organ and the next-door neighbour played the wedding music. Marlene was friends with several nurses who were dating Mounties. One of these Mounties said he was disappointed not to be invited to our wedding. Marlene jokingly told him she expected all the Mounties to come and reroute the traffic, as her parents' house was on the main road between Minto and Chipman. It was a big surprise, but they did just that. They came in their official capacity and rerouted traffic wearing their red tunics and the whole nine yards! Funny to think that my image of Canada and Mounties I had back in France came true. It was a nice wedding.

We spent a few days in New Brunswick then travelled via Montreal to Windsor, Ontario, and spent the night there. We walked across the bridge over the Detroit River to the United States. This was our honeymoon. I had purchased a Ford Mustang in Austin and took possession of it in Detroit. When we arrived at the car dealership they were just washing the car. It was a silver

Ford Mustang. It cost two thousand seven hundred dollars and I paid for it in cash. It was my first new car of my life and I was very excited.

We then travelled from Detroit to Austin in our new car. When we passed through Oklahoma it was stifling hot and our car did not have air conditioning. Marlene kept asking me to stop whenever we saw a motel that advertised air conditioning. I did not want to stop, because when I had passed through the year before, I had seen a motel just north of the Texas–Oklahoma border that was very nice and had not only air conditioning but also a swimming pool. Finally we got to that motel. I walked in and told the receptionist that I had been there a year before and liked it so much that I came back. The receptionist said, "I'm glad you liked it, but we are full today." When I told Marlene that there was no vacancy, she said, "Let's go to the nice motel a few miles back which has air conditioning and a vacancy." I refused. I did not want to go backwards. So we continued on and there were no motels until we got to Texas and then we could find only a seedy non-air-conditioned one. This is one of the many times that Marlene was right and I was very wrong.

We had a wonderful time in Texas. Marlene and I lived together for the first time. Of course, back then couples did not live together before marriage. My research went very well. My director was super. We made good friends. Marlene worked for the State of Texas Special Schools as a bookkeeper. Her parents came out to visit us at Christmas time. It was the first time they had ever been on a commercial airline. We travelled quite a bit within Texas and went to Mexico once. On our way back from Mexico I acquired a set of Texas longhorn steer horns in the border city Nuevo Laredo for eighteen dollars. An equivalent set was three hundred and fifty dollars in Texas. We walked across the bridge with the horns and when we got to the Texas side there was an elderly man sitting on a bench. Marlene was carrying the horns and he admired them and asked where we got them. Marlene told him and he asked where were we taking them. Marlene replied back home to Canada and the man said, "When you get those back to Canada, don't tell people that you got them in Mexico. Tell them they came from Texas." One of our friends had a pilot's licence and he rented an airplane and flew down to visit us in Texas. The plane was an old one with cloth wings and our friend was determined he was going to take the horns back to New Brunswick for us strapped under the wings. That would have made an interesting sight as he landed at the various airports—assuming that the tips did not pierce the canvas wings when he hit some turbulence. In the end we found that the horns could be disassembled into two parts and fit in his plane. That's how we got them back to Fredericton. They are about two metres long tip to tip.

While I was in Texas several world-renowned photochemists visited my director. His standard comment when he showed them the lab was, "This is Dr. Unger. He knows more about our work than I do, so I am going to let him show you my lab." As a result I had several offers for post-doctorates in the United Kingdom, Australia, and the Soviet Union. All sounded interesting, but I was eager to start my career as a professor and UNB had just opened the Saint John Campus and offered me a job. I was thrilled and accepted. I then received a letter of appointment from the president which stated that I would be appointed to the rank of instructor. I was not prepared to go as an instructor and I let that be known to the chair of the department by phone. A few days later I received another letter from the president of the university stating that I would be an assistant professor. I have not made an exhaustive study, but I think I may hold the record for the fastest promotion at the University of New Brunswick.

While I was at the University of Texas I had a pattern of working six and a half days a week. The chemistry department had a top-rate library and I devoted Sunday mornings to reading the most current chemistry literature. One such morning my director, Dr. Noyes, happened to walk in. "What are you doing here?" he asked me. I liked to make jocular remarks so I replied, "My wife threw me out." He didn't say anything but just left. Months later my term was coming to an end in Texas and I was to leave in a couple of weeks. I went in to see Dr. Noyes and ask him if he had any advice for me. He said, "Do you remember a few months ago in the library? Well, if you have a wife who doesn't mind you going to the library on a Sunday morning, you don't need any advice from me!"

In 1965 Marlene and I were married a second time, in Austin, in a synagogue by a rabbi. Myron and Pat Frankman were our best man and woman. They were friends from Montreal and doing post-docs in Texas. It was a very small event but a Jewish wedding, so I broke the wedding glass with my heel, according to tradition. When we left Texas we drove through Las Vegas and saw a sign saying "Cupid Wedding Chapel. Weddings $5. Free Gift for Every Bride. Open 24 hours." I was curious as to what the gift was and five dollars was not a huge amount even in 1965. I thought it would be quite a lark to get married again, but Marlene said something to the effect of, "I married you twice already. I don't need to marry you again."

The Young Professor—From Texas to Saint John

I had been in Texas for two years when I returned to New Brunswick. It was the fall of 1965 and I was just twenty-seven when I started at UNB Saint John—one of the youngest professors at the university. But UNB Saint John was a huge disappointment. It was a brand new offshoot campus of UNB Fredericton and it was very small. I went from a major American university with twenty-eight thousand students, a chemistry department of forty faculty, forty post-docs, two hundred graduate students, its own library, a machine shop, a glass-blowing shop, and even its own purchasing department ... to a school with seventeen faculty where there were only two Ph.D.s. Other than myself, no one had a research grant. There were about one hundred and thirty students—in total.

I gave my lectures at the YMCA. I did not have a laboratory and there were no library facilities. I clamoured for lab space and eventually I was offered a room in an old courthouse building that had a giant safe in it and nothing else. Since I desperately wanted to continue doing research and I did have a grant, I decided to collaborate with my former director. I took it upon myself to travel to Fredericton every week to use the library and to give a research seminar, every second week if the driving conditions were poor. I would go on Thursday evenings and stay with Marlene's parents in Minto. Marlene had a teaching job in Saint John, so she would come to Minto on Friday, and Sunday night we would go back to Saint John together. The drive back in the dark was awful and slow on bad roads.

The first year of teaching is the most difficult for any professor anyway, but for me, given the circumstances, it was even worse. There were no colleagues nearby to seek advice from. I *was* the chemistry department. All of these things led to my having severe stomach pains. It was a very trying first year and I resolved to leave Saint John. I was about to start looking for positions in other universities or even industry if need be. Then there was a fortuitous incident. At the same time I had been hired to teach chemistry at the Saint John campus of UNB, the Fredericton campus had hired a fellow called Theophanides to teach chemistry. But his wife could not stand Fredericton and they left for McGill University. He did not bother to tell anyone until late in the year. So UNB Fredericton found itself one professor short in the chemistry department. I was asked to go to Fredericton and was delighted to do so. I moved up to Fredericton in the spring of 1966, just as soon as the academic year was over, even though Marlene had to stay in Saint John until the school year was over.

When I joined the chemistry department at UNB Fredericton there were seven professors. Today there are at least double that number. The department had pioneered research at UNB, was very proud of its record, and tried to maintain it. I collaborated with my Ph.D. director. This was advantageous to both of us. The advantage for me was that I joined an established, reasonably well-equipped laboratory. The advantage for my former research director was that his publication record increased substantially. The disadvantage was that I was not viewed as independent. Also, when I was brought to Fredericton it was not because people thought highly of my research but because they needed someone to teach classes in the fall.

After a few years into my teaching career, I asked my students to evaluate me. I assumed they would rate me highly but they pointed out that I had an aggravating speech habit of using "eh" as a filler when I was looking for a word to say. I felt terrible and when I got over my bad feelings I acknowledged that the students were right and I made a determined effort to get rid of that speech habit. It took about two weeks but I did.

Later I really enjoyed teaching. I was known for doing experiments in class. In the beginning I had to teach many large basic-chemistry classes. I had, for instance, four hundred engineering students, so I would lecture for twenty-five minutes, do a five-minute experiment, and then lecture again. As an example, I would demonstrate a thermite reaction—an exchange reaction between iron oxide and aluminum, which generates a vast amount of heat. The students would get to see red-hot flowing molten iron. One time I over-heard two students talking. One asked the other, "Are you going to Unger's lecture?" "Yes, I don't know what he's going to blow up today." Another time one of Marlene's former students approached her at the high school and said, "Mrs. Unger, your husband almost burnt down Head Hall today!" That time I was illustrating some reaction and material escaped and the podium caught fire but I put it out rapidly. It was no big deal.

At that time at UNB, the president wrote all of the faculty a two-page letter at the end of the academic year. The first page discussed all the wonderful things that had happened at UNB and on the second page the last sentence stated: Your salary will be so-and-so much. Salary increases ranged from five hundred dollars to five thousand dollars. Nobody knew how the president arrived at them. My first increase at UNB was five hundred dollars, which was the smallest given that year. The next year, once again I had one of the smallest increases. A colleague in political science offered an explanation. He said it was due to my name. That's when I decided to become involved in the faculty association. I knew that I could not rely on accomplishment to advance in my profession. If I had no chance to improve my standing by myself then I felt the only way to improve my salary was to do so on behalf of the whole faculty and to try to develop some sort of rational system for salaries, promotions, tenure, and so on. I was elected president of the Association of UNB Teachers (AUNBT) in 1968. There is no doubt that at that time, if you were willing to serve, you could have the job.

I spent a lot time preparing a salary brief for the AUNBT together with Harold Sharp, the new chair of the economic benefits committee. This involved not only preparing the arguments and getting various documents together but also doing all the secretarial work because AUNBT did not have a secretary. I was very encouraged when the president said it was a good report. I went home and told Marlene that I was going to get a huge increase! Imagine my disappointment when I received my letter from the president and my salary increase did not come anywhere near the recommendation of the salary committee. That is when I realized that just because the president said that it was a good report did not mean that he was going to implement it.

Since I was eager not to let my research slip I found that I had to put in long days to prepare and give lectures, do research, talk to graduate students, write papers, prepare research proposals, and to do the AUNBT work. I worked usually from 8 a.m. to 10 p.m. Even later in my university career, one of my habits was to answer *all* letters, phone messages, and, later, emails myself. When I was a dean I told my secretaries that no matter who called, they were to transfer the call to me if I was not speaking to someone else. I answered all my phone messages in the order I received them. It did not matter whether they were from, students, professors, people outside the university, or staff.

UNB and the AUNBT experienced a severe crisis in the late sixties. An American physics professor Norman Strax became very active in protesting the war in Vietnam. In 1968, as a professor at UNB, Strax lead another protest. The university library introduced a photo identity card for faculty and students for checking out books. Strax did not like that idea, so he proceeded to try to check out books without showing his card. This produced piles of books at the checkout counter. After several confrontations, Professor Strax was suspended and banned from campus. When he broke that ban he was jailed. Student supporters occupied his office for some weeks. The faculty took sides and the Canadian National Association of University Teachers (CAUT) became involved, ultimately censuring UNB. Some faculty supported Strax; others did not. Many faculty resigned from AUNBT. The net result of the Strax affair was that Strax left the university and so did President MacKay.

In my early years at UNB there were very contentious issues and heated faculty association meetings. At one such meeting, a committee was being established. A professor stood up and exclaimed, "We don't want any 'Jewish engineers' on the committee." This was a derogatory term for accountants, I was told. Many years later I heard the same remark from a man who was being given an honorary degree at UNB. A Jewish colleague at an American university told me that he had become friends with a German professor. Once, at dinner, the German professor's wife complained that during the war her family had suffered because they did not have enough coal to heat their home and she had to wear gloves to play the piano. After I had been at UNB for several years a new faculty member in my department was speaking to me in my office about a research problem. When that conversation ended we continued on other subjects, then out of the blue he said something about "the Jews downtown." The conversation ended abruptly and he left. About ten minutes later he came back and apologized for making that remark in front of me because I am Jewish. He did not apologize because of the comment but because he had made it to a Jew. I had expected better from highly educated people.

ALS—My Father's Death

About the time I met Marlene, my father started getting sick. It was a big trauma for every one. First he had a kidney removed. The surgeon speculated that the kidney had been damaged by the kick he had received from the Gestapo in Tarnow. Then he had problems with his heart. Then Charlie phoned one day and was distraught. He said, "Father is going to die!" It was a shock! He told me that our father had this terrible disease and there was no cure. That was late 1967.

The neurologist in Montreal who saw my father was Dr. Libman and he said, "We think your father has ALS, but we are not sure." ALS, or amyotrophic lateral sclerosis, is a debilitating and fatal motor neuron disease. It is also known as Lou Gehrig's disease, after the famous baseball player who was diagnosed with it in 1939. The nerve cells in the central nervous system, which control voluntary muscles, degenerate. People with ALS usually die within three to five years. Stephen Hawking, the physicist, has ALS and has miraculously lived for years longer than that. Today, local family physicians might be able to recognize it, but at the time the disease was less known, so Dr. Libman recommended we go to the Lahey Clinic in Boston for tests.

Charlie and my father flew to Boston and I drove and met them at the airport. We went to the Lahey Clinic and they examined my father for two days. I have the highest praise for how they treat people and how efficient they were. At the Lahey Clinic they had arranged a series of appointments starting with an examination and interview with a neurologist, then tests and X-rays. The neurologist had said that in Montreal they had about one case a year of ALS, so they did not have much experience in diagnosing it. At the Lahey Clinic they had about sixty cases a year, because people come from all over the world. So they had no trouble diagnosing it. They confirmed that it was ALS. I was searching for hope and I asked the neurologist if there was any research that was going on that might help. "We are not even ten years away from finding a cure," he replied. They were very good—extremely professional, not hurtful, but at the same time realistic. It is now forty years later and there is still no cure.

My father died over a three-and-a-half-year period. He was sixty-five when he was diagnosed. Basically he worked all his life and then he got sick and died. I visited my parents several times a year after my father became sick. He had stopped working but still he would go to the Jewish Public Library in Montreal and pick up four or five books. He read Yiddish, which is written in Hebrew script. He would return with this stack of books. I had not known that about my father. Here was a man with very little formal education who treasured books and read profusely even as he was dying. I was impressed even at that time.

David Unger passport photo, circa 1951. (Israel Unger collection)

In August 1970 my father was taken to the hospital again. I went to Montreal to see him. I was scheduled to go to a conference in France and then on to Israel for my first visit. I told the doctor who was looking after my father about my plans and asked him if I should modify them. My father was having a hard time breathing, but the doctor assured me this was under control and I could travel. I decided to go but to leave out the Israel part. On the last day I was in France. I was driving to the airport and had stopped to buy gas when another motorist approached me and told me that there was a radio announcement about an emergency in my family. Marlene had managed to contact the car rental company and put the announcement on the radio to look for my licence plate and this driver recognized it. I called home and spoke to Marlene's mother, who knew my father was dying but not that he had died, so I did not actually find out he had died until I arrived back in Canada. I flew to Montreal and the next day we took my father's body to Israel for burial on the Mount of Olives.

I had a mixture of feelings going to Israel. I was sad and was concerned about my mother, who was in deep grief, and I was excited to finally be in Israel. We drove from what is now called Ben Gurion International Airport. I was impressed by the fields and I was taken by the rusting remains of trucks that had been destroyed trying to break the blockade of Jerusalem in 1948. I was just impressed that I was actually in Israel. But mostly I remember how terribly sad my mother was. I tried the religious bit and said that my father was now in heaven with the righteous, but she was not consoled. She replied, "I could have had him for a while longer."

At my father's funeral I stood there thinking of the feelings we had for one another. I had achieved a lot but I had failed him, both my parents, in religious matters. I am sure he was happy that I was successful. When I was awarded a C.I.L. fellowship, my name appeared in a Montreal newspaper. The MP for the riding that my parents lived in sent them a congratulatory letter. I know that my parents were proud of that. My father never saw me become a dean, he did not see me become the president of Canadian Association of University Teachers or the president of the Canadian Conference of Deans of Science, or the co-chair of the Holocaust Commemoration Committee of the Canadian Jewish Congress. My mother was alive, but by that time she could not really appreciate it. Still, religion would have been more important to them than all of that. If I had become a professor *and* gone to the synagogue on Saturday and kept the Sabbath—that would have been what they wanted.

After the funeral we went from Jerusalem to Haifa to my mother's cousin Shezifi to spend the night. Shezifi is the Hebrew version of the name Wittenstein. They were the relatives who sent us food to Tarnow right after liberation. It was a long way to their small apartment and we ended up sleeping on couches. We had to get up very early the next morning to catch a bus to Tel Aviv for our flight home. It would have been a shorter distance and much simpler to stay in a hotel and go directly from Jerusalem to Tel Aviv. Charlie had three thousand dollars in his pocket, so money was not an issue. But my brother and I were not really thinking straight and my mother was thinking only of her loss.

When the stewardess came by with the drink tray, Charlie lifted a few little bottles of liquor off the tray while her back was turned and just felt great about that. That was Charlie. When we got to Montreal we only had one small carry-on suitcase and customs searched it. I expect they found it strange that three people travelled to Israel with only one small bag. We returned to Montreal and sat *shiva*, the seven days of mourning for close family members. The worst part of that for me was not being able to shave. The first thing I did when the *shiva* was over was to shave.

There were twenty-five thousand Jews in Tarnow in 1939. After the Holocaust there were a few hundred survivors. My parents saved their children, five other Jews, and themselves. My father was tortured by the Gestapo to become a *Juden Polizei*, but he refused. Partisans asked my father to leave his family because if he stayed we were all doomed, but he refused to leave us. My father was a prosperous businessman and he lost every thing: he lost his business, his parents, his brothers, and his sisters, his uncles and aunts, his nephews and nieces. The same is true for my mother. When they came to Canada they had to start from the beginning. They had to learn a new language, a new culture, and they had jobs that paid very poorly. My father swept the floor in a clothing factory for twenty dollars a week and my mother worked as a seamstress. But they never complained.

I have a big regret and that is that I never told my parents that they were extraordinary and that they were heroes.

Charlie's Troubles

After Marlene and I were married we would go to Montreal especially to visit my mother, but we also visited with Charlie and his family. Lily and Charlie had three children: Rosie or Raisel was the oldest, then there was Joycie, and the youngest was Caroline. I don't think Charlie spoke to his family about his past. Charlie and I never talked to each other about our experiences and I never heard him talk about it in his own house when I was there. One time Charlie and the whole family came to Fredericton to visit Marlene and me. His middle daughter Joycie came by herself once and stayed for a week. I would not say our two families were close.

Charlie and Lily bought a duplex together with Lily's father and mother. It was a huge mistake. Charlie and Lily lived upstairs and Lily's parents lived downstairs. Right from the very beginning, after their first daughter was born, when they fought, Lily would leave Charlie and move downstairs with her parents. Charlie would take the crib down for the baby and help organize things so she could live with her parents. That would last a few days. Lily's parents would phone my parents and tell them what a bad guy Charlie was. That's how I found out about it. My father would get ideas about how to go about restoring peace. One idea was maybe we should call a third party like the Landers to mediate. After a while Lily would send a signal that she was ready to come back. Charlie would go and buy her flowers and she would go back upstairs and Charlie would bring back the crib. And the cycle would start again.

Their marriage was like a volcano, they would erupt and calm down, then they would erupt again. It was a game that Lily played whenever Charlie did something she didn't like. Faithfulness wasn't the problem. It was more lifestyle. Lily put on airs. She wanted to be a genteel lady. She joined a book club; she wanted to drink tea and be part of society. Charlie was not terribly couth. He was a meat-and-potatoes guy.

After twenty years of marriage there was a really bad fight that resulted in Charlie moving out and taking a small basement apartment in a rundown building on Park Avenue. I felt a great deal of pity for him when he phoned me and said that essentially Lily had kicked him out. After this last fight Charlie sought out my help, simply to talk to me and have my sympathy. I went to see him in that apartment and it was difficult for me to see him like that. He was very depressed. The apartment did not represent his money; it represented his mood. But he and Lily both expected that within a few weeks or a couple of months they would once again reconcile and he would move back home.

We went to dinner and drank a lot and I tried to cheer him up, tried to make him laugh. The next time I came to Montreal he was still in the apartment, but he had met Hilda. Here is my take on Hilda. She had come from El Salvador. She was a maid in, I believe, an El Salvadorian home. She became pregnant. The family then kicked her out. She took a cheap apartment. She had this very tiny baby. She had trouble supporting herself. The guy in the next apartment was Charlie. They met in the elevator of the apartment house. He was a wholesale dry goods businessman. He brought her a couple of little things for the baby. That started it.

I think if he had not met Hilda, Lily and Charlie would have gotten back together. That's the pattern they had for twenty years. I talked to Lily and she told me that friends were saying, "You have been married for twenty years. How can you let this happen?" She was definitely sending signals that she was ready to get back together. Charlie as usual would have to do some penance. But in the meantime he had found Hilda and she was fawning all over him. Shortly after they met, Charlie and Hilda started living together. Charlie was very happy and had a new purpose in life. He moved out of the rundown place to a nice apartment and gave Hilda a job in his store. The two of them visited us in Fredericton very soon after getting together. Hilda was in her early twenties and she had this darling little girl. When they came to our house and Charlie sat down on the couch, Hilda ran and took his shoes off and brought his slippers. This is something he certainly never had before.

Lily turned Charlie's children against him. It was to be expected, because Charlie was using the kids to get back at Lily. For instance, Lily would phone and say that the kids needed money to get their teeth fixed and he would not readily agree to pay. He was using money as a way of punishing Lily, so Charlie's kids reacted to the way their father treated them. Of course they were unhappy that their father left the family. I don't know if he paid alimony. I think they may have made a deal that Lily got the house and that was it. Lily continued to live in the house that they had shared. I don't know if he had visiting rights and I don't know if he cared. When Charlie and Lily divorced, it was a bitter divorce. I continued my relationship with Charlie and so his children had little to do with me. They divorced us too. At the end of Charlie's life however, they did reconcile and come to see him.

Charlie with his mother, Hinda, and son, Michael, circa 1980 in Montreal. (Israel Unger collection)

After divorcing Lily, Charlie and Hilda were married and they bought first an upscale apartment and then a house. Charlie adopted Hilda's daughter Madeleine and then Hilda and Charlie had a son, Michael, who was named after our father, whose first name was Mordechai. But Charlie's happiness did not last long.

A Mark for Canada

Back to UNB. Throughout my university career I served on many committees within UNB and on academic, governmental, research, professional association boards, and in committees in the wider community.

I think I needed to prove what I could achieve. I had a great need for acceptance, to be seen to be important. I say that about myself in a negative way. Yet I was very fortunate that I could accomplish this—no false modesty intended, I take that as a mark for Canada, not as a mark of me, that I had the opportunity to meet and work with a wide range of interesting, intelligent people in various professions across the country.

To give an example, I became the chair of the search committee for the president of UNB. It is highly unusual, perhaps even unheard of, that a professor be the chair. It was a great experience, but the best part of the experience is that I met a fellow who has become a lifelong friend, Eldon Thompson. He is a wonderful human being in every respect. We really hit it off. It was an interesting time in both our lives.

Eldon was from a small, southern New Brunswick town. He has a degree in electrical engineering from UNB. He became the president of the New Brunswick telephone company, NB Tel, and then went to Ottawa and became president of Telesat Canada. It is an international company for satellite communications for television and telephone. Eldon is a wise, gentle, thoughtful, very intelligent person.

One day he phoned me and in his typical soft-spoken way said, "I have used your name in vain." Telesat had a Canada-wide contest for high school kids to design an experiment that would be sent aboard the United States' space shuttle. I was asked if I would be one of the judges for that contest. Why did Telesat call me? Obviously through the suggestion of Eldon Thompson. I became a judge.

Another one of the judges from Telesat was John Korda. He was the launch director for Telesat, meaning he had the expertise to put satellites into orbit, and he did that not only for Canada but for several other countries on behalf of Telesat. A young man won the competition. Telesat was responsible for putting the winning idea into practice and John Korda and I talked on the phone several times to this end. Telesat built the experiment and I received an invitation to go to Cape Kennedy to watch the shuttle take off! It was the launch that preceded the one that exploded.

We went to NASA headquarters by bus from the hotel and one day I was sitting by John Korda and he introduced himself. I learned that he had come to Canada from Budapest in 1956 after the political upheavals there. "Where were you during the war?" I asked him. "Birkenau." It turns out that, as a Jew, he had been hidden as a teenager in a monastery. He came out of hiding to try to help his parents. John was caught and sent to Auschwitz-Birkenau and he was forced to see his parents taken to the gas chambers.

There were many survivors like John Korda who were now Canadians contributing to society in various fields. There were about forty thousand Holocaust survivors who ended up in Canada. Clearly my story is one of many.

Eldon nominated me and I became a member of the Council of Trustees of the Institute for Research on Public Policy, the IRPP. I would go to Canadian Association of University Teachers meetings in Ottawa and call Eldon and we would have supper together. While we ate, people would come into the restaurant and apologize for disturbing him and he would have to sign an important document. Knowing Eldon opened phenomenal doors for me.

The chair of the board of IRPP was Robert Stanfield—head of the Progressive Conservative Party of Canada for several years. In fact, he was referred to as "the greatest prime minister Canada never had." The president of IRPP was Gordon Robertson, former clerk of the Privy Council and all the members of the Board and Council of Trustees were people of equivalent stature. A short while after I had been on the council, Stanfield called and asked me to chair the nominating committee. Rosalie Abella, who became a member of the Supreme Court, was a member of the IRPP. The stature of the institute was such that Quebec premier, Robert Bourassa,

Meeting Canada's Governor General, Jeanne Sauvé, in Rideau Hall at a reception for the IRPP, 1987. (Israel Unger collection)

came for lunch once during the Meech Lake Accord negotiations. He was seeking our support for passage of the Accord. Usually academics don't get to meet these sorts of people, but I was fortunate to meet them because of Eldon Thompson.

Robert Stanfield was a wonderful, warm, and humorous person who really came across in a small group. I have a few Robert Stanfield anecdotes. We had a repartee going. One year Stanfield's term expired as chair of the board. Needless to say the committee enthusiastically agreed to nominate him for another term, but when I gave my report I said, "This was a difficult one. We debated and pondered and thought about it ..." I paused. "And after half a second, we decided to nominate Robert Stanfield." At the next meeting Stanfield was introducing new members of the board. "This is Mr. So-and-So, president of such-and-such bank in Vancouver." Stanfield listed more of the fellow's accomplishments and then said, "He is originally from Fredericton but left town when Israel Unger moved to the city." On another occasion the IRPP were meeting in Regina. The lieutenant-governor of Saskatchewan hosted a reception for us. The receiving line consisted of the lieutenant-governor, his wife, and Bob Stanfield. Stanfield introduced each member of the board and council as we came in. When it was my turn Stanfield said, "This is Israel Unger, he's a herring choker." The lieutenant-governor looked puzzled. "That's slang for a New Brunswicker." Stanfield was from Nova Scotia himself and followed up by saying, "They call us Nova Scotians Bluenosers" (after the famous schooner, the *Bluenose*). The lieutenant-governor then asked, "What do you call people from Prince Edward Island?" Without hesitation Stanfield replied, "Lobster snatchers."

Robert Stanfield and Israel Unger, circa 1981. (Israel Unger collection)

And a last story—we had a meeting in Fredericton and on the day before the meeting some fellow had gone into a rage over a parking ticket at the Fredericton airport and driven his car through the front doors. The airport put up plywood in place of the glass doors. That evening Stanfield arrived. I went to the airport to pick him up and I explained why we had plywood doors at the terminal. Stanfield said, "New Brunswickers express themselves forcefully."

Stanfield was not the only politician I met. To this day I exchange emails with the former New Brunswick Premier Frank McKenna. I have a huge respect for McKenna. When the Charlottetown Accord was being debated to make amendments to the Canadian Constitution, McKenna struck a citizens' committee to review the Accord and report to the legislature. The committee met in the Legislative Chamber to advise the government as to what their position should be on the accord. I'm sure it was all show; still, he appointed two people to chair that meeting: one was the then dean of law at UNB and the other was me. I was proud and glad to be able to do something to try to keep Canada together.

I also think it is important for the Jewish community, secular and religious, to interact with the Christian community for the benefit of both. An example of this is when I was president of the New Brunswick chapter of Science for Peace, I invited Bishop Gumbleton, who was the founding president of Pax Christi (an international Catholic peace organization) in the United States, to speak at UNB. For me, what was important was not necessarily that he was Catholic but that he was promoting a vital ideal.

Years later, when I received an invitation in the late 1990s by the Gospel, Ecumenism and Theology

Israel Unger with Bishop Gumbleton, mid-1980s, at UNB. (Israel Unger collection)

Committee (GET) of the Maritime Conference of the United Church of Canada to comment on the national United Church draft document *Bearing Faithful Witness*. I was pleased to do so. I was impressed with the document. I spent a day and a half with the committee discussing many issues. The committee consists of United Church ministers and lay people from the three Maritime provinces. A couple of months later I was invited to join the committee for a two-year term. I told them that I have no expertise in theology, and being a Jew I do not support one of their objectives, that is, spreading the Gospel. Still I was appointed and reappointed several times. I have now been on that committee for well over a decade and am the longest-serving member. I enjoy meeting the members, their earnestness and their desire to work for the benefit of all humanity. I also appreciate their sincere desire for me to be candid in giving them a Jewish perspective on issues of concern both to them and to the Jewish Community.

When I first joined GET a Catholic priest, Dan Bohan, was a member of the committee. A couple of years later Dan invited me, and I was pleased to attend his ordination as bishop. Later he was appointed archbishop in Regina. He was one of Sharon and Lee's guests at the naming ceremony for their daughter Sophie. But I am getting ahead of myself.

Sharon and Sheila

In 1967 our daughter Sharon was born. That was Canada's centennial year, so we called her our "centennial project." She was born at the Victoria Public Hospital in Fredericton. I recall sitting in a hallway in the hospital while Marlene was giving birth thinking, How should I be acting? I should be nervous. In those days only medical personnel were allowed in the birthing room. I wish I could have been present.

We were still living in an apartment then, the Ross Millet apartments on Regent Street. Marlene tells me that when Sharon was born she felt that every woman in the world was smarter than she was and could look after a child better. I did not know that at the time. It was a time when women looked after the children and men had a career—unfortunately so. Today I feel guilty that I did not help Marlene enough. She worked full-time even when pregnant. She was the first teacher at Fredericton High School to continue teaching while pregnant and she was allowed only seventeen days off after Sharon was born. Today women in Canada can have up to a year's maternity leave.

We had a traditional set-up—Marlene did the diapers, washed the kids, and so on. I did change the diapers a couple of times, but they scared me because I was afraid that I would stick the safety pin in the baby. Paper diapers had just come on the market. They were called Flush-a-byes. I thought

Flush-a-byes meant that you could flush the whole works down the flush. Marlene warned me that you could not but I went ahead anyway. Our apartment was on the second floor so I plugged up the system for half the apartment building.

Sharon first walked on Marlene's grandmother's birthday. We were at her parents' place in Minto, in the kitchen. There were quite a few people in the house. I don't remember how it started, but Sharon's first steps were towards her grandfather and when she got there she cried. She was thirteen months old at the time. It was such an intense moment and Sharon was so overcome by her success that she cried but it was clearly tears of joy.

Sharon was a very conservative little girl. When she was a year old we moved from our apartment to our brand-new house. It was clear we were going to stay in Fredericton and we did not want to rent apartments any longer. We still live in the house today. It is a bungalow that we enlarged over the years. We paid thirty-two thousand for land and house back in 1968. But when we moved in it was not quite completed. The three of us slept in Sharon's bedroom, I had a terrible toothache and poor Sharon cried all night. She did not like being moved to a strange place. She did not tolerate change well. She hung on to her favourite blanket for many years.

Sharon and Sheila Unger at Fredericton's *cheder* graduation ceremony, circa 1976. (Israel Unger collection)

In 1974, when she was seven, we sent Sharon to a *cheder*, which is Hebrew for room, and is a place where the basics of Judaism and Hebrew are taught. Marlene and I joined the synagogue at that time. Sharon would walk over to the synagogue from her elementary school. Later our second daughter, Sheila, went with Sharon and Marlene picked them up after work. The girls did not have *bat mitzvahs* because the rabbi did not do that for girls at the time.

Sharon did very well in school, although by the time she got to high school she worried a great deal about exams. To hear her tell it, she had failed everything, and then when the results came in she had very high marks.

When she graduated from Fredericton High School, Sharon ended up with the math and French prizes and a very substantial scholarship for university.

It was the death of Sharon's grandfather that motivated her to become a doctor. I was in China when Alfred died. He had had heart problems for some time but his death was sudden. They were all at the cottage together and Alfred "took a spell." Marlene took him to the hospital and he died that night. Marlene managed to reach me and asked whether they should wait until I got home for the funeral. I told her not to wait, as I felt it was best for them to get that over as quickly as possible. I hurried home and arrived in Fredericton the day after the funeral. Marlene met me at the gate. Sharon, Sheila, and Wally were in the car outside. As soon as I got into the car Sharon said, "Dad, I am going to become a doctor for Grampy." Sharon was sixteen years old at the time.

At age seventeen she went to Moncton to spend a day with a neonatologist to see what that was all about. Neonatology is a subspecialty of pediatrics dealing with newborns. Sharon decided that would be her career. She started at UNB that fall and in first year her GPA was 4.3 on a 4.3 scale. She had all A-pluses other than in English, where all she managed was an A-minus. Sharon studied for her MCAT (Medical College Admission Test) over the summer and taught herself Organic Chemisty for the exam. She had the highest score of the thirty-some students who wrote at UNB that year. Most of the other students were in third or fourth year or even graduate students and she was only in second year. Sharon applied to three medical schools and was admitted to all of them. She chose Dalhousie University in Halifax because of its proximity to Fredericton. After graduation, Sharon did a one-year rotating internship and then was accepted as a resident in pediatrics at Dalhousie University and received her Royal College Certification as a pediatrician. Then she did a fellowship in neonatology in Toronto at Mount Sinai Hospital and a year of medical research. Finally, fifteen years after that day at the Fredericton airport, Sharon was a full-fledged neonatologist and was hired by Mount Sinai Hospital. Sharon was and is unbelievably determined and once she sets a goal for herself there is little that she will allow get in her way. She will work very, very hard to achieve her goal.

After saying she would become a doctor for her grandfather, Sharon used her medical know-how to help save her grandmother's life. Wally had a nosebleed she could not get stopped so she went to the Minto hospital—a very small hospital. They took her blood pressure, which was very high, so they put her on strong drugs to reduce it and inserted a nasal balloon. This is a balloon-tipped catheter that exerts pressure to stop the bleeding. Wally's brother called Marlene. Marlene went to Minto, saw Wally, and everything seemed to be under control. Marlene went back to Fredericton and called

Sharon in Toronto to tell her about it. Sharon then called Wally in the Minto hospital. Wally told Sharon that she was not feeling well and was spitting blood. Sharon realized that the nosebleed had not been stopped but the blood had simply been rerouted. Since the blood could not run out her nose it was running down her throat and that made Wally spit blood. Sharon called the Minto hospital and asked for Wally's vital signs. They had not checked the vital signs after the initial check on arrival. Sharon said, "I will stay on the line. Please go and check her vital signs." They did and reported to Sharon that she had a dangerously low blood pressure and a high heart rate. This was a condition that could lead to a stroke, so Sharon told the people in Minto to take Wally off the blood pressure medication. She then phoned Marlene and told her to get Wally to the Chalmers Hospital in Fredericton right away. Sharon stayed on the line with her grandmother until Marlene arrived at the Minto hospital. Marlene tells me that it was the fastest trip she ever made to Minto. Marlene took Wally to the Chalmers; they stopped the nosebleed and Wally came and stayed with us for a few days. She was eighty-four years old at the time. We believe that if Sharon had not intervened, Wally would probably have died that night and people would just have said she was an old woman and died of a stroke.

Sheila was born in 1969 and is two years younger than Sharon. When she went to kindergarten, which was not compulsory in New Brunswick at the time, she missed playing outside so she was cared for by a nanny instead. Marlene then referred to Sheila jokingly as a "kindergarten dropout." One day, as I was driving with Sheila she asked me, "Daddy, is a drawboat a bad thing?" "What's a drawboat?" "That's what Mummy says I am!" She was an interesting kid.

There was an annual graduation ceremony for the *cheder*. Wally and Alfred regularly attended these events. The girls often won prizes. Afterward there would be a reception and one time when Sheila was about nine she was running wildly all over the place playing with the other children yet holding one arm stiff at her side. We asked her what was the matter and she showed us a chocolate-milk stain she had gotten on her dress. She didn't want anyone to see it!

Marlene went to Sheila's elementary school, St. Dunstan's, and came home upset. All the kids had many stars by their names but Sheila had hardly any. Marlene started working with Sheila and as Marlene has said many times since, once Sheila's motor was turned on, it never stopped. Sheila was the top graduating student at Fredericton High School.

Sheila was interested in world affairs even as a teenager. One time she attended a talk on the Meech Lake Accord with me. There was an IRPP meeting in Quebec City during the Meech Lake discussions—the failed attempt to get Quebec on board to amend the Canadian constitution. I took Sheila with me to Quebec; she was about seventeen then. Quebec Premier Robert Bourassa was our luncheon speaker. His address was about the importance of passing the Meech Lake Accord. There were questions after Bourassa's talk, all of which related to the accord, Sheila raised her hand and asked, "What are you doing to save the beluga whales in the Saguenay River?" The premier answered as seriously as he answered all the other questions and was not disturbed that this had nothing to do with the Meech Lake Accord.

In 1989, Sheila joined me when Rosalie Abella was given an honorary degree at UNB Saint John. Rosalie was born in a displaced-persons camp in Germany and moved to Canada in 1950. She became a jurist and eventually was appointed to the Supreme Court of Canada—the first Jewish woman to have that honour. Sheila and I went to the honorary degree ceremony and as it was an evening affair we booked a motel in Saint John. After the convocation there was a dinner that Sheila and I attended. I had hoped to sit at Rosalie's table, but the president had made different arrangements. The dinner was at the Delta Hotel and Rosalie was staying there. We agreed that we would have coffee in the hotel restaurant after the dinner and did so starting about 9 p.m. The conversation was scintillating and I was so absorbed I did not notice time go by. A waitress came by and said, "Excuse me, we normally close at midnight and it is already 12:30 a.m." Rosalie then invited us to her room to continue the discussion. I think we were talking about her parents' experience and my experience during the Holocaust. Rosalie's father came from Cracow. She told me he attended law school at the Jagiellonian University before the war and he had to stand in the back of the lecture room because Jews were not allowed to sit with the rest of the students. She also told me her father could not practise law in Canada because he had not passed the Canadian bar exam, and he was particularly thrilled when his daughter became a lawyer. Rosalie had a brother who was born before the war and perished in the Holocaust. Around 3 a.m. I thought we better go because Rosalie was leaving on an early-morning flight. Sheila and I went to our motel and around 3:30 a.m. Sheila, who had hardly spoken all evening, said, "Dad, can you get me a soft drink? I am so excited I can't go to sleep."

Around this same time when Sheila was either in her first or second year at UNB, a Holocaust denier came to speak in Fredericton. Marlene was visiting my mother in Montreal and Sharon was in Halifax. Normally, Sheila went with me every morning to the university and we returned home together. That week there was an announcement that David Irving, the British Holocaust denier, was coming to Fredericton and would be speaking at the City Motel on Regent Street. Someone in the Jewish community organized a demonstration to protest Irving's talk. Sheila asked me whether I planned

Israel's daughter Sheila Unger graduating from the University of New Brunswick with a B.Sc. in 1989—receiving her diploma from her father, Dean Israel Unger. (Joy Cummings photo)

to attend. I invented various excuses as to why I did not want to go. Irving's talk was scheduled for Friday evening. That morning Sheila said to me, "Dad, please pick me up early, because I am going to the protest march whether you go or not." That of course shamed me into going. There were about twenty or so people marching around in the snow in front of the City Motel. CBC-TV covered the protest. A reporter came up to me and asked me a few questions and said something about Irving being a historian to which I replied, "Irving is as much a historian as a person who pulls the wings off flies is a biologist." Sheila beamed and that was the clip the CBC aired.

I do not recall telling Sharon and Sheila directly, one-to-one, about my story of surviving the Holocaust. I made no deliberate effort to sit down and tell them. Both of them have heard me speak at Holocaust commemoration events. Both were supportive fighting Holocaust denial as teenagers and continue to be as adults. Once I took the two of them on a trip to New York and Washington, DC. In Washington we visited museums, including the Holocaust Museum. They have the original iron gates of the Jewish cemetery in Tarnow in that museum. It was gifted to them by the Polish President Lech Wałęsa in 1991.

Our daughters have ended up being highly accomplished, academically and professionally. They are both medical doctors. Sharon is a neonatologist in Toronto and she is also an assistant professor of Medicine at the

University of Toronto. Sheila is a medical geneticist in Lausanne at the Centre Hospitalier Universitaire Vaudois and has a professorial appointment at the University of Lausanne, Switzerland. They both have learned other languages. When Sharon was a student in Halifax she was on a cardiology rotation. A man was brought in from New Brunswick who could speak only French and he was going to have a heart operation the next day. No one could tell him what was going to happen. Sharon, who was the most junior person on the team, spoke to him in French and was happy to be able to ease his concerns. Sheila was working in Toronto at the Hospital for Sick Children, then moved with her husband to Switzerland, where they both worked in French. When he was transferred to Freiburg, Germany, Sheila took an intensive course in German and three months later was seeing patients and speaking to them in German. Both Sharon and Sheila are experts in their fields and enjoy international recognition.

Raising children is a great responsibility and it does not come naturally. It is easy to have children, but it takes a lot of character to raise them to be decent human beings. I often think, you need a licence for everything: driving a car, flying an airplane, and for many professions. Yet for raising children we are not required to prove we know anything at all.

The next generation. Marlene and Israel (left) look on as their daughter Sharon marries Lee Heinrich in Niagara-on-the-Lake. Lee breaks a glass for good luck as per Jewish tradition. (Israel Unger collection)

I had what I think must have been anything but a normal childhood. I left Poland as a young child without my parents and did not know if I would ever see them again. When I was reunited with them they were unfamiliar to me. Then I had to leave my parents again and live with an aunt and uncle in England because my parents could not provide food and shelter for my brother and me. Life was not normal being raised by an older aunt and uncle who really did not want to be looking after some one else's children. In all this—how was one to learn to be a parent? Fortunately, Marlene did know. When I made some silly comment about bringing up our children, she was there to set me straight.

When our daughters were in medical school we deposited monthly money into their accounts. They never asked for more. We bought Sharon a dishwasher when she was at medical school. We always thought in terms of: How can we make things easier for them?

When Marlene and I were married we agreed that we would never tell our children that they were obliged to do anything just because we wanted them to, that they could live their lives so they would be happy, not to make us happy. We tried to live accordingly. People used to tell us: Enjoy your kids because they will grow up fast. Marlene and I enjoyed our daughters from the minute they were born. We have never said, "Oh, if we had only known how fast time would pass we would have done things differently," because we had no reason to say that.

The Best Granny

Our girls had an extraordinarily good relationship with their grandparents in Minto. Alfred and Wally had three outstanding characteristics: they were very wise, they were very generous, and they were the most selfless people I ever met.

Both of Marlene's parents came from large families in Minto, about a half-mile apart from one another. Alfred was born in 1913 and Wally in 1916. Alfred went to work in the Minto coalmines at age thirteen. He worked his way to being foreman for the W.B. Evans mining company and when the mine was sold he continued on for A.W. Wasson. When Marlene was a girl, her father had a disagreement with his boss over a federal election. He was a dyed-in-the-wool conservative and used to ferry Tory voters to the polls on election day. His boss didn't like that and told Alfred so. Needless to say that was not going to stop him, so he quit and started mining coal on his own. Then he branched out and became a road contractor. That's what he was doing when I met Marlene. I tell this story to show Alfred's individualism and independence, that he would do what he considered right no matter what the consequences. I believe Marlene inherited this quality.

About the time of our marriage in 1964 Marlene's father lost his business. He was not upset or worried whether he would get another job. Within a few weeks, the Avon coal company called and asked him to be the supervisor for the dragline in Minto. A dragline is a huge piece of heavy equipment used in surface mining. One of his jobs was to get the dragline working again when it broke down. Marlene's mother was a working mother, which was not common at that time. She ran a grocery store for twenty-two years. Marlene often said that much of her childhood revolved around her mother's store. Marlene feels she learned to be compassionate from her parents. Her mother always made sure during the wintertime to have the coal furnace going at the store so kids could have a warm place to wait for the school bus. She was a very kind person. Both of Marlene's parents loved their families and their communities and they loved and doted on Marlene, who was their only child. She said she had a very loving and happy childhood.

When an old couple who ran the Minto Funeral Home died, Alfred and Wally bought it in partnership with McAdams Funeral Home in Fredericton. They did all the work in Minto except the embalming. Alfred worked there after retiring from the mines and Marlene's mother ran it until her retirement at age seventy-five.

Generally Marlene and I went to Minto for the weekends. If we needed a babysitter, invariably Marlene's parents helped out. When school was out, the girls went to Minto to be with their grandparents at the cottage at Grand Lake. One time Sharon and Sheila were with their grandparents when they were called out for a funeral in Newcastle, so they took the girls with them. When the arrangements were finished, they were on their way home and it was late. Alfred was very tired, so they stopped in Noonan and Wally took over the driving. Sharon, who was about eight years old at the time, had her favourite blanket with her. When they got to Minto, Sharon's blanket was missing and Sharon started to cry. Wally realized that the blanket must have fallen out when they switched drivers in Noonan. Wally said, "Don't cry, Sharon, I will go back and find your blanket." Alfred and Sheila went into the house and Sharon and Wally drove all the way back to Noonan and found the blanket. When they got back to Minto, Sharon said, "Granny, you are the best granny in the whole world." Sharon repeated that story at Wally's funeral and concluded with, "You are still the best granny. I love you." What Sharon did not know is that when Wally told us that story she ended by saying, "I would drive to China for that remark."

Sharon and Sheila received an allowance of two dollars a week from their grandfather. Marlene's parents were not churchgoers, although they gave money to the church and they came from a Baptist tradition. Because of the funeral home business they knew the ministers very well. In fact, one afternoon when Marlene's father was sick and in the hospital he was visited by the Catholic priest, the Baptist minister, the United Church minister, and the rabbi. The fellow sharing his hospital room asked Alfred, "What religion are you anyway?"

I thought it important for the girls to have grandparents present in their lives because I did not have mine present in my life. Sharon has a photo of Marlene's mother in every room of her house in Toronto.

My mother told Wally once that she was the lucky grandmother because she saw the girls frequently. When school was out and I was passing through Montreal, I would take Sharon with me and she would stay with my mother and then I would pick her up again on the way back home. When my mother went to Israel, she brought jewellery home for the girls, but unfortunately those gifts were lost when our house was robbed.

One time in Montreal, Marlene was admiring the matzo bag that my mother had embroidered upon getting engaged. Without any fanfare, my mother gave it to Marlene and she still has it. But it gets even better than that, because Marlene told my mother that she would keep it and give it to Sharon so that its history would be remembered. The next thing we knew, my mother went out and purchased material, made a new matzo bag, and embroidered it so there would be one for Sheila! My mother did needlework her whole life. We have several of her beautiful needlework pictures in our home and in our cottage.

That matzo bag she made for Sheila was probably the first time since her engagement that she had sewn and embroidered a matzo bag.

Part Five

Dean Unger

Dean Unger

I certainly enjoyed my university career. It was multi-faceted. One main part was of course writing scientific papers. I wrote about fifty papers in all. When I was writing these papers, at first I was struck by inertia. I would collect reference papers and prepare myself for some weeks. Then, when I decided that a piece of research was at the point to be written up and I finally put pen to paper—I could hardly stop. When I did finish writing, I felt exhilarated. One Christmas Eve, Marlene and the girls were already at her parents' home in Minto. I was at my office in the midst of writing a paper. It was a great time—students were gone, few people were around. "Don't you stay in town tonight. You come to Minto," Marlene had said to me. I started writing and was so preoccupied that the next time I looked up it was dark and snowing out. It had been snowing all day. Mindful of Marlene's command, I quickly finished up and headed for Minto, a forty-five-kilometre drive. It was such an intense snowstorm that on my way down the hill by the provincial forestry complex, the car skid sideways out of control. Fortunately no one was in the oncoming lane. It took me three hours to get to Minto, the roads were so bad, and Marlene then told me I was foolish to drive in the storm.

I also held many non-academic positions. After the Strax affair I was elected president of Association of UNB Teachers (AUNBT). There was also a new UNB president, James Dineen, former dean of Engineering. Dineen was a very decent, intelligent, thoughtful man, and a conciliator. Dineen realized that salaries were very low at UNB and that it would be a morale booster to increase them. He called the chair of the economic benefits committee and me in and said, "You have asked for the same salaries and the same lecture load as Queen's University in Kingston, Ontario. I can do one but not both. Which do you want?" Without hesitation Harold Sharp answered, "Give us the money and we will work longer hours." UNB, like all universities in Canada, had been expanding rapidly. Under Dineen we had two salary increases in one year—the first and only time. That made Dineen very popular with the faculty but not with the provincial bureaucrats!

I also spent a lot of time in meetings of the university committee that was working on a document entitled "Terms and Conditions of Employment." This was an effort to spell out the rules of the game for promotion, tenure, salary adjustment, how to process grievances, and the duties and responsibilities of faculty. The dean of law, George MacAllister, represented the university administration, Harold Sharp and I represented the AUNBT, and there were several other members on the committee. At one meeting, I argued

Dean Unger in the chemistry lab at the University of New Brunswick, date unknown. (Joy Cumming photo)

with George MacAllister that if faculty member "A" had the same record as faculty member "B" and yet "A" was promoted after five years and "B" was promoted after four years, even though "A" was given proper treatment, it was clear that "B" had been given preferential treatment and "A" had grounds for a grievance. Ultimately George conceded and said that I would make a good lawyer.

We also formed a provincial association, the Federation of New Brunswick Faculty Associations, FNBFA. It consisted of the faculty associations of UNB and St. Thomas University in Fredericton, Mount Allison University in Sackville, and Université de Moncton. I felt that if the FNBFA were going to be successful then Université de Moncton had to feel at home in the organization, so I made it a point to speak French at meetings even if the representatives from Moncton did not. I made an effort at that time to relearn my French. I proposed that we would be a bilingual association but without simultaneous translation. People could use either of the official languages and expect to be understood. I asked a professor from Moncton to draft a constitution for FNBFA. He demurred, saying that he could do so only in French and that he could not vouch for the accuracy of the English version. "That's no problem," I said. "We will write on both versions that the official version is the French one." This seemed only natural, as it had been drafted by a francophone in French. The people in Moncton were amazed. "You would do that?" they asked.

I was elected president of the provincial faculty association and as such had a seat on the board of Canadian Association of University Teachers (CAUT). I sat on that body for many years until they decided that the only way to get rid of me was to move me up. So I was elected to the executive, then vice-president, and finally president of the Canadian Association of University Teachers.

During my term as vice president of CAUT the president, David Braybrooke (a noted philosopher from Dalhousie University) and I negotiated for the Quebec association to join the Canadian one. At the time it was called the Fédération des associations de professeurs des universités du Québec (FAPUQ). FAPUQ had been a separate body until then. I think this was an amazing achievement, given that it was during the height of the Parti Québécois era under René Lévesque. The vast majority of professors in Quebec were ardent separatists. I think what helped was that our first meeting was in Montreal and we started by speaking French. Our Quebec colleagues said we could speak English and they would speak French and we would assume we understood each other. We said fine, but we carried on with the negotiations in French only. We wanted to let them know that we had a high regard for their language and for them. Also, when the first meeting wrapped up, our FAPUQ colleagues offered to have the next meeting in Ottawa, but we replied that we preferred to continue meeting in Montreal because I was from Fredericton and the president of CAUT was from Halifax, so Montreal was more convenient. We agreed that FAPUQ had a *statu special*, a special status, for voting or membership on committees. It all seemed quite reasonable but did annoy the federal government of the day, who were dead set against any special status for Quebec in anything. It's amazing how national organizations mirror national politics and national tensions.

While I was president of CAUT I worked to have the organization reach out to the wider community. I felt that speaking to business, to government, and to the media was important and that universities and professors should be part of the society they were in. To this end, I organized a conference at the Royal York Hotel in Toronto on "Business, Government and The University." I was active in university governance and represented the faculty of science on the university senate for many, many years. Then there was the work with the Institute for Research on Public Policy. The best part of this work was the people I met.

In 1984 I stood for dean of science. The incumbent dean's term was expiring and he offered to stay for an additional two years. I had no argument with the incumbent but I wanted to be dean and various people thought that the faculty needed a full-term dean. I went to see the incumbent and told him that I was going to stand but only because of the length of term. I was not selected. When I was informed, I called the incumbent and congratulated him, saying that the faculty had made the right choice. We stayed on good terms and when the faculty took on the responsibility of running the provincial science fair, the dean asked me to take care of it and I readily agreed. I used the science fair from then on to have the faculty reach out to the wider community. I would call the Department of Education of New Brunswick, the community college, the New Brunswick Research Council, and many businesses to ask them to provide judges. I had Premier Richard Hatfield come and act as honorary chief judge several times. I had the media cover the event.

When I was not selected as dean in 1984 I thought that I had had my proverbial kick at the can and that chance would not come again. But it did and in 1986 I was selected as dean of science for a five-year term. A dean was selected by a committee who would first ask the relevant faculty how they felt about that person's performance and then recommend appointment or not. Again in 1991 and in 1996 I was selected dean. I was deeply honoured by that vote of confidence.

Through being dean of science I was privileged to meet a lot of interesting people. I met several Nobel Laureates. One was Gerhard Herzberg, for decades the most eminent Canadian physicist. Of interest to my story is that Herzberg came to Canada in 1935 from Germany, fleeing the Nazis because his wife, the physicist Luise Oettinger, was Jewish.

There was a series of lectures at UNB called the Brian Priestman Lectures. Brian Priestman was a professor of physics who died trying to save a young boy from drowning. As dean, I was responsible for organizing the lecture series, inviting the speaker and being their host. I made contact with people like the American scientist E.O. Wilson. He is known as the "father of sociobiology" and was a two-time Pulitzer Prize winner. I never met Wilson in person, but we corresponded. I consider it an enriching privilege that I had the opportunity to meet such extraordinary people.

Dalton Camp, the journalist and political strategist, formed a small group who met for lunch every Tuesday for conversation at the Victoria & Albert Restaurant, not far from the Lord Beaverbrook Hotel in Fredericton. Win Hackett, Hatfield's chief of staff and a deputy minister, took part as did some professors. I was asked to participate. There were a couple of parties at Camp's place at Cambridge Narrows, too. The discussions were always political. It was fascinating to hear Dalton describe some of the inner workings of government.

I very much enjoyed my university career. It was not what I thought it would be. Initially, I had this image of a "city on a hill," and oddly enough the University of New Brunswick is literally set on a hill. But my image that it would be a place of no prejudice and that the professors sat and discussed ideas and did research to further the well-being of humanity did not turn out to be exactly as I had imagined. But it was a phenomenal opportunity to experience many facets of life and meet many fascinating people, not only in the university but in other sectors. I really do believe that teaching and learning is what advances society. The highlights of my career were receiving grants, being published and promoted, and I had a great deal of gratification too from seeing my students on the dean's list or receiving scholarships. In fact, I instituted an awards evening for students that eventually spread to all other faculties. I also had the chance to attend research conferences in the United States, Europe, Israel, and Japan. Upon retirement in 1999 I was named dean emeritus.

In spite of the fact that it was not what I thought it was going to be, I would not hesitate to choose my career again.

As dean, I had instituted a luncheon in appreciation of the secretaries for the Faculty of Science. Each year at the lunch I told them that they were an important and essential part of the work of the faculty. When I retired the secretaries in the Faculty of Science planted a crabapple tree in our back yard as a going-away present. It is just magnificent every year in late May. In New Brunswick it is the best time of the year. Spring comes very late here, but it is very beautiful once it does arrive. The trees are leafed out, the crabapple trees are a gorgeous pink, the lilac bushes are blooming. Everything is green and the weather is mild.

Struggles with Charlie

Charlie had a very bad ending. He was forty-six when he became ill. I was in Prince Edward Island on university matters and had taken Sharon along. Charlie called Marlene at home and said he needed to talk to me and so she tracked me down. I was giving an interview to the CBC in Charlottetown when Marlene reached me. I called Charlie and he said he had been told he had ALS. I was the first person he wanted to talk to. He needed my help.

Charlie asked me to help him get a second opinion, and not in Montreal. I had an exceptionally good friend, Jim Foulks, who was professor of medicine at the University of British Columbia. I called and asked him to find a neurologist in the United States. He contacted a well-known neurologist at the Columbia Presbyterian Medical Center in New York who he had gone to medical school with. Jim arranged an appointment for us. I was not aware at the time that in the United States, if you had the money, you could get an appointment immediately. I thought it was a big deal to have my friend arrange for it. I felt very good that I could do this for Charlie. I took him to New York.

That first trip to New York was the worst one. They confirmed that he had ALS and discharged him. This was the worst news he could receive. He was obviously very distraught. I thought to myself: How am I going to get him home? I took him to a bar and we had a couple of shots of gin. I tried to sedate him without telling him that's what I was up to. I can imagine what I would be like if I had just received a death sentence. We caught an earlier flight than we had originally booked, out of LaGuardia. I remember when I did get him on the plane we played cards and had more booze. I did my best so that Charlie would win the games. The flight attendant came by and I accused my brother of cheating in a jocular way. "Do you allow people to cheat on your planes?" I asked her.

Then I took my brother to doctors in San Francisco several times and, when travel became difficult, to Boston. I went out of my way to try to help him and to give him hope. I sensed that he wanted hope and I was prepared to do my best, to spend a lot of effort trying to give him hope. I found physicians, I found medicines. But he became ill very quickly. None of these trips were easy, because he could not move very well and so if he needed to go to the bathroom we had to go together, even into the stall. It was not easy getting him to and from the airport. I would have to take him down the aisle in the plane. It did occur to me that when we left Poland and when we were in Aix-les-Bains and London, I was very much dependent on Charlie. Now the circle had closed and Charlie was dependent on me. I spent weeks at a time away from my work, not taking vacations, because I was spending the time with him. At times I felt sorry for myself for having to spend so much time with Charlie.

Charlie lived ten years with ALS, but the fact that it was a death sentence was devastating to him. It was worse for my brother than my father, because he had witnessed what happened to our father.

What grieves me is that during the ALS period I did a lot for Charlie but not always with a good heart. Once in San Francisco, it was early in the morning and the windshield on the car misted up. He told me to do something about it. I was angry and I said, that's bullshit and I wouldn't do it. Sometimes Charlie made requests that made things more complicated, more difficult. One time when we were going to San Francisco, I went from Fredericton to Montreal to meet him. The morning we were leaving there was freezing rain. The house he shared with Hilda and the children had a downstairs garage and the driveway sloped down to it from the road. We called a taxi to take us to the airport. Charlie could not go down the outside stairs so I had to take him into the garage and out to the road that way. I had to open the garage door from the outside and the only way I could do that was to slip down the frozen driveway, hanging onto the wall as I went down. I got the door up and somehow got him out to the cab. Then I had to go back and get the suitcases, at which point the cab driver looked at me, scared that I was going to leave him alone with Charlie and he would have to get him out at the airport himself. "What are you doing!?" he said. "It's okay, I am coming to the airport too." So after all that I get in the cab and am settled in beside Charlie when he asked me to go back and close the garage door. "We can phone Hilda from the airport and get her to close the garage door," was my reply. No, he wanted it closed right away; he didn't want to disturb Hilda. I got out of that cab and slid down the icy driveway holding onto the wall of the house again and closed the door and made it back up to the cab again. It was a nightmare.

There were good times too. The first time I took him to San Francisco we went to a place that called itself an ALS research centre. We were there for about a week. After he was discharged we had two more days before our flight back. I wondered how I was going to get his mind off his illness. He loved gambling, so I took him to Reno, Nevada, a three-hour drive from San Francisco. It worked. He loved it. On that first trip to San Francisco they gave him some drugs, which he thought were effective; he thought he was getting better. Marlene and I visited Montreal and Charlie took us to a steakhouse for dinner. He felt good and we felt good that he felt good. When I started taking Charlie to San Francisco he tried very hard to express his appreciation. I had a Toyota Land Cruiser and I wanted to buy a roof rack for it. It was either not available or very expensive in Canada. Charlie went with me to several stores and was very interested that I get that roof rack. We found one and Charlie bought it for me as a present. On another trip he bought me a wetsuit for scuba diving.

We stopped going to San Francisco because it became impossible to go on a long flight. We started to go to Boston instead. During these trips I used to joke a lot just to try to get his mind off his illness. Then I found a doctor in Amsterdam who thought he had a drug to stop ALS. It was a known drug but not known for ALS. I contacted that doctor and he sent me batches of that drug. It was a drug that was formulated in water. The doctor in Amsterdam offered to send just the drug and instructions on how to formulate it. I did not want to get into that, so I had the pharmacy in Amsterdam formulate it and send it to me. So we paid to ship water from Amsterdam to Fredericton. When it arrived in Fredericton, customs would phone and ask a lot of questions as to what it was and they would check with Ottawa to see whether they could release it to me. In the end they always did.

Then I would deliver the drug to Montreal and Charlie would inject himself. He asked me to do it, but I wouldn't. I didn't know anything about it and was not sure it was safe for me to do it. All this trouble was worth it because my brother thought the medicine helped him.

He had two drugs at first, Baclofen and lithium. Baclofen is a drug that acts on the central nervous system. Charlie had the feeling that it helped his joints move better. In ALS you start getting stiff and he felt this counteracted it a bit. With Charlie, the doctor had prescribed, say, 10 milligrams so Charlie would double or triple the dose. The lithium fluoride that he was taking is normally used to regulate mood swings. The doctor in San Francisco prescribed this for some of his ALS patients to control their mood swings and thought he noticed improvement in their ALS symptoms, so he started to prescribe it for ALS.

Charlie wanted to get his prescription refilled in the United States because Baclofen was available in higher dosages than in Canada. I had to go to Montreal for a meeting, so he asked me to go with him to the United States. We headed for Burlington, Vermont. We got to the border and Charlie had a pile of money with him; he liked to travel that way. He put it under the car seat—why I don't know. Charlie was driving. The border police started asking Charlie questions. Where are you going? To see a friend. Where does your friend live? Charlie had no answer. Where are you going to meet your friend? In a restaurant. Where is the restaurant? Charlie had no answer. They got suspicious and told us to get out of the car and go into the customs and immigration station. They did a thorough job of searching the car. Of course they found the money. Now they were even more suspicious. This is before the age of terrorism. Until then, I had not said a word. Finally I said, "He is sick and he is going to Burlington to fill a prescription from a US doctor." So then the border officials asked me questions about the doctor, the hospital in San Francisco, and the like. I had all the right answers. The customs man asked, "Why didn't your brother tell us that in the beginning?" "He is embarrassed to say that he is sick." "Is he not more embarrassed to be caught lying?" They let us through. Charlie was visibly sick when he got out of the car. I don't know if it was really that he was embarrassed that he was sick or that he just did not want to acknowledge that he was not as capable as he had been. We got the drugs then came back via New York State. I wasn't going back through the border control in Vermont. I insisted that we declare the drugs. I was spooked after the Vermont crossing.

I felt terribly sorry for my brother. I took him to Boston to a highly respected neurology centre. We had a reservation at the Copley Place Hotel. Charlie by that time could only walk with a walker. When we got to the hotel

I went ahead of him with the valises to register. They could not find our reservation. It turns out there was a Copley Plaza and a Copley Place Hotel. The other one was just across the road. My brother was just approaching the registration desk. I told him we were at wrong place. He did not say a word. With a grim look of determination he turned 180 degrees and started for the door. We actually had to take a taxi to get to the other side of the road. The look on my brother's face made me feel awful. To see a man of his former drive and strength reduced to using a walker and having to take a cab to get across the street was dreadful.

Marlene often talks about looking at people's eyes and reading emotion in eyes. I find that difficult because eyes are eyes, but I could read things in Charlie's eyes like this time at the wrong hotel when he had that awful look of determination. Also one time in San Francisco we went to a restaurant for breakfast. He was walking with a walker and needed my assistance. It was a bit of a chore to go into the restaurant. He looked at the people all around us—he particularly seemed to look at young people—and I think what was going through his mind was: Look at these young people. They may not have much but they have their health. "I have so much to live for and I'm sick." He had a thriving business. He had Hilda, he had a new son. "Why can't they just snip a nerve and stop the disease? Just give me what I have now. Let me stay the way I am."

In the last few years I continued to do things for him like getting medicine from Holland, but the period of going to doctors was over. It lasted about five or six years. Soon after Charlie got ALS, he began having troubles with Hilda. He called me once and asked for my advice. Charlie had some money that he had socked away in various places. He said that Hilda told him that his money was coming between them and that he should give it to her and that would solve their problems. I knew if he gave her his money then she would be finished with him. I thought, surely he knows better. "Look, if you give her the money you are out the door. Why don't you write a contract with her that she has to take care of you and you will leave her everything you have but if she does not take care of you she gets nothing." Next thing I knew he turned over his cash to her and Hilda threw Charlie out, or at least made life so miserable for him that he left. She got the house, she got the business, and she got his cash. I think she pretty well had everything that she was going to get out of him and now he was a burden. One day we went to what had been Charlie's house—the one he bought for himself and Hilda—and Hilda would not let us in the door. We could see that there was another man living with her. Charlie and Hilda's marriage was not strong enough to survive the disease.

Charlie then went to live with our mother. She moved from the Jewish area to Côte-Sainte-Catherine and Mount Royal. She needed an apartment with an elevator for Charlie, who was in a wheelchair by then. She took care of him for two or three years. When she could no longer care for him, he moved into the Maimonides Hospital Geriatric Centre in Montreal for the last couple of years of his life. I did not see him often. When you go to live there, they tell you this is the last place you are going to live. Maimonides is reputed to be the best geriatric centre in Montreal. Most of its patients are Jewish.

When I went to Montreal I would go and see him, but I spent only fifteen minutes or a half hour. He did not even seem to be interested in the visit. I usually went by myself. The last couple of times I visited him he said to me, "Izzy, I want to die." At this stage he could speak but not clearly. When I got home I told Marlene about that and I said I thought that he was looking for sympathy. I had the impression that Charlie would cling with his fingernails to a cliff edge.

Charlie's children came to see him at the end of the disease. He died in 1990. Even though his struggle with ALS was long, his death was a shock. I was in Fredericton and his son-in-law called me. There really wasn't a funeral in Montreal. Charlie had made arrangements to be buried in Israel. A Jewish burial is supposed to happen within twenty-four hours. My mother wanted to accompany the casket to Israel and we had to talk her out of it. We felt that she was too frail to stand the trip. We also had a rabbi and all sorts of people tell her that she should not go. In the end we prevailed, but she was really upset that we did not go to Israel for the burial. The *chevra kadisha*, the Jewish burial society, and our two maternal cousins, Hirsh Fisch and Kalman Fisch, attended the funeral in Israel.

There was a *shiva* in Montreal. Lily's children came. The *shiva* was at my mother's apartment. It was really for my mother. I think my mother already had Alzheimer's at the time, but we did not know. There were rabbis who came for the *shiva* and I had them tell her that it was okay that she did not accompany the body to Israel and that the burial had been carried out according to *halacha*—Jewish law. But it didn't help. It would have been awful to drag that frail old lady to Israel for one day for the burial: she was in her mid-eighties by then. Charlie is buried on the Mount of Olives in Jerusalem.

I was Charlie's executor. He left an insurance policy to his daughter Caroline. Rosie and Joycie were more or less established already. By then, the oldest was thirty-two, the next thirty, and the youngest about twenty-five. His second wife and children did not come to the *shiva*.

We don't know how Charlie managed to live ten years with ALS. Maybe it was the drugs, but the other possibility is that when my father got it he was age sixty-five; when Charlie got it he was forty-six. In the end, Charlie was only fifty-six when he died, younger than my father had been at his death. At my brother's *shiva*, people came who knew my parents. Through this I got in contact with a woman who was also hidden in Tarnow, in a closet. I had known nothing about her story. She lived in New York and I spoke to her once or twice, then I lost her phone number.

At Charlie's *shiva* one of the guests called me a *Sanzer Einikel*. I had heard this before. Once when I went to one of the small Montreal synagogues, a rabbi there told a few people that I was a *Sanzer Einikel*. My father had said it a few times too. "Sanz" refers to the southern Polish town of Nowy Sacz (also known a Nowy Sancz or simply Sanz in Yiddish), home of an important Hasidic Jewish dynasty. "Einikel" means grandchild. The most famous offshoot of the Sanz dynasty was in Bobowa, a town south of Tarnow. A *rebbe* is the Yiddish word for rabbi and means a mentor or a learned person and is used as the name of a leader of the Hasidic movement. The title is passed down in a family line and one of today's Bobover *Rebbes* (the title for the current *rebbe* is under dispute) is a man called Rabbi Mordechai Dovid Unger. My father's name was Mordechai David Unger. I guess this is why I have been called a *Sanzer Einikel*—it means we, Charlie and I, are descended from that line.

My Mother and Her Backbone of Steel

Back when my father died, my mother tried living in Israel with her cousin's widow, Tzipora Fisch. That lasted about three months. It turned out to be too much of a culture shock; she returned to Canada, directly to Fredericton, to live with us. Again, this did not last long—about two weeks! She could not imagine why anyone would want to live in a small town—she liked the big city. Also, she could not go to the synagogue in Fredericton because it was too far away to walk from our house and orthodox Jews don't drive cars or let themselves be driven on the Sabbath. We were not religious. We tried to accommodate her. Marlene bought special dishes. We koshered the stove and had the rabbi come in and testify that it was kosher. But we still watched TV on Saturdays and answered the phone. It was not for her. She returned to Montreal but later came for visits. Unfortunately, religion remained the big thing that always stood between us. She never lost hope that I would become religious, and then Marlene and the kids would be more religious too.

I then made more of an effort to spend some time with my mother in Montreal. I would go every couple of months. I would stop by whenever I travelled for a business trip to Toronto or Ottawa or Montreal. The university's and the school's March breaks did not coincide. During the university break I would travel somewhere with Sharon and Sheila, skiing or to New York to see a play. During Marlene's March break, she would go and visit my mother. My mother told her things about the past that I never discussed with my mother. In fact, that is how some of the stories have come together for this book—from the things my mother told Marlene.

When I went to see my mother, I usually did not stay more than a day or two. As Marlene would say, my mother nattered at me. "Go wash your hands." That was the first thing she would say to me when I entered her apartment, because Jews wash their hands ritually before eating. Then she would say, "Wear this," and hand me a *yarmulke*. Then she would make me coffee whether I wanted it or not and put milk and sugar in it. "You need sugar." I never took sugar. After I drank the sweet coffee she would say, "Go visit Mrs. Goldfarb. I want her to know that you are here."

My mother and I spoke Yiddish when we were together.

My mother was in her mid-seventies when Charlie became ill. Still, she did all his personal care for those years when he moved back in with her. My brother was self-medicating. He was on a couple of prescribed drugs but a dosage that he increased himself. My mother had to go and get the additional drugs without a prescription. She went from drugstore to drugstore and would make such a nuisance of herself that the pharmacist would finally give her the drugs. In one instance, at least that we know of, the pharmacist gave her the pills and very firmly asked her never to come back.

Then, when Charlie moved to the Maimonides Hospital Geriatric Centre, my mother went every day of life except Saturday for another few years. She had to change buses twice to get there. For a while he was at the Montreal chest hospital. She visited him every day there too and on Saturday she walked there and back—about an hour's walk in each direction. I am amazed that she could even find it. One time there was a flood in Montreal. I was there on university business and it was so bad that they closed some of the freeways. My mother made it to the nursing home that day. At one point she was carried from one bus to the next. By then she was well over eighty.

Charlie's death made my mother's Alzheimer's either more acute or more pronounced. Charlie's daughter Rosie and Marlene and I noticed it after the death. This is probably medical nonsense, but I think that her going to see Charlie every day and taking him things gave purpose to her life and she controlled her Alzheimer's by force of will. Once he was dead, the purpose was gone and the Alzheimer's became visible. She was eighty-five when he died.

Because of her Alzheimer's she became very afraid. She would walk up and down the halls of her apartment building. I found a Russian immigrant woman who was my age who couldn't speak English but could speak Yiddish. Her name was Mrs. Derrish. She needed a job and we needed somebody.

My mother did not like people doing work in her apartment, but she did like meeting people right to the end and this lady would spend time talking to her and doing small chores. We learned from Mrs. Derrish that my mother was having panic attacks.

My mother developed diabetes, and that is when the doctor said she could not live alone anymore. One day I had a call from social services in Montreal and they were taking my mother to the Jewish General Hospital against her will because of her diabetes. We went to Montreal right away. We thought we were doing the best for her when we found a place for her in a religious home that took about ten older people. We arranged for her to go there when she came out of the hospital. At that home she could still light the Sabbath candles. She had her own room. We thought it was something made in heaven for her. When my mother went into the home Mrs. Derrish used to go at 9 a.m. and stay until lunchtime and then went back for supper and stayed in the evening. She was with my mother every day except the Sabbath. But my mother did not like that place. She went downhill fast. She took sick. She was moved from there to the Jewish General Hospital, where they have a long-term-care unit that is really like an old people's home. This was not a long-term solution, but they were building a brand-new home and that's where these people were going to go. "If you have good bread you don't change the baker," my mother said. She liked it there. Mrs. Derrish still went to see my mother. She would call Marlene or me and say your mother needs this or that.

About three or four days before my mother died Mrs. Derrish called Marlene and said, "I would like your mother to have a pair of sneakers. We are going to go walking. We will walk in the neighbourhood where she used to buy her groceries." She gave a list of this and that, which we collected. It was right at the end of the school term and the next week we were planning on going to Montreal. A day or two later at work about 10 a.m. I received a call from the Jewish General Hospital. They said my mother was dying. I called Marlene and said I'm going to try to get tickets right away for us to go to Montreal. I called Sharon and Sheila, who were both in Toronto, and they flew immediately to Montreal before my mother died. I think that is quite a testimony to how our daughters cared for their grandmother Unger that they both made the effort to be there as she was dying.

My mother had picked up a bacterial infection in the hospital and it killed her rapidly. Marlene and I did not make it before she died. I'm glad we did not. I think it would have torn me up to emotionally to see her die. The girls were there, but my mother did not know they were there. My mother's death was a very big shock to us because it was sudden and unexpected.

Both my parents are buried side by side on the Mount of Olives in Jerusalem. I have not seen my mother's grave, because it is dangerous for Jews to go there now. They had bought their plots a long time before, in 1968. Marlene and I have no particular intent to be taken to Israel. I'm a chicken— the whole idea scares me.

My mother had a backbone of steel. After the Holocaust her right hand shook constantly. When she drank tea, don't ask me how she did it, but she never spilled a drop. When she decided to do something she was unstoppable. She was a person who could feed her family for two years on flour, barley, and water. She was an extraordinary cook and was always sending us parcels by air of cookies, pies, and hamburgers. There was a naming ceremony for Sharon's first girl, Rebecca, and Sharon and Lee decided that her Hebrew name would be Hinda—named for my mother. Her second little girl has the Hebrew name Baila, named after one of my mother's sisters.

Marlene

My wife is an extraordinary person. I think she is a fantastic mother, grandmother, and wife. I am more impressed with her every day, if that is possible. She is kind and generous and she has a phenomenal sense of justice. If she pursues a cause, she does her homework, she is determined, and she never gives up.

One of the major things Marlene did was to fight Malcolm Ross. In 1978 Malcolm Ross, a teacher in Moncton, New Brunswick, sent a copy of his book *Web of Deceit* to the New Brunswick Teachers' Federation (NBTA) and it was given to Marlene to read. She was outraged. She could not believe that in the 1970s someone would try to peddle hate like that. When Marlene found out that Malcolm Ross was a teacher, someone in her profession, she was even more outraged. My advice to her at the time was, "He's a crank, he'll go away, ignore him." Fortunately she did not accept my advice. She read all his books, his letters to the editor, and she watched his interview on television. His books copied materials from the *The Protocols of the Elders of Zion*, a fraudulent anti-Semitic book from the early 1900s. Ross questioned the fact of the murder of six million Jews by the Nazis and claimed *The Diary of a Young Girl* was not written by Anne Frank.

One day Marlene was shopping at a local grocery store called Tingley's and saw Ross's book on display. She went to see the owner and he was as shocked as Marlene to see anti-Semitic material on his magazine rack and removed the books immediately. Marlene started to look at the bookstores in Fredericton for his book. Hall's Bookstore had *Web of Deceit* and they refused to remove it. At Westminster Books they told her they would not carry such a book. A small Christian bookstore in the Fredericton Mall told her they had it and carried it because they believed it. The public library had his books. One of them, titled *Christianity versus Judeo-Christianity*, was catalogued under Comparative Religion, Marlene fought that and was successful in having the cataloging changed.

In 1991 there was a Human Rights Inquiry investigating a complaint from David Attis, a Jewish parent from Moncton who said the New Brunswick School District 15 was encouraging racism and bigotry by continuing to employ Malcolm Ross. The teachers' union supported Ross and that is when Marlene began to get vocal.

The union said they had to provide legal counsel for Ross, even though Ross had his own lawyer, Doug Christie from Vancouver. Christie was also the lawyer for other Holocaust deniers such as Keegstra and Zundel. Marlene was told by the union that she was the only one to complain about the union providing a lawyer for Ross. She and a fellow teacher at Fredericton High School, Eric MacKenzie, then polled the teachers and ninety-eight out of about one hundred and forty signed a petition saying they did not want Ross supported with their union dues. It did not help.

The teachers of Fredericton High School petitioned the union about how the union lawyer should act during the inquiry. During the inquiry George Filliter, the New Brunswick Teachers' Association lawyer, cross-examined David Attis and, in referring to the Holocaust, spoke of "both sides of the story." He questioned whether six million Jews had been murdered during the Holocaust. Marlene was very upset by this line of questioning and immediately went to the NBTA to protest. The NBTA then appointed one of their staff to sit with Mr. Filliter to ensure that such lines of cross-examination, which gave the impression that the NBTA supported Malcolm Ross's views, were not repeated.

What Marlene achieved in her battle against Ross is that she was able to have a resolution passed by the New Brunswick Teachers' Association recognizing Holocaust denial as a virulent form of anti-Semitism. Marlene wrote to the president of every local teachers' association asking for their support on the resolution. It was passed with all locals voting in favour except Moncton and Saint John. Ross was from Moncton, but why the Saint John local voted no, I have no idea. Another resolution she was instrumental in having passed was that the union lawyer should adhere to the New Brunswick Teachers' Association resolutions on racism and anti-Semitism in adducing and deducing evidence at the human rights inquiry.

In May 1993, a professional development workshop on the Holocaust sponsored by the History Council of the New Brunswick Teachers' Association was held. It was held in fact in the Saint John synagogue. Malcolm

Ross and his brother William attended the workshop. One of the presenters at the workshop was the cartoonist Josh Beutel. Ross sued the New Brunswick Teachers' Association and Beutel for defamation of character, because several of Beutel's cartoons critical of Ross were shown. It was during this trial that Malcolm's brother testified that he shared his brother's views on the Holocaust. Several years later Marlene discovered that William Ross was a member of the provincial anglophone curriculum advisory committee. Given his publicly expressed views on the Holocaust Marlene felt it was wrong for him to be on such a committee and went to the media with her concerns. William Ross was then voted off the committee.

Malcolm Ross charged Marlene with a violation of professional conduct, specifically Section 2 (d), which deals with the ethics of a teacher criticizing a fellow teacher. A letter had been written to the *Telegraph Journal*, a Saint John newspaper, with the rhetorical question: "Why can't Ross believe whatever he wishes to believe?" Marlene responded to that letter stating that Ross promoted hatred toward Jews and Ross then charged her. The NBTA processed the charge at two levels. At the first level, Marlene was not allowed to bring support with her to the hearing but Malcolm Ross was; he brought his brother. At the next level Marlene was accompanied by Reverand James Leland, a very vocal opponent of Ross. The ethics charges were dismissed.

Marlene thought that the best way to combat Holocaust denial would be by educating students. We both believe that teaching about the Holocaust is teaching basic human rights. Marlene was delighted when Holocaust education became a mandatory part of the grade eleven history curriculum. In September 1988, grade eleven students in the English-language high schools were to get a two- to three-week program on the Holocaust. The Holocaust education curriculum was to focus on the historical reality of the Holocaust and its continuing relevance. The program made New Brunswick a leader in Holocaust Education in Canada. Unfortunately, almost simultaneously with the last in-service of teachers on Holocaust education, a new and revamped modern-history course was introduced in grade eleven. The study of the Holocaust was reduced from ten to fifteen hours of classes to one to four hours at the discretion of the teacher. Marlene was very upset and immediately began working to get the Department of Education to have a workshop for teachers on Holocaust education. Although it was promised, nothing occurred by the time she retired in 1995.

Upon retiring, Marlene became the Fredericton representative on the Atlantic Jewish Council (AJC) and then the chair of the Holocaust Education Committee. When Eric MacKenzie was a member of the New Brunswick government, she asked him to sponsor a bill to commemorate the Holocaust. Eric was pleased to do so and in November 1999 the New Brunswick legislature unanimously enacted a bill to commemorate the Holocaust annually in New Brunswick.

In her role with the AJC she successfully lobbied the provincial Department of Education for a teachers' workshop on Holocaust education. That workshop, titled "Human Rights and the Holocaust," was held in Moncton in April of 2001. The organizers had planned for a maximum of one hundred and twenty-five teachers and the workshop was overfull. Subsequently I joined the AJC Holocaust Education committee and together we requested the Nova Scotia Department of Education to hold a similar conference. They agreed and a very successful conference attended by over three hundred teachers and administrators was held in Halifax in 2003. We both believe Holocaust education is tolerance education, because it shows people what happens when hate is permitted to go unchecked. We want to remind people they have to be careful; we are not immune to racism and bigotry.

When Marlene fought Malcolm Ross she always thought of Ross and company as a lunatic fringe, but today that type of anti-Semitism has morphed into anti-Israel feeling. When something happens in Israel then synagogues and Jews get attacked the world over. The attackers don't ask whether those Jews are pro-Israel or not. Anti-Israel feeling is just a cover for anti-Semitism. Often, if you change the word Zionist to Jews then you have some of the same expressions that were made by the Nazis. Western anti-Semitism is thinly disguised as anti-Zionism by many.

I might criticize aspects of Canadian government policy; people in other countries may do so as well, but they distinguish between the *government* of Canada and the *people* of Canada. I have heard some British academics say that Israeli academics should be boycotted—*all* Israeli academics, regardless of their political views. When it comes to Israel, critics frequently condemn all Israelis or call for Israel to be boycotted or for the country to be abolished. They would not do the same while criticizing Canada.

In May 2008 in Fredericton a local middle school put on a play based on the novel *Three Wishes: Palestinian and Israeli Children Speak*, by Deborah Ellis. The book had already been banned by the Toronto school board as being anti-Semitic. It was a virulently anti-Israel play. A parent was directing the play with full cooperation of the school. It had scenes with girls, representing Israelis, holding wooden replicas of machine guns standing in a circle and pointing the guns at two cowering girls representing Palestinians. When the parent was interviewed by the paper, she said: Wasn't it wonderful what you could teach children through drama and music? Marlene found out about it. She read the libretto. The play had been taped so she watched the whole thing twice. Then she went to see the school board and had the play stopped. I couldn't sit and listen through that thing. Marlene is thorough.

Later that year at St. Thomas University in Fredericton a professor arranged for a panel discussion and one panelist gave a PowerPoint presentation comparing Israelis to Nazis. There was no discussion possible because questions had to be pre-submitted. Marlene complained to the vice-president academic, but it lead nowhere. In the summer of 2010 there was a Gay Pride parade in Fredericton and a group was allowed to march holding up a sign saying "Queers Against Israeli Apartheid." Marlene tried to get a hold of the marshal, but her calls were not returned. So this type of serious anti-Semitism marked by the demonization of Israel is alive and well in Fredericton. Unfortunately anti-Semitism did not go away in May 1945. It has re-emerged as anti-Zionism.

It takes a lot of intestinal fortitude to do what Marlene does. I think she inherited strength of character from her parents. One of Marlene's uncles, her father's brother, a major in the Canadian army, was killed at the end of the war, so the war had been discussed a lot in their home. She says she remembers the adults following the war on her grandmother's radio and that she remembers when the state of Israel was declared. Marlene inherited a sense of justice, of right and wrong, and a determination and single-mindedness to do the right thing no matter how much work, how much effort, or whether she would suffer as a result.

Marlene and I both worked outside the home, which was unusual for the sixties. She taught school the entire time. She loved it. She had originally planned to stop teaching after my salary alone would cover our monthly expenses—the biggest item being our mortgage. After starting to teach she did not dream of stopping.

She began her teaching career 1961 and taught in Chipman, Minto, Saint John, and then she taught math at Fredericton High School for thirty years. She loved and cared for her students. She never came home before 5 p.m. The kids called her "Mama Unger." She often had students in late for extra help. One time a student was acting up and Marlene got furious and said, "If you keep that up I won't let you stay in after school!" Marlene told her students, "Only my friends get to stay after school." After retiring from Fredericton High, she taught a few semesters first year math at UNB but stopped when it interfered with attending the Josh Beutel–versus–Malcolm Ross trial.

Marlene converted to Judaism even though she was not very religious. She felt that our children should be born Jewish. She is part of the *Chevra Kadischa*, the Jewish burial society in Fredericton. The community in Fredericton is very small, so when the rabbi asked her to help out she did. We celebrate Jewish holidays with festive dinners either at our home or at friends' homes.

I do not attend synagogue services frequently. Marlene did not go for years, because in the Fredericton synagogue men sat in front and women in back. Marlene said that she did not believe in African Americans sitting in the back of the bus in the sixties in the United States and she would not support segregating men and women in the synagogue. For some years we went to Toronto for Yom Kippur and attended services at Holy Blossom Temple. It is Reform and women and men sit together and participate equally in the service. For a person like me, brought up in orthodox Judaism, to attend a Reform synagogue is quite an experience. Still I like it a lot better than the orthodox synagogue in Fredericton. In recent years the Fredericton synagogue has changed its policy and men and women can sit together, Marlene and I now attend services.

We have five grandchildren. Sharon and her husband Lee have three girls, Rebecca, born in 2001, Sophie in 2003, and Meira in 2005. Rebecca, like her dad, loves sport and is the goalie on her hockey team. Sharon put Rebecca in ballet when she was four, but at the final performance all the other little girls were dancing around and Rebecca was on all fours. When Sharon asked her what she was doing she said, "I'm pretending to be Scooby-Doo." So Sharon let her quit ballet and enrolled her in soccer instead. Sophie, not to be outdone by her sister, plays forward on her hockey team and has inherited her father's and grandfather's love of hiking. Meira is the most girlie one

Grandchildren! Left to right, back row: Meira, Rebecca, and Sophie; front row: Luisa and Viviana. (Andrea Superti Furga photo)

and enjoys ballet and receiving dresses as presents. Our friend Nancy makes delicious cinnamon buns and one evening Meira ate these and the next day she could not stop talking about "cinnamon bums." That is what we call them in the family now.

Sheila and husband Andrea have two girls, fraternal twins, Luisa and Viviana, born in 2008. When they were born, Marlene stayed three months with them. I call Luisa Super Activa. She is in constant motion. I call Viviana Super Rida for her big smile. *Ridere* is "to laugh" in Italian. She has a killer smile. Marlene is the proverbial Yiddishe Mama—both for our girls and now for our grandchildren.

My life has been enriched by my sons-in-law. Andrea, who is proficient in Latin and who became our second son-in-law, I have nicknamed *Secundum*. He has become our official photographer and keeps us supplied with lovely pictures of our granddaughters and family portraits of all of us. As an added bonus, he has taught me the joys of Italian cuisine. Lee, at times referred to as *Primus*, has taken me on numerous spectacular hikes that I could not possibly have undertaken on my own. Lee also knows his way around a barbecue and stove. There is a downside—both daughters and both sons-in-law are physicians and yet none of them show any sympathy when I complain about personal medical problems.

Marlene received an award from Friends of Simon Wiesenthal Center for Holocaust Studies in recognition of her long-standing promotion and advocacy of Holocaust studies and human rights education. She was presented the award in 2006 with a plaque that reads: "In honour of the work you have done in the fight against intolerance for the benefit of all Canadians." At the ceremony I was asked to say a few words and concluded my remarks with

Marlene Unger appears in Fredericton local paper upon receiving the Simon Wiesenthal Center for Holocaust Studies award, 2006. (*Daily Gleaner*, 1 July 2006)

the following: "It took me four years to get a B.Sc., two years to get an M.Sc., and three years to get a Ph.D., but it took me five years to convince Marlene to marry me. So that was clearly my most challenging task and my most rewarding. I am proud of Marlene and proud to be her husband."

Making Up for Lost Time

As an adult I would learn a sport and then try to transmit it to my daughters. In my mid-thirties I learned cross-country skiing. At first it was like skating as a boy in Montreal—I did not know you had to *learn* to ski. I bought some skis and took off behind the house in Odell Park and I could not get up a slight incline! Soon I was skiing more. Once I took part in a two-day ski marathon from Woodstock to Fredericton. Marlene ran all over Fredericton to get me a full-face mask cap because it was minus thirty-five degrees that weekend! The first day ended at Crabbe Mountain. A top skier froze the tip of his lungs. All during the marathon I worked my fingers to get them warm. I made it.

During another two-day marathon, I had to work, so could not ski on Saturday. The only way I could participate was to be a sweeper on Sunday— that means to follow along at the end of the race and make sure no one has fallen behind and perhaps needs help. I was with another fellow and towards the end of the sweep we came across a woman who was lying in the centre of the trail wearing a very heavy sweater, looking up at the sky. We asked her if she was okay and she said she was. We asked what she was doing and her reply was that she was having a rest. We asked her to ski with us and she did not want to, so we decided that we needed a snowmobile to take her out. There were no cellphones then, so I stayed with her and the other fellow skied to the next checkpoint and called for a snowmobile. The young woman we took out on the snowmobile was Carolyn Gammon's sister, Jennifer. When I first met Carolyn, mistaking her for her sister Jennifer, I said to her, "I think I rescued you during a cross-country ski marathon."

In my fifties I learned to scuba dive. Sharon said she was going to go diving in Costa Rica and asked me to come with her. I needed to learn scuba diving, so I took a course at the university pool. The next person to me in age was twenty years younger. I was making up for lost time, taking on challenges. The fellow who taught scuba was an RCMP instructor. You had to go thirteen feet under without gear and then put the gear on. I did things I didn't know I could. There was a test where you had to find the equipment underwater while blindfolded. I said I couldn't do it. The instructor said, yes you can. And I did do it! The open-air test was in the Bay of Fundy in November, when the water temperature was about four degrees Celsius. Then I dove with Sharon in Costa Rica. In Belize Sheila got her certification. On a vacation in Kozumel

Marlene and I snorkelled, and in addition to some great daytime scuba diving I even went on an amazing night dive.

Marlene's grandmother had a farm at Wuhrs Beach on Grand Lake, New Brunswick, and that is where Marlene spent her childhood. Marlene's father bought two adjacent lots there in the 1950s, one for themselves and one for Marlene. In 1960 Marlene asked her father to move a changing shack he had originally built for his workers down to the lakeside at Wuhrs Beach so she would have a place to change her bathing suit for swimming. That was the start of our cottage. Alfred built it for us. If it was within his means, Marlene's father did anything he could for Marlene that she wanted or needed.

In the beginning we did not have an indoor bathroom at the cottage. One time Marlene's mom went to the outhouse and encountered a moose. She came back in a hurry and said, "Alfred, if you want me to keep coming here you better build an indoor bathroom." He did. We also had a classic skunk encounter. Alfred took to feeding a dog when its owner was in hospital and then the dog adopted Alfred and would not go back to its owner. One afternoon at the cottage we heard Marlene's father cursing to the effect of, "I'm going to kill that dog!" and he came running out of the bedroom after the dog. The dog had chased a skunk under the cottage and the skunk did the usual thing when cornered. Marlene washed the dog with tomato juice, but he smelled like skunk the rest of the summer.

I enjoy the cottage because it gives me opportunities to build outdoors and indoors. When Alfred was alive he did the construction and I helped. We've built additions, decks, changed the inside, built a shed, and shingled it. We built a fireplace. We cleared the land. I poured the concrete for the footings for the additions and patios. We did most of the fixtures ourselves and even when we hired people I still did some of the work such as building the railing for the deck. I built a swing set for the grandchildren. All this work gives me a lot of satisfaction. The cottage has grown as our family grew. In fact, we just added to it for the grandchildren. So we started with an eight-foot-by-twelve-foot changing shack and now we have five bedrooms, two patios, kitchen, den, computer room, living room, enclosed patio, two bathrooms, and four sheds!

There's the seasonal work like cutting the grass or pruning trees that have grown too close to the cottage. I use the tractor to maintain the grounds. We have to get ready for our grandchildren, our daughters, and their husbands. We get all of the food ready and the toys and so on. Then when they arrive we cook and entertain them, but of course we enjoy doing that. Just sitting on the beach or boating does nothing for me.

Sheila lives in Europe now and the cottage is where it is comfortable for the entire family to get together. Marlene and I both learned kayaking at

The extended Unger family. Back row: Sons-in-law, Lee Heinrich and Andrea Superti Furga; 2nd row: Sheila, Meira, Israel with Viviana on his lap, Rebecca, Marlene with Luisa on her lap, Sophie and Sharon at Wuhrs Beach, Grand Lake, New Brunswick, summer 2012 (Andrea Superti Furga photo)

the cottage. After Alfred died we tried to include Wally in everything. We bought three kayaks so that Marlene, Wally, and I could kayak together. Wally kayaked until she was over eighty. I still like kayaking. Recently my son-in-law Lee and I went out kayaking into the Bay of Fundy at Hopewell Cape. I hoped to see some whales, but they did not cooperate. Also in my fifties I learned windsurfing. I learned on Killarney Lake in Fredericton from the guy who sold me the board. Then I tried it at Grand Lake. I wasn't good at it. I would sail away from the cottage and then try to get back to it but always landed thirty metres to either side.

When Marlene and I retired, we decided we wanted to go south for a portion of the winter. We briefly considered buying a condo, but we did not want to be tied down to one place. Years before, when we had been on our way back from Texas, money was in short supply so we camped as well as staying in motels. In one campground we met a couple who showed us their Airstream trailer. We thought it was great and said at the time that when we retired we would buy one of these and repeat our trip in style. In 1999 Sheila was in Los Angeles on a post-doc fellowship and we were going to visit her at Christmas. Marlene's mother was with us and we thought of buying a Ford van to be comfortable on the drive. Then one day there was a recreational vehicle (RV) show in Fredericton and we spontaneously decided to buy an

RV, which we then did in Smithville, Ontario, and the three of us took off for Los Angeles.

A motorhome is a complicated instrument, a house on wheels, so there are a lot of things that can go wrong and usually do. It has its advantages and, of course, disadvantages. Marlene and I are happy we took that route and it has given us a lot of memories, though we would have been happy not to have a blowout on a Sunday in New Mexico, an alternator failure in West Virginia on an Interstate, and another alternator failure just outside of Minto, New Brunswick!

The first few years we tried different motorhome campgrounds in the Florida Keys. Marlene loved the Keys, but they are very expensive and I was allergic to the mosquitoes, which were plentiful. We tried Tucson. Then one time Sharon was coming to visit us by herself with her two babies. We wanted to find a place that Sharon could fly to in one hop. So we looked for a resort and picked one out of a book and it was Pleasant Harbor Resort in Peoria, Arizona, not far from Phoenix. From the picture it looked like we could use our rubber dinghy that we had bought for the Keys. This proved not to be true, but we really liked the place and we still go there each winter. It is a six-thousand-four-hundred-kilometre drive diagonally across the continent from Fredericton. Driving a motorhome is much more comfortable than driving a car, but it can be quite nerve-wracking, particularly when driving through big cities and having to make many lane changes. There is one road that has eighteen lanes! Because of that we eventually gave up driving the motorhome back and forth between New Brunswick and Arizona. We parked it in Arizona and take our car. We thought it would be safer, though in 2011 we hit a cow in Arizona and totalled the car.

We like the set-up, the climate, and scenery in Peoria. There are no biting bugs. I can hike. The cultural and shopping opportunities are great in Phoenix. We take advantage of the art museums, the ballet, and the opera. There's a Jewish

Marlene and Israel in their motorhome, 2010. (Carolyn Gammon photo)

film festival. Nearby in Flagstaff there is the Lowell Observatory. We have friends in the park who we bike with. I like reading, doing my emails. We have entertained many visitors.

When I was seventy Lee and I hiked down to the bottom of the Grand Canyon and back up. Lee thought I wanted to do it to prove I wasn't getting old. I was very excited about the hike but also worried whether I would be able to do it. It is about sixteen kilometres from the rim to the guesthouse at the bottom and 1.4 kilometres from bottom to top in height. In February there is snow and ice on the trail at the top, so you have to have crampons on your boots. As you descend, the snow disappears and at the bottom there are palm trees.

I practised for it by hiking an hour or two a day. Once I saw a rattlesnake, about half a metre long, with four rattles on its tail—a young one. It wasn't coiled or shaking its rattle, but Lee reminded me that the small ones are more dangerous than the adults because they inject all their venom at once whereas the grown-ups inject only a small portion of their reservoir. Scorpions are actually more dangerous. You have to be careful not to pick up stones, and if you spend time in the Grand Canyon you are supposed to check your shoes in the morning. But it wasn't rattlesnakes or scorpions I was worried about on the hike with Lee, it was having to be strapped to the back of a mule to get back up the canyon! There are about four hundred people a year who have to be rescued from the Grand Canyon. That didn't happen to us. We actually made it faster than we thought, just four hours down and then, to my amazement, it only took us five and a half hours to get back to the top. Lee carried our equipment. We spent two nights at the Colorado River at the bottom of the canyon in the guesthouse. It was the most spectacular hike I have ever been on. When I look at the photos Lee took, I'm surprised that we did it!

Airplane Accident

One of the challenges I took on for myself was learning to fly. I wanted to see how it worked technically, how to navigate and communicate with the ground. I took flying lessons at the Fredericton airport. I enjoyed learning to fly and progressing at it. In 1976 I received my pilot's licence. I took the girls up with me and Marlene and her parents. We would fly to Saint John for a coffee and come back. We would fly over Grand Lake and spot the cottage. There were incidents occasionally. One time I went with Marlene and Jack Wetmore and his wife in his plane to Montreal. He was a senior pilot. On the way back the weather was bad. We kept flying lower and lower and finally we had to land in Woodstock because the cloud ceiling was too low. We then had to rent a car to get back to Fredericton. Once I flew with a fellow named

Menzies to St. Stephen, New Brunswick. Weeks later he asked me to fly with him to British Columbia. I had an urge to accept, as I thought it would be a great adventure, but I declined because it was the middle of the academic year. He crashed and was killed just outside Calgary.

My own crash came some years after. Two of my colleagues, George Semeluk and Doug Brewer, and myself had a meeting in Halifax. We thought it would be more enjoyable and no more expensive if we flew with a rented aircraft rather than driving or flying with a commercial plane. The Fredericton Flying Club had recently acquired a new, or at least new to them, airplane. It was a Piper with a variable-pitch prop and retractable undercarriage. I had qualified on that plane, so I reserved it. We were scheduled to leave around 9 a.m. or 10 a.m. When we got to the airport the clouds were too low but expected to lift, so we waited. I checked the logbook for the airplane and noted that it had just had a fifty-hour inspection. I remarked to the person who was doing the paperwork that I was the first person to use the plane after the inspection.

Around midday we took off and I noticed immediately that the plane was not flying normally. It was sluggish and was not cruising at the speed that it should have been for the power setting and the revolutions per minute (rpm) that were showing. It did not want to climb. I checked that the undercarriage was up, that the pitch on the prop was correct, and so forth. As we were approaching the Bay of Fundy in the Alma area I decided to turn back rather than cross the bay with an aircraft that was not performing properly. I executed a left turn. As I did so, the airplane shuddered and started to lose airspeed and elevation. I decided instantly to head to Saint John, which was the closest airport. I called the Saint John tower and advised them that we were having problems and asked them to cancel my flight plan. They asked if I needed help when I got to Saint John. I replied, "If I get there I do not need help."

I was so busy trying to keep the plane up and make it to Saint John that I did not have time to get scared. I tried various things to see if I could get the plane to fly, but nothing helped. I allowed it to slow down to just above the stall speed. The plane had various alarms, which went off. The undercarriage came out on its own—a safety feature—so I cranked it up by hand. It became apparent that we would not reach Saint John.

We were over woods and I recalled from my training that, if given a choice about where to make an emergency landing, between field, water, highway or trees, that the best place was trees. I told my colleagues to brace themselves and I turned off all the switches so no fires would be started when we crashed. I let the plane glide over trees and in the last few seconds I pulled up on the control column so the front of the plane would not be the first contact point. I recall thinking to myself as this was going on that it could be the end and that people had said that when death was near their whole life flashed by. That was not happening. I thought to myself that I should be thinking about Marlene and our girls.

The tail of the aircraft snagged some trees. One wing was ripped off and we slid down to the ground. When we stopped I told my friends to get out and I turned the switches back on to see if I could get the radio working. The antenna had been ripped off so the radio would not work. I turned off the switches again and got out of the plane. Doug was sitting by a tree—he had twisted his ankle. George was standing and he said, "I wonder what the Boy Scouts do when they want to find out where they are." I looked in the opposite direction and saw a farmhouse. "I don't know about the Boy Scouts, but there's a farmhouse over there, so that is where I am going," George came with me; Doug stayed in the woods.

When we got to the farmhouse I knocked and a woman told us to come in. She was giving her boy a bath in a tub in the kitchen. I told her that we had just had an airplane crash and needed to call the RCMP. "Oh, it was you making that noise back there," she said. "I would let you use the phone but I don't have one." She told us that her mother-in-law, who lived up the road, had a phone. We walked up the road and stopped at the first house. The phone was a party line and two women were talking on the line. I told them why I needed the phone and one of them on the party line said, "How are you dear?" I told her I was fine but I needed to call the RCMP so they got off the line and I called. The line was busy.

Going on to the next house, three young men were having a beer. I asked if someone could drive over and inform the RCMP office. "I would," said one, "but I lost my licence last month." Then he thought it over and said, "What the hell," and jumped on a motorbike and took off. A short while later an RCMP car arrived. We picked up George and Doug and headed to Hampton. On the way Doug said to the officer, "You have a new golf course in Hampton," and the RCMP officer offered to show it to us on the way to the office! We declined. He filed a report on our crash and then took us to the hospital in Saint John. George and I were dealt with rapidly and had nothing wrong. Doug had X-rays because of his ankle. While we waited for the results Doug was in a bed next to a man who was severely injured. He was wrapped from head to toe. George asked what had happened to him and he replied, "It was my day off so I was painting my house and I fell sixteen feet down off the ladder. What happened to you?" George said, "Oh, we fell two thousand feet!"

The accident was announced on the radio, but fortunately Marlene and the kids were at Grand Lake and heard nothing about it until they got back to Fredericton. I ran out to tell them what happened and since I was standing there right in front of them, obviously they could see that I was fine. It was not a great trauma. The next day I called a flying instructor who went up with me to make sure my flying skills were still okay.

Telling My Story

I was first asked to speak about my experience during the Holocaust in the late seventies to a religious studies class at Saint Thomas University in Fredericton. In the mid-1980s a school in Oromoto, a town just outside of Fredericton, asked me to speak. I have never sought out the chance to speak, but I have never turned down a request. I have spoken in every province in Atlantic Canada, at Mount Sinai Hospital in Toronto, in Berlin, and in Tarnow. The groups have been school groups, service clubs, Holocaust commemorations, university classes, at November 11th Remembrance Day ceremonies, to teachers' conferences and church groups. Marlene has come to these events whenever she can.

Whenever I speak I have been greeted warmly and respectfully, but never more so than at the Social Justice Conference for teachers in Sydney, Nova Scotia. I very much enjoyed my interaction with the teachers and I was impressed by their commitment and knowledge. I was their keynote speaker and they kept me there for almost three hours! There were over three hundred teachers from all over the province. Many of them came and spoke to me warmly afterwards, but perhaps the most touching thing was that a First Nations woman gave me an eagle feather.

From my various talks, two questions particularly stick out in my mind. One is: How did they know who was a Jew? For boys, the most obvious answer is, Jews are circumcised. In general, Jews did not have baptismal papers. Their neighbours knew. The Germans ordered all Jews to register as Jews and failure to do so was punishable by death. Since Jews did not know from the outset that the Nazis planned to murder them, they registered.

Another question that sticks out is: Do you hate Germans? My answer to that is, I have always believed you cannot blame one person for the wrongdoings of another. In every country in Europe at the time of the Holocaust you could divide the population essentially into three groups: those who knew what was happening and approved and cooperated—whether that was 30 percent in Germany and 15 percent in France and 10 percent in Hungary, I don't know. But these people existed in every country in Europe. Then there was a group of people who knew what was happening and perhaps approved but did not participate themselves—again, what the percentages are, I don't know. And third, there was a tiny fraction in every country in Europe who knew what was happening and were prepared to risk their lives to save their Jewish neighbours. Those people existed in Germany as well as in other European countries. It is irresponsible to blame the people of today for what happened then. I do believe that Germany and Germans have a responsibility to themselves and to Jews and to humanity in general to learn the lessons from the Holocaust. I am aware that many Germans regret what happened and that the government has done much to ensure that the Holocaust is remembered and taught. I am aware that Holocaust denial is illegal in Germany and the country has provided compensation to survivors as far as this is possible. That all said, when I am in Germany I think all the time that this is where the Holocaust was initiated and planned. And that is not a good feeling.

One time I was asked to speak to a philosophy class. They had been studying the book written by Simon Wiesenthal called *The Sunflower: On the Possibilities and Limits of Forgiveness*. Wiesenthal described how, when he was a concentration camp inmate, a guard came and took him from his work detail. Wiesenthal thought he was going to be killed, but he was not. He was taken to a hospital room where a young SS man was lying badly wounded, about to die. The SS man told Wiesenthal this story. His unit was in a village in the Ukraine and they rounded up all the Jews, over one hundred fifty people, and herded them into a house and made the men carry cans of gasoline inside. He described the look of fear and anguish on their faces. Then, when the house was packed, they shut the doors and threw in hand grenades. From a second-storey window a man and a woman and a child jumped out. When they fell to the ground, he shot them. At the end of his story, the SS man said he wanted a Jew to forgive him and so he asked Wiesenthal to forgive him. Wiesenthal did not say anything. He left the room. I was asked to comment on this story and I said, I believe one can only forgive the person who has hurt *you*. You do not have the right to forgive for someone else. Sometimes I am asked a question that usually comes from a religious Christian. They want to know if I feel it was God's plan that I was saved. I say no, and then I tell them about Primo Levy, who went into the concentration camp as an atheist and came out as an atheist. Elie Wiesel went in as an observant Jew and came out as an observant Jew. I tell them there is no single reaction by survivors about their survival.

I am also frequently asked, "Why do you speak?" From every tragedy we must learn so that we can try to prevent future tragedies. The former West German president, von Weizsäcker, said, "Those who close their eyes to the past are blind to the present." The Spanish American philosopher and writer George Santayana said, "Those who cannot remember the past are condemned to repeat it." The Holocaust is the most atrocious crime ever committed in human history, and among all the tragedies within the Holocaust

I think perhaps one of the greatest was that it could have been prevented, if only decent people had spoken up. There is a good deal of evidence that when decent people did speak up, the Nazis backed off.

Perhaps even those who perished would like to think some little bit of good came out of that. That little bit of good is if we can prevent it from happening to anyone, anytime in the future. Physicians do autopsies not because they like to slice up cadavers but because they want to learn so they can help others. We have inquiries when a bridge collapses or an airplane crashes so we can prevent other bridges from collapsing and other planes from crashing. So we must too investigate and learn from the Holocaust. That's why I speak.

I have been honoured a few times for my work in Holocaust education. In 1998, in connection with the fiftieth anniversary of the Universal Declaration of Human Rights, the Canadian government honoured fifty Holocaust survivors from across Canada who had contributed to Holocaust education. I was among those honoured. There was a ceremony in the parliament buildings in Ottawa, which I attended. They read the name and citation for each person and because it was alphabetical, I was very near the end. I was very pleased that the Government of Canada saw fit to hold such an event. Marlene and Sharon were with me in Ottawa. The horrors of the Holocaust lead to the passage of the Universal Declaration of Human Rights, so it was fitting to honour those active in Holocaust education.

In 2010 I received the first ever John Peters Humphrey Human Rights Award at a ceremony in Hampton, New Brunswick. John Peters Humphrey was born and grew up in Hampton. He had a distinguished legal career and was the first United Nations Human Rights Commissioner. In this capacity, with the help and encouragement of Eleanor Roosevelt, he drafted the Universal Declaration of Human Rights. Hampton is a town of about five thousand people and three hundred of them showed up for my talk. I was treated with great hospitality. Again they stayed for hours and I had at least two standing ovations. Many asked for my autograph!

New Brunswick, which is a province with only seven hundred fifty thousand people, unanimously passed a bill in the provincial legislature to commemorate the Holocaust. All provinces in Canada, as well as the federal government, passed similar bills. New Brunswick was the third province in Canada to pass a Holocaust commemoration bill. That this bill passed, that a small province like New Brunswick has such a devotion to the issue of human rights, that adults and school children display such a great interest in the Holocaust—all this gives me a great deal of hope.

When I was president of the Fredericton Chapter of B'nai Brith I initiated the annual Holocaust Commemoration event for Fredericton. The event is held on *Yom HaShoah*—the Day of Remembrance of the Holocaust annually in spring. In Fredericton it is held at the Sgoolai Israel Synagogue, in the sanctuary. It begins with a reading from the Book of Joel, one of the prophets: "Has such a thing happened in the days of your forefathers? Tell your children and let your children tell it to their children." Then there is the lighting of the six candles by various people, including one by a Canadian veteran and one representing a Righteous Gentile. A seventh candle is lit by a young person from the Jewish community to signify our hope for the future.

Israel lighting a candle at the *Yom HaShoah* ceremony in the Fredericton synagogue, 2009. (Carolyn Gammon photo)

We then have a keynote speaker, usually a Holocaust survivor. There is the singing of *Ani Ma'amin*. This is a prayer that basically says "I believe" and is used in daily prayer but has become associated with the Holocaust and Holocaust commemoration as it is said that many chanted the *Ani Ma'amin* on the way to the gas chambers. The 23rd Psalm is also recited as well as the *El Maleh Rahamim*, a funeral prayer, a version of which is for remembering victims of the Holocaust. We end with the prayer for the dead, the *kaddish*. There is a reception in the social hall. The attendance in past years has been about two hundred people, which fills the synagogue. The event is open to the wider community and it is exceptionally well attended by people who are not Jewish.

The keynote speaker is a vital part of the event. We have had Sally Wasserman from Toronto, who was a survivor of the Dombrova ghetto in Poland. She was given to a gentile couple at age seven and saved by them. She was the only surviving member of her nuclear family. David Korn from Halifax and his brother were given by their parents to a Lutheran monastery in Miklus, Slovakia, and sheltered there. They never saw their parents again. Judy Cohen, originally from Hungary, is a survivor of Auschwitz and lives in Toronto. She was motivated to start speaking about her story in 1993, when she ran into a group of neo-Nazis in downtown Toronto. Philip Riteman, from Poland, also survived Auschwitz and found his way to Newfoundland after the war. Max Eisen from Toronto survived numerous camps and was liberated by the 761st Black Panther Tank Battalion—Black troops who were not allowed to serve with white ones but were part of General Patton's third

Israel Ünger and Philip Riteman (middle) after telling their stories on the Day for the Elimination of Racism at the Canadian Forces Bases Gagetown, Oromocto, New Brunswick, 28 March 2012. (Deby Nash photo)

army. Esther Bem and her parents fled from Yugoslavia to Italy by foot. They were saved by a Catholic priest and poor farmers in a tiny village. They took on false identities as Italians. Dorota Glowacka from Halifax spoke about her father, who survived the Holocaust on "Aryan papers" hidden by Righteous Gentiles. He remained in Poland after the war and in 1968 was victim of anti-Semitic violence again under the Polish communist government. It was through having Dorota speak that I became acquainted with her, and she has helped with this book as translator and research assistant.

Doing this book is part of telling my story. I had an unexpected surprise and pleasure during the final edits. I had given the manuscript to my two daughters to look over. I called Sharon and she was just reading the part about Aix-les-Bains to Sophie who was eight at the time. That makes the whole project worthwhile.

Part Six

"They Know My Name Is Srulik!"

Return to Tarnow

I did not want to go back to Poland. From the time I left Poland I wanted to forget Poland. I did not want to think of myself as Polish. I did not want anyone to suspect I was not born in Canada. At university in Montreal I took a course in English diction so that I would not have a foreign accent.

I did not spend much time thinking about the Holocaust until that first time I was asked to speak in Fredericton. It was not until my parents passed away that I realized I did not even know the names of my uncles and aunts on my father's side. I had made some minor efforts to find out the names. The search led nowhere, which only reinforced my bad feelings that I had not done more. All I had to do was to ask my father when he was alive.

It was Marlene who persuaded me to return to Poland. She was always very interested in learning more. She wanted to see where I was born. I agreed to go only to see if I could find the names of my paternal aunts and uncles so that their memory would not be forgotten forever. I did not look forward to going.

For a while Sheila worked as a doctor in Freiburg, Germany, Marlene and I went to visit her and her husband Andrea. At the time they were both working at the Universitätsklinikum hospital. We used the trip to Freiburg to go to Tarnow for the first time since I left Poland as a boy. It was October 2006. We travelled from Freiburg to Tarnow via Berlin and Cracow. The train to Berlin was superb. The trains in Poland were not nearly as comfortable. The ride was very long, over twenty-four hours in total.

We missed our connection in Cracow and that was upsetting. I am usually quite calm and in control, but that upset me. We found out there was a later train to Tarnow, but at the last minute they switched tracks. In a panic we scrambled with our luggage down a flight of stairs, then up. We had two large suitcases and two carry-ons, because after Tarnow we were returning to

Canada. Ultimately, we ended up in a crowded train compartment, with no friendly people. Or so it seemed until we met a young man on the train who offered to take us to our hotel on arriving in Tarnow. We gratefully accepted.

We stayed three nights at the Tarnovia Hotel, a large hotel in the city centre built in the communist times. Breakfast was not good. I was surprised by how fast I found *ulica Zydowska*, Jew's Street, and recognized the house we had lived in when we came out of hiding. We saw the remains of the destroyed synagogue, the *bima*. There are just four pillars left and a protective roof over it. This is the *bima* I remembered seeing from our window with the weeds growing out the top.

It had been a very old synagogue, dating back to the 16th century. The Tarnow government put a wooden roof over the remains in 1987 and this is what Marlene and I saw. The impression of the *bima* was much starker before they built this protective cover over it.

I did not feel any particular emotion being in Tarnow—certainly not nostalgia. I did not feel an urge to cry and that surprised me. I did not feel any relationship to Tarnow. It was no different to me than if we had gone to any other town where the Nazis had committed atrocities. I noted with some dismay that the former Jewish area of Tarnow is now a place attractive to tourists. Perhaps the most depressing feeling was seeing the huge church next to the town square where Jews had been assembled and tortured prior to being murdered. We saw priests and nuns walking to the church. One was an older priest and I thought he might have been there in 1942. It was very rare that the Catholic clergy protested against what was being done on their doorstep.

We went to the city registry office and found my parents' wedding certificate and that of my uncle Abraham, who went to England prior to the war. I was very glad to find those documents, but we found no information on the other relatives. We went to an archive and met Jan Chmura, who spoke good English and made an effort to be helpful.

Usually one needs a key to the Jewish cemetery, but it happened to be open as workers were there fixing it up. We asked if we could enter and they readily agreed. There is a monument made from one of the columns of the destroyed Jubilee Synagogue. It was a synagogue with a large golden dome that could be seen throughout Tarnow. In 1946 a sculptor, Dawid Beker, placed this broken column where mass executions took place and where the mass graves are. There is an inscription: "And the sun shone and was not ashamed." This is actually from a poem by Nahman Bialik referring to the slaughter of Kishinev Jews in the Ukraine in 1903. Another inscription in Hebrew, Yiddish, and Polish reads: "25,000 Jews, murdered by German thugs between June 11, 1942, and September 5, 1943, are resting in this grave."

This is the memorial column where my brother and I had our photo taken as children after the war with the few remaining Jewish children of Tarnow. To think that the Kielce pogrom took place not even a month after the erection of this monument.

I had seen photos of this monument in a very rundown state, but by 2006 it had been fixed up. I was pleased to see that both the cemetery and this monument were being preserved. Marlene was upset that people had placed pictures of Catholic saints and Christian candles at the memorial. She questioned the motives

Israel at Holocaust memorial in Tarnow cemetery, 2007. (Carolyn Gammon photo)

of people who had done that—were they trying to "save their souls" as non-Christians? She asked, "Shouldn't your aunts and uncles, some of who are probably buried here, have Jewish memorial candles?"

I tried to say the mourners' *kaddish*. It is a prayer I often recite in its entirety, but I could not remember it past the first line.

Marlene finally persuaded me to visit the regional museum. It is on the main square in Tarnow. Every time we had passed it, she had stopped and said, "They're having a display on the Hassidim," I replied sarcastically, "Now that there are no more Jews, they are putting on displays about Jews." The museum director, Adam Bartosz, was not in. We spoke to a historian, Janusz Koziol, who later told Bartosz that we had been there. It turns out that Adam Bartosz has done much to help Jews returning to Tarnow for a visit. Over the next years he did a lot to help me confirm my story.

We had heard about the current-day anti-Semitism in Poland, but still it was shocking to see anti-Semitic graffiti from the train on the way back to Cracow. Then we took the overnight train from Cracow to Frankfurt and in the middle of the night, as we were crossing the border, two men burst into the room in full gear, carrying rifles, demanding to see our passports. They were Czech border guards and gave us quite a fright.

After returning to Canada I received an email from Adam Bartosz. There were photos and drawings of our hideout. It turns out that in 2001 the old Dagnan flour mill was to be demolished. Bartosz received a call from Augustyn Dagnan's son-in-law, Dariusz Dworek, who knew the building and had noticed a strange extra wall construction in the attic, which concealed a space behind. There was a small opening that lead to the hideout and because there was so much junk and machine

Adam Bartosz crawling into the hideout, 2001. (Tarnow Regional Museum)

parts, this entry was hidden. He had then questioned his mother-in-law about it. Mrs. Zofia Dagnan, Augustyn Dagnan's widow, was ninety-one at the time, but she remembered the Jews in hiding and later gave an interview to Bartosz. She knew the name Unger and she knew the couple called Aleksandrowicz. Bartosz hurried over to the mill and made the photos and drawings just a few days before demolition. I was very glad to see the pictures, as they confirmed my memory some sixty years after the fact. They were exactly how I remembered the hideout to be. Receiving those pictures from Bartosz made that whole first trip worthwhile.

Front of the hideout, 2001. (Tarnow Regional Museum)

158

Back wall of the hideout with the opening to the chimney on the wall,
2001. (Tarnow Regional Museum)

After the first visit I decided to have a memorial stone made for my
mother's family killed in the Holocaust. At the cemetery, Marlene and I had
seen that other survivors had done similar things for their lost families. I
began that process by contacting Adam Bartosz and arranging for a stone to
be made in Tarnow.

In 2007 I met Carolyn Gammon. She had called me because she was
organizing a book tour for her book about Johanna Krause, a survivor from
Dresden. I was wary at first, because I thought I was dealing with someone
who wanted to use me to sell books. We met at Tim Hortons doughnut
shop and the meeting changed that to the opposite. She was genuine, smart,
and with a conscience. Carolyn was born and raised in Fredericton. She
studied at UNB and at Concordia in Montreal. So we are both alumni of the

same university because Sir George Williams University became Concordia University. She studied literature and writing and has lived for over twenty years in Berlin, Germany, where she works with a Jewish tour company. Through her work she has met many survivors and knows a lot about the Holocaust. Her book about Johanna Krause shows her dedication to recording the stories of the Holocaust.

It turned out that Marlene knew Carolyn and taught her sister high school math. Carolyn came to know my story and we decided to make a book out of it. I have seen the project as an attempt to record not only our family's story of surviving the Holocaust in hiding but as an example of what happened to some survivors after liberation. She interviewed me and Marlene and others. I did much of the transcription work. Helpers translated interviews from Polish to English. Carolyn took photos and we did research in archives. It was a long process, about five years in total.

That fall we returned to Freiburg, Germany, to visit Sheila and Andrea. We then flew to Berlin and visited with Carolyn and her family. She had arranged a talk for me sponsored by a museum called "Otto Weidt's Workshop for the Blind." It deals primarily with the topic of Jews in hiding. Otto Weidt is recognized as a Righteous Gentile for trying to save Jewish workers, many of whom were doubly jeopardized by being both Jewish and blind. The original site of his broom and brush factory is a museum on Rosenthaler Street in Berlin's Mitte district. The talk was co-organized with the Anne Frank Centre next door, a partner centre to the one in Amsterdam. That is where my talk was held. It was the first time I told my story to a German audience.

When I think of Germany I often think of a famous poem by Gray called "Elegy Written in a Country Churchyard," in which the poet imagines what the people who died young might have contributed to humanity. The Holocaust was a tragedy of unimagined proportions in many ways. For the Jewish people it was a catastrophe from which we will never recover. Only recently did the worldwide Jewish population reach the same number as in 1939. For Germany, it was also a disaster; Jewish Germans contributed enormously to German and world science. Twenty-five percent of German Nobel Laureates were Jewish. Jewish Germans contributed far beyond their numbers to German theatre, music, medicine, German literature, and art. All that is gone forever, and who can even guess what other contributions might have been made?

I was interested in how a German audience would react to my story and I was interested in the questions they would ask. It turned out that the questions were pretty well the same as those asked in Canada. One exception was a question about what relations were like between Jewish and Gentile Poles in Poland before the war. I answered by saying that Poland had a long and complex Jewish history. There were times when it was better and times when it took turns for the worse, but that at the time I was born it was very anti-Semitic, like much of Europe. I answered that Jewish Poles were not considered Poles by many. There would have been business relations but very little, if any, personal contact. But I also told the audience that after the war, although things were very difficult for us in Canada, my mother would send packages to a non-Jewish family in Tarnow. There was no monolith. I think what the person who asked this question wanted me to say was that there was lots of anti-Semitism in Poland and that anti-Semitism was not unique to Germany.

After this, Marlene and I flew to Cracow and from there we went on to Tarnow. Carolyn came along to document the process. Flying was much better than the long train trip. We were there for five days. We stayed in a nicer hotel, the Villa Krzyska, a short distance north of city centre. Carolyn did interviews with eyewitnesses. Every evening she did extensive interviews with me. She had asked me to write down my story. I did so and the section on Tarnow was a page. I remember she said, "Izzy, I can't make a book out of a page." Needless to say, the visits to Tarnow, seeing the places I had known as a child, trying to answer Carolyn's many questions—it all added up. By the time she was finished we had twenty-five pages on my time in Tarnow.

A Modern Righteous Gentile: Meeting Adam Bartosz

After having corresponded with Adam Bartosz on and off since our 2006 trip, we now met him in his office at the regional museum. His office was full of paraphernalia of his various interests and occupations. He told us he began by being interested in the Roma community—known as gypsies. In fact, he had instigated a Roma museum in Tarnow, which we visited. Through getting to know the story of the Roma people and their fate under the Nazis he came to have an interest in the Jewish history of Tarnow. He clearly became quite passionate about it, and there were photos in his office of him with various Jewish people and groups in Tarnow and in Israel. At the time his daughter was living in Israel.

Even before I had returned to Tarnow, Adam Bartosz knew the name Unger. He knew an Unger family had been in hiding. But he also said that it was a big family name in Tarnow, Dąbrowa, and Żabno. He spoke of the *Tzadik* tradition that ran through an Unger dynasty. *Tzadik* means righteous and refers to a spiritual leader. There were Ungers who were leaders of the Hasidim. He was confirming basically what I had always heard about Charlie and myself being *Sanzer Einikel*. I told him that my father was clean-shaven—that he was very religious but not Hasidic. Bartosz also said that the name

Unger most likely comes from the country Hungary—someone who lived in Hungary or came from there. He said there are Ungers buried in the Tarnow Jewish cemetery.

When I told him my grandfather Fisch had worked for a nobleman in the wood business, Bartosz said he was pretty sure this would have been someone from the Sanguszko family. They were a big, wealthy family whose ancestors had founded Tarnow. They owned much of the forests around the city.

I specifically wanted to know the names of the people I had been with in hiding. I had not remembered them from my early childhood, and because our family never discussed the time in hiding, I no longer knew the names except for Mrs. Bochner. I thought the two girls could still be alive—if only I had their names I might be able to trace them. I had, in fact, made a few efforts to find them on various websites but had not had any results. Bartosz did not know the names of the girls either, but he did know about the Jews in hiding from a few sources: from Augustyn Dagnan's widow Zofia, from Dagnan's son Aleksander, and from another Tarnow survivor who had escaped to the Soviet Union before the liquidation of the ghetto, a man called Franciszek Jachimowicz (later Federico). Jachimowicz lived in Buenos Aires after the war.

Bartosz had spoken to Jachimowicz by phone in Buenos Aires and learned that he returned to Tarnow after liberation in 1945 and found out from my father about the Jews in hiding. He had met my father on the street looking terribly thin. Jachimowicz told Bartosz that Dagnan was known for being friendly to Jews before the war. Other than my father, he knew the name of the Aleksandrowicz couple but no others. That is how I found out the name Aleksandrowicz—from Bartosz, who had learned it from Jachimowicz.

Bartosz, in his capacity as Regional Museum Director, had initiated a project called "Memories Saved from Fire." It turned into a website and a book about the fate of the Jews of Tarnow. He published an article called "The Secret of Dagnan's Mill in Tarnow," based on his interview with Zofia Dagnan back in 2001. He writes of the Dagnan mill and our hideout. Because Zofia Dagnan was very elderly at the time and maintained she knew very little of what went on in the mill, she did not provide many details, but it is essentially the skeleton of my story. The son, Aleksander Dagnan, also wrote an article for this book where he talks about personally witnessing a *wysiedlenie* as a teenager. He notes that helping a Jew was punishable by death and yet, for a few, there was a place to hide. He then describes the hideout in his father's mill.

When I returned to Tarnow, I was the first and only one of those of us hidden who ever returned. Adam Bartosz facilitated our research in many ways: by providing us with photos, with the transcripts of interviews he had

Adam Bartosz and Israel in the Tarnow Regional Museum, 2009. (Carolyn Gammon photo)

conducted, and by setting up meetings for us with Dagnan's son. Bartosz became part of the history himself through all his help.

There is a term given people who helped save Jewish lives at the time of the Holocaust. It is a designation given by the officials at Yad Vashem, the Holocaust Museum in Jerusalem. These people are called "Righteous Among the Nations," or Righteous Gentiles for short. Adam Bartosz fulfills the appellation of a modern Righteous Gentile.

On the way out of the regional museum, Bartosz showed us a place on the stone archway of the building where there had once been a *mezuzah*. A *mezuzah* is a small casement containing a piece of parchment inscribed with a verse from the Torah. It literally means "doorpost" and is placed on the upper-right side of a door frame in many Jewish homes. There are "shadows" of where a *mezuzah* used to be on many doorframes throughout Tarnow—and Poland for that matter.

Meeting Mr. Dagnan

Bartosz arranged for us to meet Dagnan's son. There were the two Dagnan brothers: Augustyn and Antoni. Aleksander Dagnan was Augustyn's son. According to the son, Antoni was absent during much of the German occupation of Poland, constantly travelling and moving and never sleeping at home because he was afraid that he would be arrested. He was not married and so could travel around. Augustyn Dagnan had a family, his wife, Zofia, and children, and he ran the mill.

In Adam Bartosz' office at the Tarnow Regional Museum, 2007. Left to right: Adam Bartosz, Israel, Marlene, Aleksander Dagnan, and Carolyn. (Carolyn Gammon photo)

Aleksander Dagnan is seven years older than I am. So at the time of this meeting in 2007 I was sixty-nine and he was seventy-six. That means he was fourteen or fifteen when the war was over and so was quite aware of what was going on. We also met him again in 2009 and spoke with him at length both times. It is through these meetings that many of the details of my story were confirmed. The second meeting when he came in he kissed Marlene's hand in the Polish custom.

Dagnan knew my family. He knew my father and my mother. He knew most of the people involved in my story. He said about his father, "My father's relations with the members of the Jewish community who lived around us were very good. To be honest, they lived off each other. There was another big flour mill owner, Szancer, but he did not do small deals. He was into big business. My father delivered flour to all the little stores." Flour was precious at that time. I asked Dagnan what relationship my father had to his father and he said, "Business partners." Dagnan's father made the flour and my father sold it to the Jewish bakeries. Dagnan's father would have visited my father in his bakery, though they would not have socialized. "They collaborated to create market opportunities. My father took care of the mill but not the sales. Your father made it possible to sell flour in the Jewish community."

He also knew Eliasz Unger who had a glass tiling and roofing workshop in Oak Square. There is a photo of an advertisement for that shop.

Dagnan told us that the Jewish men had not built the hideout themselves but paid the Drozd brothers to do so. That was the first time I heard about the Drozd brothers. The Drozds were a team of father and sons, a master builder and three brothers. They were responsible for renovations, painting, building, and bricklaying. They had signed the *Volkslist* when the Nazis came. That meant they claimed to have German heritage in hopes of gaining privilege under the Germans. The Drozds built the wall, he said, but also provided food for us, for money. When the money ran out, the Jews in hiding paid with flour, he said.

Aleksander Dagnan also knew about Mrs. Bochner, the older woman in hiding with us. "This older lady used to visit my mother after liberation. She felt guilty that she survived when her son and closest relatives all died. She survived in their place. "What is the point of being here?" she would ask. "It should have been one of my children who survived, not me." He also said that Mrs. Bochner was quite old, over seventy at the time.

He knew that Mr. Aleksandrowicz had been a galvanizer for the Dagnan factory, that he had graduated from the Polytechnical University before the war and was an educated man. The galvanizing shop was located by the tool storage, which was directly under the hideout. The machinery was powered by steam, which made noise during the day and muffled the sounds that might have come from the attic.

Mr. Aleksandrowicz spoke to Dagnan after the war and told him that we obtained food in different ways. Next to the transmission belt it was possible to sneak into the mill and take flour. He said my father and Mr. Aleksandrowicz did this, which is exactly what I remember.

Once, according to Dagnan, Mr. Aleksandrowicz was seen downstairs in the factory looking very ill, his body swollen and he had nothing to wear. They put a jacket around Mr. Aleksandrowicz and got him quickly out of sight. Bartosz said Mrs. Zofia Dagnan had told him this same story and that Aleksandrowicz was green in the face and could barely stand. She said she did not ask questions because she knew what the punishment would be for hiding Jews. "My parents lived through this trauma," Dagnan said to us. "Each time someone knocked on the door at night, we thought ..."

Bartosz added that there were posters with the warning that anyone who helped a Jew would be killed. He said they had originals of these posters in the museum.

Carolyn asked if there were a list of workers like in *Schindler's List*. Dagnan said yes, not only of the Jewish workers but all workers. The list had been lost when the office was broken into by burglars looking for money. "The records of the employees were well kept until the beginning of the nineties. Everything was destroyed in very stupid circumstances."

Carolyn asked Dagnan if he thought his father was like Schindler. "At that time I didn't. Later I knew how much he had done. When he came home after work, he prayed all the time, non-stop. His life situation forced him to take a position. And every position was a bad one. Prayer was the only solution. I did not understand the situation of my father then. I understand it now."

He told us that the factory also processed barley, which I remember we mixed with water to make soup. He said the Jews who were working at the Dagnan factory had no real set jobs, and that having the papers to work there meant they would not be deported immediately and it allowed them to obtain some supplies for their families. "They had brooms and were pretending they were doing something, but really it was an opportunity to escape. It was chaos, everyday new people, working groups from the ghetto. The machine shop was a repair shop, a garage for the *Wehrmacht*, and this is why the factory had the right to have a few Jewish workers. It was an alibi for having these workers."

Dagnan knew Skorupa well. Boleslav Skorupa was a master locksmith in the factory and a manager in the workshop. He had an apartment on the factory premises. He had four sons: Jurek, Zbyszek, Antoni (known as Tosiek), and Adolf, the oldest. According to Dagnan, the father, Skorupa, had been the driving force behind the whole thing of hiding Jews and it was for money.

Boleslav Skorupa (fourth from right front row) with machine shop workers, Dagnan factory, during the war. (Kalman Goldberg collection)

He said that Boleslav Skorupa had a "business attitude" toward everything. Zbyszek Skorupa was the one who brought us food in the beginning despite the fact that he had a disability. Dagnan said he was missing a leg from an accident on the mill property years before, when he had fallen and driven a chisel through his thigh. He used a crutch and walked with a limp, but I do not recall any of that. I only knew that "Skorupa" brought us food.

The Skorupa brothers were also involved in smuggling Jews over the border into Hungary for a fee. They would use a truck from Dagnan's factory. One time, near Nowy Sacz, the Germans stopped the vehicle. The driver, Tadeusz Kaplon, was captured and taken to Auschwitz and a series of camps and eventually he was killed while a prisoner during the bombing of Dresden. Adolf Skorupa got away, but Zbyszek Skorupa, who was sitting next to the driver and could not move fast because of his disability, was shot and killed.

When Dagnan told us this, I finally knew the details of why the young Skorupa suddenly stopped coming to the attic and bringing us food, and why my mother sent packages to Mrs. Skorupa from Canada. Bartosz said that the oldest brother, Adolf Skorupa, was still alive and he had interviewed him and spoken to his wife. His wife told Bartosz that Adolf could not talk about what happened at the border because he, as the oldest brother, had taken the younger brother along on this dangerous action, despite his disability, and the mother had never forgiven Adolf that the younger brother was killed. She held him responsible for it the rest of her life.

Dagnan said that my parents lived across the street from the mill on the other side of Lwowska Street in a long wooden house on the corner of Lwowska and Ochronek. About one hundred families lived there. The house is now gone. I take it that was where they lived in the ghetto, as I later located my parents' house where they lived when Charlie and I were born and it was not near the ghetto but on Krasinskiego Street.

Dagnan spoke of witnessing the *wysiedlenia*. "Things went on in the Czacki School. On the ground floor they were told to undress and then they would take them into the field and shoot them. I was lying on the ground in a potato field there and saw it happen. And in the market place in Tarnow, it was such a slaughter that blood was flowing into the sewers. The fire department had to come with their hoses. During the liquidation of the ghetto I saw a young girl walking along. I was looking through the window and a soldier just took out a pistol and shot her. So many people."

Dagnan also confirmed details like the Germans milling around the machine shop to have their cars repaired, which explained what we saw out the cracks of the walls from our hideout. He said that we did our cooking not only upstairs but also down in the galvanizing shop, where there was a stove. That is also where our water supply was.

Carolyn asked Dagnan if his father knew about the Jews in hiding. Dagnan replied, "How could he not know? It was a public secret." If things went missing in the factory, his father did not react. But, Dagnan said, everyone was very very tense about it and it was hardly mentioned at the time or even after the war. "We could have all died. And you wouldn't be here, and I wouldn't be here.... We all knew that if someone denounced us, we would all have ended up in the oven. Despite everything, even though quite a few people knew, there was not a single swine who told."

Dagnan remembered seeing us when we came out of hiding. He said Mr. Aleksandrowicz was emaciated, a "human scrap," when he emerged from hiding. "Your father was swollen because of the poor nutrition and bad living conditions." Carolyn asked, "Do you remember seeing a little boy come out of hiding?" "Yes, I remember him. There were two of them." Then he said to me directly, "You were a lot smaller than now."

He also said that after the war either the Ungers or the Aleksandrowiczs had given a house to his father as a thank-you for hiding all of us. I knew nothing about this. We asked where the house was. He said it was on the corner of Lwowska and Goslar streets, where a Mr. Kozicki had had a drugstore on the ground floor. He said that it had been part of the ghetto and by the end of the war there were no windows, or doors or floors left—that everything had been ripped out and it was a ruin. But it was given to his father and uncle as remuneration for hiding the Jews. His uncle and father fixed up the house after the war. By total coincidence, Janus Koziol, who was acting as a translator for the interview, said, "I live in that house now." We saw it on our 2009 trip to Tarnow.

Dagnan had a question for me. "One thing that really puzzles me, is why these people, even once, would not give a sign of life—where they were and what was happening to them. I know it was a huge trauma, and from talking to people in Israel I know that they didn't want to talk about what was happening during the war." Still, he wanted to know why none of the people in hiding had contacted him. I said I could only speak for myself, that in our family we never spoke about the Holocaust or even about Tarnow, that at the supper table we only talked about the present and the future.

Conversely, when Carolyn asked Aleksander Dagnan why not more was said about the Jews in hiding after the war, he said that no one spoke about it because, if it were known you had helped Jews, then people would assume you had been paid to do so and had lots of money. In Bartosz's interview with Jachimowicz, the survivor in Beunos Aires, he had put it like this: "You know what it was like after the war. People would not admit that they had been hiding Jews. It was not well looked upon. People were afraid of the returnees, the survivors. They were afraid because in the meantime they had taken over the Jewish homes." Dagnan said, "For sure those who helped construct the wall took some money. Those who were bringing food didn't do it for free either. After the war nobody would talk about it because one could be suspected of having become rich and be a target for other Poles. But mostly, what we got out of it was ... fear."

Then Dagnan gave another reason too. "There was nothing to brag about. It was normal, a simple civic duty. Nobody asked, nobody was interested. Everyone was relieved that is was over, this stressful situation was finished." Carolyn asked Dagnan if their family realized that having nine Jews survive in hiding was something extraordinary. Dagnan said, "It was not anything extraordinary. What happened was a colossal German crime." As a teenager he had witnessed horrors during the liquidation of the ghetto, people slaughtered in plain sight. "We were all relieved we were not executed."

I asked him about the box that my mother had stored with someone, the box from which we recovered the matzo bag and a few other items. I wondered if perhaps my parents had left it with the Dagnans, but he did not think so, that if it had been stored with his family he would have known about it.

I said that my mother had kept in touch with Mrs. Skorupa after the war. I said that our life after leaving Poland wasn't so easy. He asked me what my profession was and when I told him he said, "Your father was selling flour and you are selling knowledge." Dagnan himself had worked as a psychologist and other professions. He also said, "Congratulations, because after everything you have gone through, you achieved much." I told him that it was Canada that gave me the opportunity to achieve.

I asked Dagnan what happened to the mill after the war. He said that his father was transported to the Soviet Union and he added ironically, "As a thank-you for helping people." Under the Soviet system Dagnan's father was seen as a capitalist factory owner. Augustyn Dagnan spent nine months in a prisoner-of-war camp working in the mines. Skorupa then ran the mill. His father was not happy about that. When he returned to Tarnow the mill was nationalized, taken over by the state—a "communist revenge," he called it. It was later let go to ruins and demolished in 2001. He quoted from Shelley's poem *Ozymandias* about the decline of all great man-made things. We agreed it was not the buildings that are important but the people.

At the end of the meeting Mr. Dagnan said to me, "I am very happy that you still remember the language." I could understand some of what he said. He told me that he saw my father in the shape of my face and said that meeting me was a huge gift. We agreed that the history of the Unger family and the Dagnan family is important. That yes, money was involved but also risk and humanity. He told me about his three daughters, five grandchildren, and one great grandchild, and I told him of my family. He wished me a very long

Aleksander Dagnan, son of the factory owner, with Israel at the Tarnow Regional Museum, 2009. (Carolyn Gammon photo)

life. I told him that we will try to do the book in Polish so his grandchildren will know about their great grandfather.

Skorupa

After my first visit to Tarnow I mentioned the name Skorupa in the email contact with Bartosz. He then contacted Adolf Skorupa, the last of the brothers who was still alive. In January 2007, Bartosz interviewed Adolf Skorupa at his house in Tarnow. Dorota Glowacka in Halifax translated the interview from Polish to English for us, but it was after we had met Dagnan so it ended up being a confirmation of much of what Dagnan had told us. Skorupa also knew the names of the people in hiding—Unger, Bochner, and Aleksandrowicz—but not the two girls in the attic. He mistook them for the daughters of the Aleksandrowicz couple. He also did not remember my brother—that we were two children in hiding.

He spoke of being witness to the *wysiedlenia*, or "actions," as he called them, and described it in much the same way as Dagnan. He was hiding in some new apartment buildings on Praca Street when, across the street, the Germans went from door to door checking every house. If the Jews had a "good" *Kennkarte* or *Judenpass*, they would be spared, and if not they were shot on the spot. He says about seventy people were murdered from just three apartment buildings. He was driving a truck as a job and during one *Aktion* he said he could not get up the hill to the old market in the truck because the road was so slippery with blood. He called the massacre "macabre." I have read a very depressing history of the Holocaust in Tarnow. The brutality of the Nazis was horrific, particularly toward children. Small Jewish children were killed by smashing their heads against a wall. My father witnessed that. I wonder how such incredibly cruel people could exist and how they could be made to do such brutal acts.

Skorupa confirmed that the Drozd brothers had built the false wall, that they were Dagnan's construction crew, jacks-of-all-trades about the factory. He said because of that, no one would have noticed whether they were carrying bricks around. According to Skorupa the Drozds fixed us up so we could cook in the hideout. He said, "When the Jews still had money, the Drozds helped."

In the interview with Bartosz, he and his wife spoke briefly about the brothers smuggling Jews across the border and about the skirmish near Nowy Sacz that killed his brother Zbyszek. After that Adolf Skorupa could not return to Tarnow and so he joined the partisans. At the end of the war, in the last couple of months when it was clear things were coming to an end and everything was quite chaotic, he returned to Tarnow and also had to hide out in the Dagnan factory complex. Before the war, the Skorupas lived on the factory premises, so this is where he returned to hide himself. He maintains that he would come up to our hideout on occasion and talk with us. I have no recollection of this and can hardly imagine it. But he did comment on the dreadful conditions we lived in, that our clothes were in rags. In fact, he called it a "hole"—and said, "How could a boy live there and not cry?"

Skorupa said that after the war the Dagnans were chased out of their factory as capitalists by the Soviets and so he took over running the factory for a while. In this capacity he worked with my father after the war, when my father tried to get back into business and needed flour. "I had it good with Unger," is how he put it. His interview is hard to take because of anti-Semitic remarks peppered throughout his comments and inaccuracies, so it is hard to know how much to trust it. Bartosz told Skorupa that "the boy" who had been in hiding, referring to me, had returned to Tarnow and Skorupa commented that perhaps we could meet. When we travelled to Tarnow in 2009 Bartosz set up a meeting with Adolf Skorupa, but on the day when we were to meet, his wife called to say he was not feeling well and was not up to it. If I had met him, I would have asked him who was the Skorupa who brought us food, just to confirm that.

On the Tarnow trip in 2007 I agreed to speak at a Polish high school about my story, the II Liceum Ogólnokształcące on Mickiewicza Street. The teacher had prepared the students for my visit. It was, in fact, an English class.

In the hallway of the school there were posters showing the school had sponsored the fixing up of certain gravestones of rabbis in the Jewish cemetery. I told my story as I had previously done. It was no different than speaking in Canada, except I believe the students could not follow me as well,

Israel speaking at the Polish high school Liceum Ogólnokształcące in Tarnow, 2007. (Carolyn Gammon photo)

so I did not feel the usual connection with them. After the talk three students gave each one of us, myself, Marlene, and Carolyn, a rose. The student who gave one to Marlene kissed her hand. Obviously that tradition lives on in Poland. One student said to Carolyn, "We are ashamed for what happened in this country." We gave the roses to the women who ran the Tarnow tourist office, as I had gone there every day to do my emails.

The most important thing about going to Tarnow again was meeting Adam Bartosz in person. He is very interested in preserving the Jewish history of Tarnow and a genuine friend of Jews. Bartosz is not an apologist, as some even well-meaning Poles we met were prone to be. He, more than anyone else, helped me to confirm my story. He confirmed the names Dagnan and Skorupa and through his research and contacts I eventually learned the names of those of us in hiding who I had forgotten in the long years of silence. The additional information filled some gaps. I had thought that my father and the three other Jewish men built the wall, but they would have to have been stonemasons, so it makes more sense that it was the Drozd brothers who did the job. After so many years, and given that I was very young at the time, I sometimes wondered whether my memory was reasonably accurate. It was comforting to have Dagnan corroborate my recollections.

I still did not know the names of the two girls I had been in hiding with. That took more research and time.

Kalman Goldberg—Outside the Hideout

Carolyn and I continued to do research to learn details about my time in Tarnow. For instance, at the Holocaust Museum in Montreal, Carolyn met a survivor who knew *the* expert for the Jews of Tarnow, a man called Howard Fink, who was living in Massachusetts. He accessed records from the town of Bochnia, which is on the road between Tarnow and Cracow. The records were part of a project indexing Jewish records in Poland. He discovered the name of one of my uncles, Nuchym Hersch Unger, whose parents are listed as Josef Pinkus Unger and Hana Leia Lesser—my grandparents. There was the marriage record and a record of the births of his five children. I finally had the name of one of my father's siblings.

I placed a search on the website All Generations for Holocaust survivors and their relatives. My query asked about information pertaining to my story. It read: "From Israel Unger, a survivor in Fredericton, New Brunswick, Canada. My name is Israel Unger. I was born in Tarnow, Poland, in March 1938. My nuclear family: father, mother, older brother and I, along with five other Jews, survived the Holocaust in Tarnow in hiding. Our hiding place was behind a false wall in the attic of Dagnan's flour mill." I named my family members and Mrs. Bochner and the Aleksandrowiczs.

First I heard from a woman called Felicia Graber, whose father had worked at Dagnan's and had written his story down. She sent me a page of text pertinent to my family's story. Her father had been part of the scramble to try and obtain the life-saving identity cards at Dagnan's flour mill. According to her father, the Gestapo had issued an order that every business employing Jews had to have a letter assigned to it and Dagnan's was assigned a "Z." At some point most Jewish workers were deported and only ten remained. Each was to have this special identification (ID) card with the letter "Z." Without it, you had no work and would be shot. Her father did not receive one and someone told him it was because a Mr. Unger had paid Dagnan a diamond ring to get the special ID. When her father approached Dagnan with this information, he claimed he had received only nine allowances for Jewish workers. Felicia's father said Dagnan was a swindler. He wrote that Mr. Unger interceded on his behalf and so he, Felicia's father, continued to go with the group of workers although he had no legal papers to do so. The daughter did not know more about this story than that one page, so that was the end of that lead.

Then I had a response from Kalman Goldberg in New Jersey. He had worked for Dagnan in the machine shop of the flour mill. First his daughter Sandy wrote to me, that her father had known a David Unger. Soon after I spoke to him personally on the phone. He was born in 1923 in Tarnow. He had a high regard for Dagnan and compared him to Schindler. He worked at Dagnan's mill until September 1943. That means during the early period of being in hiding he

Kalman Goldberg as young man in Poland. (Photo courtesy of Kalman Goldberg collection)

Kalman Goldberg and Israel at Kalman's house in New Jersey, 2010. (Carolyn Gammon photo)

knew what was going on *out-side* the hideout. We wanted to go to the Yeshiva Archives in New York anyway, so in April 2008, Marlene, Carolyn, and I drove from Fredericton to New York.

Kalman Goldberg is fifteen years older than I am and he was eighty-six when we interviewed him at his home in New Jersey.

His parents were Chaim and Sarah Goldberg. "My father was orthodox. He was a *gabbai* in a *shul*; he wore a *shtrayml*." To translate: his father assisted in the synagogue and wore a fur-edged hat. Before the Nazi period, his family manufactured soap in Tarnow—and, he noted, soap was like gold in wartimes. Like all Jews at the time, he had to do forced labour. He was assigned to the Jewish hospital, but he wanted to work as a mechanic at Dagnan's flour mill. His father knew the chief of police, who was also friends with Dagnan, and so Kalman got a job working at Dagnan's in the machine shop and as a chauffeur for a German soldier.

Like my father, he was escorted each morning at 7 a.m. from the ghetto to the Dagnan mill. Later he lived at the garage. Working for Dagnan meant you were protected. He respected Dagnan, but said that Dagnan "played at both ends," quietly helping Jews but at the same time having business connections to the Germans. He personally saw a lot of SS coming and going from Dagnan's and wondered what they were doing there.

He says he knew about our hiding place. He thought perhaps that it had been made by Dagnan for some of his workers. He did not know about the Drozd brothers building it. According to Kalman, some of the Jewish workers at Dagnan's returned to the ghetto, but a couple did not—they stayed in the hideout at night. This corresponded to what I

Kalman Goldberg (below the "x") working in the Dagnan factory machine shop circa 1942. (Kalman Goldberg collection)

knew about the men taking turns to stay overnight. "I knew about the hiding place, but we didn't talk about it because it was dangerous. It was a big secret. The two who worked for Dagnan and stayed overnight in the hideout, they thought nobody knew about it." I asked him how this open secret worked. He said not everyone knew about it, just the people who had contact with the ones in hiding, who took them food and such. "Whoever knew about it kept the knowledge to himself." Everyone was aware that if the Gestapo found out it would be a tragedy, that everyone involved would be executed.

Carolyn asked how he thought nine people could get enough to eat in hiding. He said that the farmers would bring food from the farms and that someone was smuggling it into the hideout. When I asked if he had heard the name Skorupa, he said, "Maybe." He knew that some Jews had escaped to Hungary. He had great praise for the engineer who was in charge of Dagnan's garage, Styryjski Władziu, who helped him obtain Gentile papers and told him, "Save yourself, run away."

Kalman knew the name Bochner—that must have been Mrs. Bochner's son. And he knew about a worker named Weksler, who had two daughters who were hidden there. That is how I finally found out the names of the two girls I had been in hiding with—Weksler. He said the Weksler father was caught in the ghetto at the time of the liquidation and then disappeared in the Plaszow concentration camp in Cracow. He said that the two girls survived and went to Palestine after the war. This is how I found out what happened to the girls' father. I knew as well that the girls had gone to Palestine.

When I asked Kalman if he knew the name Unger he said, "Yes, I knew about Unger because I spoke to him once in a while. He used to come in and out of the ghetto. Your father was dealing in flour before the war." He thought my father was also working discounting vouchers. I could not understand exactly what he meant, but he said that they would send goods to Bochnia and be paid by cheque, say one hundred Zlotys. My father would give cash, say ninety-five Zlotys, for that cheque and take care of going to the post and cashing it. He called this being a *bukher*, like a bookmaker in Yiddish, or a *veksler*. He also knew an Unger who was a locksmith in Tarnow. I showed him a photo of my father and he said he recognized him, "No question about it." I was pleased that he remembered my father. He knew we had moved to Canada.

Kalman Goldberg had photos from Dagnan's mill, the workers, and the garage where they repaired the SS vehicles. He said the German army was going to the Russian front and had their vehicles repaired there at Dagnan's garage. There was one photo of a large hook and pulley for lifting heavy engines out of the trucks. He had another of the field behind Dagnan's factory called Kapłanówce. In the photo he is wearing the mandatory armband with the Star of David.

It turns out that Kalman Goldberg was on Schindler's list. When the Tarnow ghetto was liquidated he was deported to Plaszow concentration camp. He worked for Schindler right to the end; that is how he survived. Most surprising were his views of Schindler. He did not have a good opinion of Oskar Schindler. He said that Schindler raped a girl he knew at the factory, that the film is not accurate, and he had called Spielberg and told him so. He said Spielberg accepted his story but did not want to know more about it.

Kalman's mother died before the ghetto was set up and they were still able to bury her and put up a stone. Of seven children, Kalman was the only survivor in his family. "I am overwhelmed about how I survived." He said his father had looked at our hideout one night and the next day said, "Charlie, I don't want to stay there. I don't want to live there." His father and brother tried to survive on "Aryan" papers in Lemburg, but they did not survive. In email correspondence with Kalman's daughter, she remarked that if Kalman's father had stayed in the hideout he might have survived.

Rescue Children, Inc.

During the same trip in April 2009 when we met Kalman Goldberg, we visited Yeshiva Archives in the Yeshiva University of New York. I had written ahead, and Deena Schwimmer was very helpful in preparing files for us to look at.

When my father left my brother and me in Cracow with a large group of Jewish orphans, we were given to organizers of what I now know was a vast effort to rescue Jewish children in postwar Europe. Because I remembered the name Aix-les-Bains, when Carolyn and I began the research and put the name Aix-les-Bains together with "Jewish orphans," it became clear through Internet research that Charlie and I had been part of something called Rescue Children.

In 1939, a group of American and Canadian rabbis formed an emergency committee to try to rescue Jews from Europe. Their group became known as *Vaad Hatzala*, Hebrew for "rescue committee." They worked throughout the war raising money and using it to try to save people. Funds were provided by the Joint Distribution Committee, the World Jewish Congress, the American Jewish Congress, and other international organizations. They raised funds for the passage of Jewish refugees who had transit visas to Japan. They sent funds to refugees who had made it to Shanghai. They lobbied the American government to procure visas for rabbis and students. They alerted officials to the systematic extermination of Jews in Nazi-occupied Europe. They worked behind the German lines trying to save people any way possible, including paying the Germans to release some people from concentration camps.

After the war, the work focused on helping survivors and a branch formed dedicated particularly to Jewish children survivors. This branch, called Rescue Children, Inc., was headed by Herbert Tenzer in New York. He was a lawyer as well as in the candy business, Barton's Candy. In fact, he was the first to produce kosher candy for *Pessach*. He took time off his law practice to organize Rescue Children. The concept was two-pronged. In Europe, people would try to find these children and, on the American end, sponsors would be found to "adopt" the children by paying one dollar a day. A sponsorship cost three hundred and sixty-five dollars a year. Rescue Children did fundraising in the United States. We saw an interview with Tenzer in the *New York Post* 1946 entitled "The Saddest Things Left in Europe Are These Children." He says in this article that in the years 1945 to 1946, the first year of its existence, one thousand four hundred fifty children had been "adopted." There was a letter to Eleanor Roosevelt in which it was clear she had expressed interest in "adopting" a child. New York's then mayor, William O'Dwyer, "adopted" a child. So it was clearly high-profile.

First, the on-site organizers in Europe had to find the children. They came from all over Nazi-occupied Europe and had survived all different ways, often in incredible circumstances. They had survived in hiding like myself and Charlie, or with the partisans, or with Christian families, or in orphanages that had been paid to take them, or with people who did it out of humanitarian reasons. Some were in monasteries and convents, some had survived in the woods. How did

Herbert Tenzer, organizer of Rescue Children Inc., in a *Post* article, 1947. (Yeshiva University Archives)

they find the children? They gave out cigarettes and chocolate and money to get information. "We have heard there were Jewish children in this village." The children had been schooled not to reveal that they were Jewish, so it was hard to identify them. One way was to speak Yiddish and see if the child understood. Another way was to see if the child knew the *Shema Yisrael*, the basic prayer. Most of them had had no education in years. Some no longer knew their original identities. In one letter Tenzer writes that he needs to raise money for false teeth, because 60 percent of the children are in need of such dental work. In one document it estimated that of the one million Jewish children in Poland before the war, only five thousand survived.

On the European side there was one particular man who, with funds from the Joint Distribution Committee, went to liberated Europe to find and help children. Dr. Isaac Herzog was originally from Lomza, Poland. His family had moved to Ireland at the turn of the century and he served as the chief rabbi of Ireland for some years before going on to be the chief rabbi of Palestine. Immediately after the war he went to Europe to find children in Poland, and it could be that Charlie and I were in a group brought out of Poland by Rabbi Herzog in late summer 1946.

Rescue Children set up homes in France, Belgium, and Sweden for the found children. Ours in Aix-les-Bains was only one of many. In fact, at the Yeshiva Archives I learned that there were four homes in Aix-les-Bains organized along religious orientation. Charlie and I were in one called Hôtel Beau Site.

The archives had records of me and my brother. They had the forms filled out with our names, birthdates, and so on. The forms were in French, under the title "Protection des Enfants de Déportés"—protection of children of people deported. Rescue Children worked in France with a French government agency called Comité des Oeuvres Sociales de la Resistance, who had helped families during the war whose relatives had been part of the resistance and deported or executed. I found reference to our entire family in the files.

Israel and other children listed as being at the Hôtel Beau Site on the list of Rescue Children, Inc. (Yeshiva University Archives)

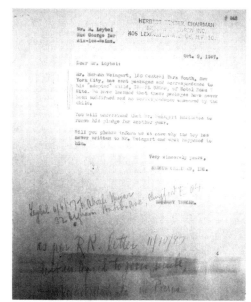

Israel's document of registration with the Rescue Children,
Inc. program in Aix-les-Bains under the auspices of the
Protection des Enfants de Deportés in France. Note Herbert
Tenzer's stamp, bottom right. (Yeshiva University Archives)

Document saying Israel had been "adopted" by Mr. Weingart
in New York. Handwritten note says Israel has left to "join
uncle." (Yeshiva University Archives)

One letter was very interesting in that it said I had been "adopted" by a Mr. Weingart in New York. In a letter from Tenzer to the local organizers in Aix-les-Bains, the sponsor asks why he has not heard from me, his "adopted" child. There is a handwritten note dated 11 June 1947, saying: "left to join uncle" and my uncle Abraham's address at 32 Higham Station Avenue in London is given.

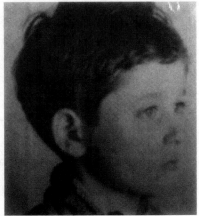

Israel at the age of nine, circa 1947, in Rescue Children Inc. archives. Photo used for sending to prospective sponsors. (Yeshiva University Archives)

The Rescue Children organizers sent the prospective sponsors photos and a biography of the child and the sponsors were encouraged to develop a relationship with the children by sending them, for example, a gift at Rosh Hashana or Chanukkah. I do not remember receiving anything like that, but this could explain what I remembered about being issued new clothes only to have them taken away right after a photo was taken of us.

Looking through the Yeshiva Archives Rescue Children photos I recognized a few things. I did not find myself or Charlie, that I know of, in any photos except the one official photo of me. (There is no photo of my brother.) I recognized the main room in the Hôtel Beau Site and the chequered tablecloth in the dining hall. Also there is a photo of a sink in a bedroom, which looked just like the room I shared with Benzion Singer. It was just that type of room and sink I recall the time I was so tormented by the hair lice that I ran and combed my hair into the sink. There was also a photo of a communal bedroom and the boy in the lower-left corner sitting on a bed could be me. Marlene thinks so too. What would I have been doing in a communal bedroom? Visiting my brother perhaps. We saw photos of children learning Hebrew, putting on plays and other activities, but I do not remember anything of those activities. There were photos of the Rescue Children and *Vaad Hatzala* organizers sending boxes of matzos to Europe. Those were the Manischewitz square matzo I remember well right after the war in Tarnow, when we were so astonished that they were square.

Through the All Generations website I made contact with a woman, Shoshana Drizen, who was also in the Hôtel Beau Site. She was three years older than I and remembered the big hall on the ground floor and a park in front of the building. Marlene and I went to Aix-les-Bains after this and I recognized the building. It is now an apartment block.

Ryglice and Dąbrowa

During the 2009 trip to Tarnow I wanted to see where my mother's and father's family were from. I was curious to see what these places would look like. This time I travelled without Marlene. I went via Berlin to meet Carolyn. She had arranged that I speak at her partner's intercultural centre, Joliba, in Kreuzberg. It was November 9, so they had advertised it as part of memorial events for *Kristallnacht*. There I met a German non-Jewish woman I had been corresponding with for some time, Amelie Doge. For years she had been trying to help a Berlin survivor living in the United States, Leo Gerechter, trace his sister, who had been deported with her husband to Tarnow. Amelie had contacted me after my talk at the Anne Frank Centre in Berlin two years before. She thought I might have some information about the sister. Amelie has spent an incredible amount of time trying to find out what happened to Leo's sister. I was not able to assist her further, though Carolyn and I did check the archives in Tarnow for her. I met Amelie at my talk in Berlin in 2009.

There is a memorial initiative in Germany, now all over Europe, called *Stolpersteine*—Stumbling Blocks. They are small brass plaques placed in front of houses where Jewish people lived before deportation. These plaques state the names, birthdates, the date of transport, and where the person was murdered. Amelie Doge arranged for Stumbling Blocks to be placed in front of the house where Leo's family lived—the very house and apartment that Amelie herself now lives in. Amelie is a woman who makes every effort to commemorate the Holocaust. I am encouraged there are people like Amelie in Germany.

Before my talk in Berlin I asked myself, as I always do: Why am I doing this? I do not enjoy it. I don't need this. But then when the talk is over I am always pleased I did do it. So it was in Berlin this second time, even more so, in fact, as I enjoyed the discussion period—much more than the talk. Someone asked about the relationship with my brother, which was a new question for me. It was all done in English–German translation.

Carolyn also used the opportunity of my being in Berlin to do more interviews. Then we flew to Cracow and took the train to Tarnow. Adam Bartosz's office helped us out yet again by providing us with an apprentice named Maciek. He was quite shy, but he helped us find a taxi driver for the day, a fellow who had worked in Tipperary, Ireland, on a pig farm for a few years and spoke some English.

We headed south of Tarnow, about a half-hour drive, to Ryglice, where my father was born. It is very rural. Ryglice itself has about two thousand inhabitants. When my father lived there as a boy about 10 percent of the population was Jewish.

On Maciek's suggestion, our driver went directly to the town hall and asked how we might get a key to the Jewish cemetery. A woman actually accompanied us to the cemetery with the key. It was very overgrown and our search for Unger graves was not successful. The stones were mostly in Yiddish and without last names.

Carolyn and Israel in the Jewish cemetery, Ryglice, 2009. (Carolyn Gammon photo)

Then we met Adam Szczech, a local historian at the city hall. He explained that the Jews of Ryglice would have lived around the *rynek*, the town square. He was helpful and even brought up on his computer a document signed by a Chana Unger from Ryglice dealing with property. The names, which were transliterations of Hebrew, were often spelt in different ways: Chana, Hanna, Hana, and so forth. So that could be my grandmother. He printed out a copy for us. Later, via email, he did some research for me to try to find out what property my family would have owned or where my father might have lived.

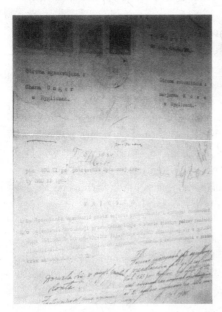

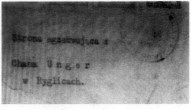

The one document (with blow-up) linking Israel's father's family with Ryglice—a legal letter about a house and monies owed with one party being Chana Unger—perhaps Israel's grandmother. (Ryglice City Hall archives)

We ate at the restaurant on the town square. It was an old one and Carolyn said perhaps my father had eaten there. As I ate I noticed a fellow who was hanging around on the street corner who was obviously a drinker. He had rosy cheeks and was quite chubby. He was looking for acquaintances to drink with. When someone came by, the two of them would come in for a shot. Then he would go out again. This happened two or three times while we ate lunch.

Dąbrowa Tarnowska, where my mother's family was from, is larger, about eleven thousand people and a short drive north of Tarnow. It seemed like a city compared to the village of Ryglice. The main synagogue and the Jewish cemetery were right next to each other in city centre. There were hardly any stones in the cemetery. I think we looked at them all. This time we were looking for the name Fisch and found none. A large synagogue was under renovation. I was impressed by the size of the synagogue and that it was being restored.

State Archives and Registry Office

On that trip too, Carolyn and I visited the Tarnow Registry Office and the State Archive in Cracow, Tarnow Branch. We could not have had two more opposite experiences. The one experience was of hostility and the other was friendliness. I had been to the registry office in 2006 with Marlene and obtained a printout of my parents' wedding certificate, but this trip I was hoping to find more Ungers, perhaps even records of my father's siblings. The Tarnow Registry Office is not only an archive but is an office used today as well for things like getting a driver's licence. They have birth and marriage records going back about one hundred years.

I asked to see my own birth certificate. It was a handwritten entry in a large ledger. It had my full name: Israel Mendel Menachim Unger. It named the circumciser, or *mohel*, Salamon Blaugrund. It stated my father's occupation as *robotnik*, or worker. The witnesses—I take it this means at the circumcision—were Lazar Unger and Majer Geld. Lazar might be one of my father's brothers. It stated that we lived on Krasinskiego Street, number six. That was the first time I knew where my family had lived before being forced to live in the ghetto.

I also saw my parents' wedding certificate. It said that Markus Dawid Unger, aged twenty-eight years and seven months, married Hinda Fisch, who was twenty-six years and six months old on 15 June 1931. It names my paternal and maternal grandparents. The rabbi was Isak Rapaport and the witnesses Gerson Roger and Salomon Singer of Tarnow. There was a marriage certificate of the one uncle I knew from London, Abraham Unger,

Israel's father's and mother's wedding certificates, listing the names of his paternal and maternal grandparents. Note that the Polish version of Mordechai is Markus.

born 1897. His first wife was Beile Bogen of Tarnow. These were all important sources of information for me about my family.

At the registry office you could order a printed version of the birth and marriage certificates for thirty-three Zlotys, or eleven dollars, per document. The problem was that the printed documents had only about half the information that was recorded in the registry book. Carolyn asked, therefore, if she could take photos of the documents so we would have the complete information. Her request was refused. We were told that written permission had to be obtained from Cracow and that we should write in Polish. We asked whom we might appeal to for the allowance to take photos on that day, as we were leaving Tarnow the next day. We were told that the person who could make that decision was not in. Was there another person, we asked? Yes, in Cracow. Could we call him or her? No, not on their phone. On and on it went. It got quite nasty when the woman helping us, whose English was quite good, told us that we should have come with a Polish translator! As if they could not imagine why I hardly speak Polish. It went from bad to worse as we were told really they should not even be showing us the ledger without written permission from Cracow. Although the woman we were dealing with had some sympathy for our request, her superiors were openly hostile. They clearly did not want us in the office and did everything with body language and talking about us in Polish—some of which I understood—to make us feel unwelcome. There was obvious resentment.

I had wanted to search for the names of my father's siblings, but they made it so unpleasant that we decided to leave. I had to wonder what benefit they had from denying one of the few surviving Tarnow Jews a photo of his own birth certificate. Until this point our on-site research had gone fairly smoothly, but this encounter brought us back to Polish reality. I later wrote to the Polish ambassador in Canada asking for his help in obtaining a photo of my birth certificate and other family records in the Tarnow Registry Office. I explained to him what had happened. He did not reply to my letter.

We had a very different experience at the State Archives. It is officially called the State Archive of Cracow, Tarnow Branch. There we were met by Jan Chmura, whom I had met with Marlene in 2006. He could not have been more helpful. He understood how important such a visit is to a survivor who manages to make it back to his hometown. He brought out bundle after bundle of archival material. He did not even take the time to rebundle the files before bringing out another. He thought of things himself to check. He found documents about properties my father owned. There were documents from 1946 about my father selling property without houses on them in Ryglice. From another document I found out that my father had owned a two-storey house on Walowa Street, number twenty-three, and sold it in 1946 to a man named Pawel Zielinski.

Israel and Jan Chmura at State Archive of Cracow, Tarnow Branch, 2009. (Carolyn Gammon photo)

My father was obviously making preparations to leave Poland. It gave me a different perspective on my father. Obviously, after coming from the small town of Ryglice, he really made his way in business in Tarnow, enough to own property. The documents were filed under the particular lawyers who took care of the case. There is no way we could have located these without Jan Chmura's help. By the end of our two- or three-hour visit his archival room was scattered with open bundles of documents. He had really gone out of his way to be helpful.

In Cracow, on the way out of Poland, Carolyn and I went to the state archives. A Mr. Slawinski, an official at the archives, had contacted me some time before seeking information about Tarnow. When I knew I would be in Cracow, I had written ahead to Mr. Slawinsky and he offered to assist me when I came to the archives. I told him the date in advance but he did not show up. One fellow tried to be helpful. After a long wait, he retrieved files for us from the Institute für Deutsche Ostarbeit (IDO index)—Institute for German Workers in the East. Six boxes were labelled "Tarnow," which we proceeded to go through. There were endless questionnaires about the slave labourers: where they were from, occupations, and so on—most of them Catholic Poles. Then there was a shock. There were dozens of unlabelled sealed envelopes from Tarnow. The archivist opened one of these for us. It contained human hair. Very macabre. The visit to that archive was useless and a disappointment that Slawinsky did not follow through on his offer to help. We stayed one night in Kazimierz, the former Jewish quarter. Everything looks Jewish but there are hardly any Jews.

The three visits to the three separate archives show various aspects of Poland today. The Tarnow Registry Office showed how much resistance and resentment there is to Jews returning. Jan Chmura in the State Archive of Cracow, Tarnow Branch, represents how helpful and considerate some people can be. And the last archive in Cracow shows how hard it is to do research without help.

My Birth House

Based on the information on my birth certificate I now knew that my family had lived on Krasinskiego Street, number six. We went to the house I may have been born in. In those days in Poland, middle-class people had their children at home. I believe I was born at home. From the archives I had learned that my parents lived there before Charlie was born as well. Krasinskiego Street is west of city centre but within walking distance—not within the traditional Jewish neighbourhood of Grabowka. The original house still stood.

I would not have done it, but Carolyn rang the doorbell. She explained over the intercom in English that a person who used to live in the house was there and a voice told us in Polish to wait a moment. Then a girl's voice came over the intercom in English inviting us up. Mother and daughter came to the door. There were four apartments in the house and of course I had no way of knowing which would have been my parents' apartment, but it was interesting to see the stairwell and the apartment with its coal ovens (left there as antiques). The apartment was beautifully furnished in a modern style. The mother served us coffee, and Carolyn had German choco-

Israel at his birth house, Krasinskiego Street, number six, Tarnow, 2009. (Carolyn Gammon photo)

lates that she offered them. I told them a bit of my story. Carolyn showed them photos of the hideout. The girl was in grade eleven and her English was very good. She translated for the mother. The mother asked strange questions like, "Were your parents Jewish?" or "Did your parents miss Poland?" I think she found it hard to accept that people left Poland and she did not want to think that Jews had been subjected to rampant hostility after the war.

We went to the house on Walowa Street that my father had sold in 1946. It is very central, and, as the document said, a two-storey house. The façade was renovated, but when a woman opened the door we looked in. It seemed somewhat derelict on the inside. Carolyn wanted to go in, but there were two dogs that growled at her.

Based on the documents, I now knew for certain that my family lived on *ulica Zydowska*, Jew's Street, number twelve, after the war. Carolyn and I went to house number twelve and it was exactly the house I had pointed out to Marlene the very first trip in 2006. The back upper apartments overlooked the broken *bima*.

We also went to the empty lot where the Dagnan factory had been demolished in 2001. I had been before but had not realized what I was looking at. In fact, one wall of the hideout is still standing! Carolyn and I compared photos of the old factory and the drawing of the hideout and concluded that

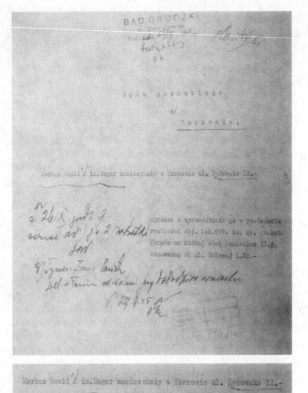

Court document from the *Sad Grodzki* court with blow-up showing that Markus David Unger lived on Zydowska Street, number 12, dated 25 September 1945. The document is a request to get back property on Walowa Street, number twenty-three, and is witnessed by a Catholic priest. (State Archive of Cracow—Tarnow Branch).

the chimney we could still see on a big blank wall was indeed the chimney that had gone up through the hideout! It actually belonged to the adjacent building. We confirmed all this with Bartosz.

All told, I was able to confirm even more details of my story on this last trip. I now know where my family lived when I was born. If Dagnan is correct, I know approximately where we lived in the ghetto. I have the proof of where we lived after the ghetto. I know that my father owned property, one house on Walowa Street and the one on Lwowska Street, which he gave to Dagnan. And I know that the one wall of the hideout is still standing.

Israel in front of Walowa Street, number twenty-three, a house his father once owned. (Carolyn Gammon photo)

Matzevahs for My Family

Another important part of these trips to Tarnow was to commemorate my family who had been murdered in the Holocaust. One of the things that I missed in my life was having an extended family—uncles, aunts, cousins. I deeply regret that I did not question my parents about the relatives who were murdered by the Nazis. I feel it is very important that at least their names be known, that they should not disappear from history. I know the names of aunts and uncles on my mother's side because an uncle had inscribed them in a *siddur*, a prayer book.

Survivors from many former *shtetls*, small Jewish towns, produced memorial books called *Yizkor* books to remember the dead. *Yizkor* literally means "to remember" and is part of a prayer for the dead. The *Yizkor* books are in Hebrew or Yiddish. The one for Tarnow was done by a survivor, Avraham Chomet, in Israel in 1954 and then expanded and redone in 1968. It is called *Tarnow; kiyuma ve-hurbana shel ir yehudit—The Life and Decline of a Jewish City*. It was published by a group in Israel called the Association of Former Residents of Tarnow. I received a copy of the Tarnow *Yizkor* from my parents. My father's family are not recorded there because they were from Ryglice. The Tarnow *Yizkor* is in Yiddish and it gives the names of my maternal grandparents, aunts, and uncles and states that they were killed by the Nazi murderers. It also says: "In everlasting memory."

After my first trip to Tarnow, Mr. Bartosz had written me and invited me to be their guest of honour at the next "Days of Remembrance of the Galician Jews," which is held annually in June. I thanked him, but I did not really feel like going back to Poland for that, even though I do feel that the good work he is doing should be encouraged.

The primary purpose of my trips to Tarnow in 2007 and 2009 was to "unveil" and bless the memorial stones, the *matzevahs*, for my family. In 2007 I had the stone for my mother's family made. The cemetery was a short walk from our hotel. We met with Adam Bartosz at the cemetery. He had made the arrangements for me with the stonemasons. I was pleased with the *matzevah*. It has gold print on black granite in English and Hebrew. My three cousins participated in the *matzevah* project. My cousin Renee's husband, Chaim Kaufman, in Belgium, checked the Hebrew. When we arrived at the Jewish cemetery the first day, the workers were just installing it, so we went back the next day. I had it inscribed as if my mother and her brother, the two who survived from the family, had done it. It says:

In memory of our parents,
brothers and sisters murdered
by the Nazis and their collaborators.
Our Father Chaim Ben Eliyahu
Our Mother Raizel Bat Kalman
Our Brother Eliyahu, his wife and their two children
Our Sister Baila, her husband and their three children
Our Brother David, his wife and their two children
Our Sister Hanna Temeral and her husband
May the Lord be gracious unto them.

Yakov Fisch
Hinda Unger Fisch

This time I had the mourners' kaddish written out and I spoke it at the stone with Marlene at my side. I was pleased that their names were being remembered. I later told my cousins in Belgium that I said the *kaddish* at the *matzevah* for the Fisch family. It made a difference to them.

Israel's maternal grandparents, Raizel and Chaim Fisch. (Israel Unger collection)

Hanna Temeral (née Fisch) and her husband, pre-war. (Israel Unger collection)

In 2009 I did the same for my father's family, even though I do not have many of their names. That one reads:

In memory of my grandparents,

Josef Pinkus and Hana Leia (née Leser) Unger of Ryglice

And their eight sons and daughters.

Josef and Hana and six of their children were murdered by the Nazis.

Two sons, Abraham and Mordechai David, survived.

Abraham moved to England prior to the war.

Morcdechai David, my father, saved his wife

And children and himself by hiding in Tarnow.

After liberation he and his family settled in Canada.

Israel Unger

It is also in English and Hebrew and I said the *kaddish* there during the 2009 trip. Even without the names at least it indicates that they existed.

Israel saying the *kaddish* at the *matzevah* for his maternal relatives in the Tarnow Jewish cemetery, with Marlene at his side, 2007. (Carolyn Gammon photo)

"They know my name is Srulik!"

"Do you know this?" That was the one-liner sent to me by email in 2009 by Adam Bartosz that led to me finding the Weksler sisters at long last. After I had learned the name Weksler from Kalman Goldberg, I had again put out a notice on the All Generations website, but without their married names it was impossible to trace them. During the 2009 trip I had told Bartosz the name Weksler, and some months later came this one-line email referring to a website called sztetl.org.pl, about the Jewish communities, the former *shtetls*, of Poland. It was mostly in Polish, but he sent me a link to an English resumé of an interview in Hebrew that took place in Israel years before. The woman interviewed was Anna Riwka "Hanka" Sarid, née Weksler, from Tarnow. She was born in 1928 and her sister Czesia in 1931. This was it, I had at last found the Weksler sisters!

Anna and Czesia Weksler with their parents, Lazar and Rozia, pre-war. (Shoshi Macam collection)

In the interview Anna tells of her family's life before the Nazi period. Her family were Zionists and they learned Hebrew as preparation towards

Anna Weksler (second from right) while doing forced labour in a shoe factory in Tarnow, 1942. She is wearing the mandatory arm band with Star of David on her right arm. (Shoshi Macam collection)

immigrating to Palestine. Her father, Lazar Weksler, was from Dąbrowa near Tarnow, where my mother's family came from as well. Her mother, Rosa Siegman, came from Tarnow. When the Germans attacked Tarnow, the father escaped to the east, but the mother refused to leave her parents so he returned to help the family. He arranged the all-important stamps for their papers and Anna worked in a wooden-shoe factory.

When new documents were issued, the mother, father, and sister received the vital papers, but Anna did not. She was rounded up in the first action and witnessed the massacre in the town square. She writes that the sight was an "indescribable hell." Anna managed to escape, and life continued in the ghetto until further actions and mass murders in which her mother's parents were murdered.

Anna describes how her father was part of building the hideout already in 1942, taking straw, food, blankets, and clothing into it. She and Czesia moved into hiding and other Jews and their families without documents joined them. In this article she named the Ungers: my father as being a flour merchant, my mother and two children, the Aleksandrowiczs, and Mrs. Bochner. "The hiding place was upgraded. They ... connected the electricity." Anna lived in the hideout even though her father suggested returning to the ghetto. In another *Aktion* of December 1942, her father heard that the ghetto was surrounded by Germans. He decided to go to the ghetto anyway to try and save Rozia. He did not return. When the liquidation of the ghetto came, no news was heard from their mother and father.

Anna names Zbyszek as the man who brought food to the hideout. She says he did not want money for that. "Suddenly he disappeared. There was nobody to help." They took turns going to the mill and bringing back flour and so survived on a type of bread, hard as rock. Needless to say, when I read this for the first time, it sounded exactly like my story. It was my story.

After liberation, Anna and Czesia tried to find their parents—without results. They went to a kibbutz in Czestochowa that accepted orphans. Then they went by foot over the Carpathian Mountains to Czechoslovakia, Hungary, Austria, and Italy. The Jewish Brigade soldiers from the British Army helped them to reach a port near Genoa and eventually they made it to Haifa.

Anna's written interview confirmed all that I remembered. The interview had been done in the year 2000. It was accompanied by photos of both sisters and family members. One of the photos showed Anna's sister Czesia with her son, Shamai Opfer. Knowing this name would be quite uncommon I looked him up on Google and found him in Israel. I had no idea if his mother or Anna were still living, but I wrote him an email in August 2010: "I believe your mother may have been hidden with me in Tarnow, Poland, during the Holocaust."

It was truly amazing! He confirmed that he was the son of Czesia and nephew of Anna. He said that both Anna and Czesia were "Relatively okay ... but not getting younger." Oddly enough when he received my email he was just flying home to Israel from the Netherlands, where he had visited the hiding place of Anne Frank. He wrote that he had told his family the story of his mother, "Which is also your story." He asked if I knew if the hideout still existed and I wrote that the factory had been demolished in 2001. He suggested we talk on the phone, which we did soon after.

First I spoke with Shamai's wife and then with Shamai himself. Afterwards I was so excited I called Carolyn in Berlin and said, "They know my name is Srulik!" They knew my brother's name, Kalman. Shamai's wife said they had heard the same story from Czesia. They wanted to know about my brother and if I knew anything about the Aleksandrowiczs. I told him that Charlie had died and I sent him the pictures of the hideout. Czesia called Anna, who was also happy. Then Anna's daughter, Shoshi, contacted me too and was excited and curious to meet me. She sent me a photo of herself with her mother.

I knew Marlene and I were going to visit our daughter Sheila again, who by then had moved back to Lausanne, so we talked about a visit. Shamai said his mother would be happy to meet me in Israel. This surprised him, because the subject of the Holocaust had hardly been talked about in their family. In October of 2010 I flew from Lausanne to Tel Aviv to meet the Weksler sisters, sixty-five years after I had last seen them.

We met at my hotel and the next day at Shoshi's house near Rehovot. In some ways it was like meeting a relative whom I had not seen for a very long time. After hugs we sat down. Anna, who is called Hanna, started to speak and spoke in Polish. For a very brief time I was overwhelmed and almost cried. I have no idea why.

After that, my next thought was that it was a bust. I thought for sure they would know Yiddish, but they spoke Polish. The next generation could speak English and they translated some and I could understand a lot of the Hebrew too. I thought I could not understand Polish, but I could understand

Czesia, Anna, and Israel in Tel Aviv, 2010. (Israel Unger collection)

about 80 percent or 90 percent of what Hanna said. So I spoke Yiddish and she spoke Polish and somehow we understood one another. Hanna, the older sister, was very communicative and Czesia was less so. Though on a 2012 visit with Czesia, we talked more together. She asked me how I found them and questions about the hideout. Hanna says she remembered me as an exceptional, bright little boy who never cried or complained, that I understood that I had to be quiet. She said she would make up stories for me and I was satisfied to hear them.

I had some questions for them to both confirm some of what I had recalled and learned more recently from Aleksander Dagnan and others. The first thing I wanted to know, "Was Dagnan a good guy?" "Yes, definitely," Hanna said. "Did he hide us for money?" "No," she said. When her daughter had picked me up at the airport she brought that up immediately too. "Should Dagnan be named as one of the Righteous Among the Nations?" I answered that I could not say that because I was too young at the time, that if he were to be nominated it would have to come from her mother. They had a high regard for Dagnan.

Hanna said that the Drozd brothers built the wall and were paid for that by my father. Anna and Czesia were the first to enter the hideout, then my mother, then Charlie and I. They entered about three months before us. We all agreed there were nine people in the hideout. They did not know Mrs. Bochner's first name, but they did know her son's name, Chaim. The Aleksandrowiczs were Filip and Bertha, but she was called Blima.

The elder Skorupa was a manager in the mill and there were three or four brothers and it was Zbyszek who brought us food for the first three months. They did not know that Zbyszek had been shot and killed. According to Hanna, it was my father, Mr. Aleksandrowicz, and herself who left the attic to go for the flour and water downstairs. I asked who knew on the outside and they said: the Dagnan brothers, all the Skorupas, and the Drozds. They said that one time Dagnan saw Aleksandrowicz downstairs and said, "I don't know you. I've never seen you." This corresponded to the same story I had heard from the son, Aleksander Dagnan.

I asked how we cooked and they said that Zbyszek Skorupa hooked us up with electricity and we had an electric hot plate. I had always remembered we had a hot plate and we did! I just had not recalled that we were hooked up to electricity.

Then they told me an amazing detail. At some point in the winter, the Skorupa father—whom she called "*Meister* Skorupa" (meaning a master of his trade)—warned us that the heat from our stove was melting the snow on the portion of the roof tiles over the hideout. He said we had better stop doing that or people on the outside would suspect something.

We then only ate dry food. We cooked the flatbread on a metal plate over a gas stove in the workshop downstairs. In the hideout, Hanna said, we had two barrels, one for water and the other for the flatbread. I had remembered that we stored the flatbread in a barrel but had forgotten about the second barrel for water. I remember thinking the rats probably came to get our supply.

Hanna said we had to be quiet all the time. Their father had brought books to the hideout and the sisters read to me and told me stories. My mother did not like Blima, Mrs. Aleksandrowicz, to sing because she was afraid that someone might hear. Mr. Aleksandrowicz did not like my father to speak Yiddish because he was afraid that someone might overhear. If someone overheard Polish being spoken they might think it was a Gentile, but not so with Yiddish. Hanna said my father spoke Polish poorly, but my mother spoke it well.

Hanna said one time there was an accident and boiling water was spilled on my brother and he was badly burned. He had boils on his body from the burns. He was in great pain and scratched the walls from the pain but he did not cry.

She also said several people came up to the main attic room at different times. They did not know we were behind the false wall. We were very afraid on these occasions and stayed behind the wall except for the incident where my father went out and gave the man some money and jewels to not tell on us.

I asked them how they experienced liberation and the answer was a surprise. They were happy to be alive but not overjoyed, because they knew that their family had perished and there were no Jews left. They left Tarnow in 1945 and basically *walked* from Poland to Italy! They said that my parents visited them in 1967. My parents had been visiting a cousin of my mother's in Haifa. This cousin's son-in-law, knowing that Lazar Weksler was from Dąbrowa, told Hanna's husband, "There are some Jews here from Dąbrowa." That is

Israel's parents, David and Hinda Unger (right), at the Western Wall, Jerusalem, 1967, with Hinda's cousin Peretz Fisch and wife, Tzipora. This was the visit that they re-met the Weksler sisters. (Israel Unger collection)

how they met again in 1967. I had no idea about this. That is how little my family discussed the Holocaust.

I visited with Hanna, Czesia, and their children and grandchildren over two days. We were all excited to meet one another. They were all very warm and exceptionally gracious. Some of them came from as far away as a kibbutz in Galilee. Shamai took the two days off work.

Shamai became very interested in the process of uncovering more of the story and in fact later went to Tarnow himself. He gave us a report in Hebrew written by his mother decades earlier. It was, once again, my story with new details. Czesia mentioned, for instance that when the wall was built they made the new wall dirty and put spider webs on it to make it look old. She writes that we slept on straw—that part of the hideout was taken up by straw and blankets for our beds. She said that Blima Aleksandrowicz was about thirty years old and very beautiful. Czesia calls her Blimka in the report. Adding "ka" to a name is an affectionate Polish diminutive. In the same vein, she refers to my mother as Hindazia. She also said that Blima would sing songs in the hideout, particularly songs from the Verdi opera *La Traviata*. Luckily, she comments, the noises from the factory below were louder than our noises. She writes that we heard noises in the house next door! The high side of our hideout shared a wall with the adjacent building and when the people in that house went up into their attic to hang clothes to dry, we could hear them and of course we were very frightened and kept absolutely still. She said sometimes children ran on the factory roofs looking for pigeons and that too made us very nervous. Czesia's report added a detail to the snow melting on the roof episode. We were so concerned about it, she said, that we put snow back on the spot where it had melted so no one would notice!

Czesia called the summer heat and stagnant air in the attic "insufferable"—that the brick tiles on the factory roof made our attic like an oven and we had to strip to our underclothes to survive it, that "the sweat ran off us like water." She said there were arguments amongst ourselves because of the terrible conditions. Mrs. Bochner complained she was getting hit by elbows, but as Czesia writes, "no one was to blame, the place was so cramped." To contrast, one day, the Dagnans held a birthday party outside in the yard and we could see it from the cracks in our hideout walls. "It all looked so beautiful from our attic.... We could see his guests sitting and laughing. We were envious and sad and helpless."

The liquidation of the ghetto was a huge blow for Czesia and Hanna. For some time their father had tried to convince them to go back to the ghetto, as he felt the hideout could never work in the long run. Hanna insisted they stay and Czesia backed her up. Czesia writes that from the hideout we could hear the ghetto being liquidated—screaming and machine-gun fire. Their father, who had been coming and going from the ghetto, never returned. Of course they hoped their parents might somehow have survived the deportation.

Food was scarce. As I remembered, she talks of getting bits of rye bread that, compared to our usual fare, tasted like heaven. Also that we went to the guard's cellar at night and took frozen potatoes. The scarcity of food became unbearable after Zbyszek Skorupa disappeared, and she writes that we took the desperate measure of Filip Aleksandrowicz going down into the factory and exposing his presence to a worker called Milinovsky. Aleksandrowicz hid in a big tub, and when Milinovsky came in Aleksandrowicz called out his name. The Polish worker was going to bolt, but Mr. Aleksandrowicz gave him some money and convinced him to help us. She repeats often in this report how risky it was being dependent on the people who knew about us. As time went on she believed that many workers knew about us, among them anti-Semites. After liberation factory workers said they had heard noises above and would say that ghosts were up there in the attic. So it was an open secret, as Dagnan said, but everyone kept quiet about it.

Czesia writes that during the battle for Tarnow the water in the factory was cut off and so we had to melt snow to make water. Here is how she describes liberation: "One winter morning in 18 January 1945, we heard soldiers, the sound of soldiers passing by—singing. The song was in Russian! We could not believe what we heard. For a moment we were frozen. Then we started applauding. We were laughing and crying. Dreams became reality. We were free!"

Hanna was seventeen at the time of liberation, Czesia was fourteen. Clearly they had more of an understanding of what was going on than I did. They also remembered different details of life in the hideout. Their contribution to confirming my recollections of life in the hideout and to the book in general has been invaluable.

Meeting the Weksler sisters, meeting Hanna and Czesia, was like meeting long-lost family. Or, as Hanna said, "Four children living together like that for two years is *more* than family."

A page from Czesia Weksler's report about how she and her sister survived the Holocaust, with details of living in the same hideout as Israel Unger. (Shamai Opfer photo)

"How did the Holocaust affect you?"

I have been asked many times, "How did the Holocaust affect you?" I always answer, "I don't know, but I think not very much, because I was a child at the time." I was protected and looked after by my parents. I was saved rather than having to save myself. I was lucky to be so young. I believe that Charlie was affected much more by the Holocaust than I was, simply because he was older and understood more of what was going on. He was tough, he was self-centred.

I want to believe that it did not affect me, because I do not want to believe that my life was changed because of it. I don't like when historians say: "What if? What if Hitler's mother had a miscarriage?" But Hitler's mother gave birth to him and we cannot go backwards, so what is the point of thinking that so much misery might have been avoided? What if Roosevelt had agreed to bomb Auschwitz? It is like trying to remake history.

Several years ago our daughter asked us to buy her a skirt at a store in Phoenix the day we were leaving. We did, and because of that we left Phoenix at 10 a.m. instead of 8 a.m. Then we had an accident near Tucson. When I told my daughter, she started to blame herself because, she said, if we had left at 8 a.m. we would not have had an accident. But the accident had nothing to do with her and, who knows, maybe if we would have left at 8 a.m. we might have had a worse accident.

I think you can never know how you will react in a situation until you actually experience it. And you certainly cannot tell how others will react. I try not to say: "I would have done so and so," when discussing a situation unless I have actually faced such a situation. For example, I really loved the first new car I bought in 1964, the Ford Mustang. Several years later, after we had had Sharon, Marlene came to my office and was crying. I asked her what was wrong. She said that she had had an accident with the Mustang. "Are you hurt" I asked. She said no. "Is the baby hurt?" She said no. "Is the person in the other car hurt?" She replied, no. I said, "Don't worry about it. It's only metal." I feel very good about that even today.

A psychologist told me once that it is impossible for people, even very young ones, *not* to have been affected by the Holocaust. To this day I have some personality traits that I think may have something to do with my early childhood experience. For instance I have a strong need to have a supply of whatever I may need. Before I run out of anything I buy the next bunch. I seldom let the gas tank on our car get to a quarter before I fill up. When we drive the motorhome I usually fill up when it is half full. I had, and perhaps still have, a great need to have security in almost everything. Time has made improvements.

I've always had a strong sense of not being dependent on others, of doing things myself. I always try to fix things myself, around the house or on our motorhome. And I have a habit of trying to figure out alternatives. I don't know whether this is normal or whether it is due to my experience, but I have a habit of saying, "We need to go to 'X.' Now we can do this either by plane or by train or by car. Here are the advantages. If we go by train, we can change here or there. If that does not work, then this is what we can do." If we are driving down to Phoenix, Marlene and I will talk about it and I will start looking at a map and I will say, "We can drive via the number forty or the number twenty. If we go via the forty it's a bit longer, but we avoid Dallas and Fort Worth. If we go the other way it is eighty miles more, but there will be less traffic." I want alternatives.

Because we nearly starved in the attic, I have been asked what my relationship to food is. I love food. The only issue I have had with food is that I cannot stand seeing food wasted. I have a great difficulty throwing away food even if it is spoiled. When we were first married, Marlene would wait to clean the fridge when I was not home because I could not bear to watch food being wasted. Like other things, I have a need for a secure supply of food. If the coffee can is half full I buy another can of coffee. Most items that we have in our pantry, we have two or more of, and when we get to only one left, I resupply. I drink tonic water and there are usually six or more bottles in the house and I don't let it get under that. I cannot budget on food. If I want to eat cherries, it does not matter what the price, I buy cherries.

Another thing is crying. Crying could have meant death in the hideout. I didn't cry in the hideout. I didn't cry as a child, not even with physical pain like when the children pushed me and I got the gash on my head in Tarnow after the war. Nor when my father left Charlie and me in Cracow. I have difficulty with that even now.

One occasion that I did cry occurred at Yad Vashem, the Holocaust Museum, in Jerusalem. In 1985 Marlene, Sharon, Sheila, and I visited Israel. We travelled around visiting family, friends, and historical sites. Before we left Canada Marlene had said that she wanted to visit Yad Vashem. We started with a building that recorded the history of the Holocaust, then we went into a memorial building that consisted of a large hall with an elevated walkway. In the centre there was a memorial flame. On the ground there was a map of Europe with the names of all the concentration camps and death camps marked in Hebrew and English. By each camp marked, there was a red memorial light. I felt as if all the six million people were buried there and I could hear them weeping. I was overcome with grief and nearly collapsed. I leaned on Marlene, buried my head on her shoulder and sobbed. Marlene took me out of the hall and insisted that we leave Yad Vashem. I did not want

Sharon and Sheila to see me in that state. Marlene says she never saw me weep like that.

I can get very emotional about some things, like when I see a hurt animal or when I see people being hurt on television. I don't know whether I inherited this from my parents, but I have a huge problem with tragedy. When I see some misery whether it's human or animal it really gets to me. A trivial example is one time I had taken my mother to the Jewish General Hospital. We came out and there was an older lady at the entrance and she was very distraught and crying. Her daughter was supposed to pick her up and had not come. Well, I took her in our car and I drove her home. I think my parents would have had that kind of a human reaction when they learned that Skorupa's father had died and he did not have the resources for a funeral. I won't say I never cry—but it is rare. In fact, I enjoy humour and try to bring it in to all my activities. I very much enjoy laughing and have others laugh with me.

Marlene says I have a very keen sense of justice. Some of the changes I made at the University of New Brunswick came from this: founding the Academic Freedom and Tenure committee, or starting the Status of Women Committee for the teachers' association. I was instrumental in getting UNB unionized. She also feels I put down deep roots. Marlene wanted to buy a new home in Fredericton at some point but I did not.

I believe that forgetfulness is perhaps Nature's way of making sure that we survive, because some memories for people who experienced the Holocaust are too painful to bear. Marlene and I visited Yad Vashem again a few years ago. The guide was a man of about thirty-five. I asked him how he managed to go through that museum day after day, looking at those exhibits and speaking to people about them. He replied that the guides work only three days and then have a rest because it is simply too difficult to do it for a longer time.

Every survivor story that I have heard is unique and extraordinary and they all show the unbelievable brutality of the Nazis. It seems that many survivors continued to have a lot of tragedy in their lives after liberation, but I was very, very lucky. Although it was difficult for the years immediately after the war, in the end I had an education and a marvellous career, I have a wonderful wife and two wonderful children and now have five grandchildren. I could not have wished for more.

I have had a very good life.

Afterword
Writing *The Unwritten Diary*

I first met Israel Unger in a Tim Hortons doughnut shop in Fredericton. We hit it off. We both sensed an immediate affinity. I was born in 1959 in Fredericton, New Brunswick, to non-Jewish parents and grew up knowing very little about the Holocaust or the Second World War the entire twenty-one years I lived there. So how did it come about that Israel and I spoke the same language that day in 2007?

In 1991 I was invited to Berlin, Germany, to perform my poetry. I fell in love and stayed. My student activism days had left me with a yearning to find out about oppression and overcoming it. In Germany in the early nineties the silence around anything Jewish was oppressive. I had German friends who could barely say the word "Jewish." By 1994 my German was good enough to attend a weekend educational at the former concentration camp Ravensbrück, now a memorial site. There I met and befriended the Holocaust survivor Johanna Krause. Not only had she been persecuted as a Jew under the Nazis, but after surviving the camps and returning to Dresden after the war she suffered persecution a second time as a Jew under the communists in East Germany.

Through my friendship with Johanna I suddenly became very involved in the Dresden Jewish community. Being secular I had hardly entered a church since early childhood and here I was regularly attending synagogue with Johanna as her companion, singing songs in Hebrew and learning about Jewish culture and religion intimately. Johanna asked me to write down her life story and after finding a German co-author, Christiane Hemker, I took on this tremendous responsibility. Johanna's story was published in German in 2004 and in English as *Johanna Krause—Twice Persecuted—Surviving Nazi Germany and Communist East Germany*, in 2007.

During my years in Germany I have heard many Holocaust survivors speak. I have become a member of a Berlin association that deals with survivors and their helpers (*Blindenwerkstatt* Otto Weidt). I became friends with children of survivors. My work began to evolve around Jewish life in Germany. In my work as a tour guide I was keenly interested to learn the Jewish history and Holocaust history. I began working for Milk and Honey Tours, a Berlin-based Jewish tour company and slowly but surely what had begun as a friendship with Johanna turned into a lifelong passion and commitment.

In looking for a suitable venue for presenting Johanna's book in my hometown during a cross-Canada tour, I met with Fredericton's rabbi, who said, "You need to speak to Israel Unger. He organizes the Holocaust Memorial Day in Fredericton." Soon after, Israel and I met at the doughnut shop.

I was amazed to find a survivor living in my hometown. Fredericton had become Israel's hometown even before I was born! By the time I met Israel I had been living fifteen years in Berlin but my two worlds had remained separate—the world of Germany with its heavy history of having perpetrated the Holocaust and its ongoing efforts at reconciliation—and Fredericton where I annually go for carefree summer vacations. Friends in Fredericton could scarcely understand the work I did in Berlin.

My two worlds met that day in the person of Israel Unger.

The next meeting was at Israel's home. I rang the doorbell and the woman answering the door said to me, "Are you Jennifer or Carolyn?" I said, "Mrs. Unger!" I was flabbergasted. Marlene had been my sister's grade eleven math teacher! As I sat in Israel's kitchen listening to his story, I thought this was meant to be. I have the knowledge and ability to write such a story and Israel's story needs to be written. When Israel told me a few months later that he and Marlene were planning a trip to Tarnow to unveil a memorial stone for his mother's lost family, I thought: It is now or never to take on Israel's story as a book project.

My first act in gathering the sources for *The Unwritten Diary* was to ask Israel to write his own story down, which he did in installments by email. His spare and succinct writing style became the voice of the book. On the time in the attic there was a single page. I recall telling Israel, "We can't make a book out of a page."

En route to Poland in 2007, Israel and Marlene came to Berlin. I arranged for him to talk at the Anne Frank Centre in Berlin. One could not help but notice the similarities between the stories. Anne and Margot Frank and their parents were like a mirror image of Israel, Kalman, and their parents. In both groups there were others sharing the attic, thrown together by fate. There were helpers on the outside and people who knew. Both groups hid for about two years—the Franks in a few rooms spread over three floors, the Ungers in a crawl space. The most glaring difference of course was that the Franks' group was exposed and all but one murdered in the Holocaust.

When Israel spoke at Berlin's Anne Frank Centre he was advertised as speaking on surviving the Holocaust by hiding in an attic, and yet during the talk he skipped from going into hiding to being liberated in one breath! I quickly realized that Israel could not talk about the time in the attic with a simple series of interview questions. We had to somehow investigate that early childhood time from many different angles. Over the next years we went to Tarnow, we went to the site of the hideout, we interviewed eyewitnesses, and I interviewed Israel

Israel gives a talk at Berlin's Anne Frank Centre, October 2007. (Carolyn Gammon photo)

in Tarnow, in Berlin, in Fredericton, and on the phone. Whenever a new detail surfaced I wrote it down. I'll not forget meeting Israel at his cottage at Grand Lake, New Brunswick, where my family also has a cottage. It was a fabulous sunny summer day and my son and his granddaughters were going swimming. And there were Israel and I crouched over the Tarnow *Yizkor*, the Holocaust commemoration book. He was translating the Yiddish for me and I was writing it down.

In four years we transformed that one page into fifty.

The core of the work was the trips to Israel's birth town. Israel and Marlene had been to Tarnow once before in 2006. Although they had not met Adam Bartosz that first visit, the contact had been made. Israel was the only one of the nine Jews in hiding who ever returned to Tarnow.

Adam Bartosz was the director of the Regional Museum in Tarnow. He began as a champion of the rights of the Roma people, setting up a Roma museum in Tarnow. He also became very involved in the Jewish history of the city. Anyone travelling to Poland with a Jewish story will tell you how mixed the reception can be. One can be cursed at or one can encounter brave and amazing people like Adam Bartosz who do everything in their power to help out.

The three of us arrived in Tarnow, an hour by train east of Cracow, one cold crisp November day. Our hotel was in the north of the city—a short bus ride, it transpired, from the Jewish cemetery. That was to be our first stop, to see if the memorial stone was ready. We got on a bus but wondered if it were headed in the right direction.

Suddenly Israel spoke some Polish! (He had claimed he did not speak it anymore.) *"Cmetarze zydowskie?"* "Jewish cemetery?" he asked. All faces in the bus turned to us. Tarnow might once have had twenty-five thousand Jews, half the population in fact, but that day there were probably only two Jews in the city: Israel and Marlene. *"Cmetarze zydowskie?"* said a friendly young man. "No, no," he indicated, "you are going in the wrong direction." To make sure we found it, this fellow stepped out with us at the next stop, had us hop on the right bus, came with us, and lead us to the cemetery gates.

The Jewish cemetery in Tarnow is huge. Much of it in 2007 had not yet been disentangled from nature. As far as the eye could see there were stones buried among bushes and weeds. Only the front part of the cemetery where the main Holocaust memorial stood—a large pillar from the destroyed Jubilee Synagogue—was free of overgrowth.

We were met by Adam Bartosz and his colleague Janusz Koziol. A hard-working crew of men were slowly making headway in freeing parts of the cemetery from decades of neglect. Israel asked Janusz who these men were who were doing the strenuous work. We were astounded by his reply. "They are all criminals." What he meant was, there was an agreement with the local jail that prisoners could work to clean up the cemetery!

Israel's maternal family stone, which he had ordered ahead of time, was not quite ready to be erected. When it was finished the next day, Israel stood hand in hand with Marlene and recited the mourners' *kaddish* over it. We all felt a profound moment of at last honouring his lost family.

Every day we went to the cemetery. It became familiar and somehow, with the *matzevah*, like visiting Israel's family.

We walked from the hotel to the Jewish cemetery to Adam Bartosz's office as if nothing else existed in Tarnow. Israel was not there on vacation and had no desire to sightsee.

I wanted at least to see the site of Dagnan's flour mill, which he had seen before, so I went off alone down Lwowksa Street one day. I found an empty lot with slabs of cement and high grass. That a wall of the hideout still existed I did not have the knowledge to see—that would have to wait for our 2009 trip.

Bits and pieces of Israel's story were revealed to us. Sometimes by hard work and research, sometimes by happenstance or the dropping of a casual side comment that would lead to an incredible new discovery. What amazed me over and over was that Israel's childhood memories, even though they were memories forged in extreme trauma, were confirmed every step of the way.

Adam Bartosz arranged for Israel to meet the son of Augustyn Dagnan, who ran the Dagnan flour mill. We were all incredibly nervous and excited. What did he know? What if he were anti-Semitic? What if he wanted gratitude? What if he wanted Israel to wave a wand and erase the collaboration of so many Poles by "absolving" his father? We did not know what to expect.

Adam Bartosz stepped briefly out of his office. A huge man came to the door. He seemed at least twice the size of Israel. Was this Mr. Dagnan, we wondered? We were not sure and the man could not speak English, so we all stood there awkwardly. No one offered a hand. The man was clearly as nervous as we were. Adam Bartosz joined us soon after and made introductions—it was indeed Mr. Aleksander Dagnan. Still no handshakes. It was all too strange and unpredictable.

Mr. Bartosz offered Mr. Dagnan a chair. He sat and as he did the chair exploded into dozens of pieces and Mr. Dagnan crashed backward onto the floor! We all bounded up from our seats. Mr. Dagnan was lying staring up at the ceiling. Had he had a heart attack? Was he okay?! He lay there for a moment coming to his senses. I offered a hand and he slowly got up. He was seventy-six at the time and that was a bad fall even for someone much younger.

Mr. Dagnan was all right. And not only the chair but the ice was broken. It was as if the tension in the room exploded in that wooden chair and brought us all back to a human reality. The encounter could begin. That conversation was key to understanding Israel's story, corroborating it.

I'll never forget when Aleksander Dagnan said, "I remember seeing a little boy come out of hiding."

Before meeting Dagnan, Israel's story had been just his. After meeting Dagnan Israel's story had an eyewitness—the first of many we were to find on our journey.

Every evening in Tarnow I interviewed Israel. The Tarnow interviews became the basis for *The Unwritten Diary*. Imagine, as an interviewer, asking about Israel and his brother being sent out of Tarnow as orphans. Imagine asking the same questions after having been that day to the very Tarnow train station that they left from. The immediacy of the day's experiences became the immediacy of Israel telling his story. It wasn't easy. In fact, on tape I have a hallmark bit of humour when Israel compared my interview questions to a rectal exam! Five evenings, up to two hours per session—by the end of the Tarnow interviews, Israel remarked: "Now the story has legs."

As we left Tarnow, Israel spoke to the taxi driver in Polish. I had learned a few words myself, among them *wysiedlenie*.

I tried to follow every lead and found myself searching till wee hours in the morning in obscure databases with lists of Jews from Tarnow, Ryglice, or Dabrova. Any name dropped casually by one of our contacts I checked out. I called a Tarnow survivor, Franciszek Jachimowicz in Buenos Aires, only to learn that he had died just that week. I briefly told the reason for my call and gave condolences. I called another survivor, Rose (Zimmerman) Dubinsky, who had just celebrated her 90th birthday, and after saying *Mazel Tov* I asked her about Tarnow. She painted a picture of pre-Holocaust Tarnow right there on the phone. "Tarnow," she said, "was a place you could live in dignity—before the Nazis." Ungers? Yes, she knew the name. "But the ones I knew weren't bakers. There were a lot of Ungers in Tarnow."

One day in Montreal, after visiting Israel's old neighbourhood to see the house he and his family had lived in on Jeanne-Mance Street, I stopped by the Holocaust Museum. In the foyer I recognized two older women immediately. I did not recognize them personally, but I heard the accents and knew they were survivors. I asked about Tarnow. "The expert on Tarnow is Howard Fink in Massachusetts." A call was made, a phone number given. Howard Fink had the yet-unpublished database with the name of one of Israel's uncles.

With the help of Polish translators I reviewed archival material. I even tried to locate the Drozd brothers, who had built the false wall in the attic. With a translator, I called all the Drozds in the Tarnow phone book today. Yes, someone had heard about the Jews in hiding—I should call another

Interview with Israel in Adam Bartosz' office, Tarnow. Marlene looks on, 2007. (Carolyn Gammon photo)

number—which was out of order. Slowly I began sorting the vast amount of material we were gathering.

That Israel himself did the arduous task of transcribing the interviews was an invaluable part of the project, adding layers of insight. As he transcribed he recollected new stories, corrected, and reworked the original oral history. With a series of emailed questions based on the transcriptions, I could piece the entire story together. Working with Israel was a joy, even if the subject matter was so difficult. At one point he wrote me: "We had a lot of laughs during the interviews."

It was like a Ping-Pong match of questions and answers and comments shooting back and forth across the ocean electronically. Sometimes I would ask a complicated question and receive a yes or no answer. I would ask again in a different way and suddenly I would receive an eloquent, detailed paragraph that fit into the book like a missing puzzle piece.

We developed a friendship over continents and time, working and getting to know one another wherever we met, in Fredericton, Tarnow, New York, Berlin, or Arizona. We even hiked the Grand Canyon together in winter!

In 2009, Israel and I returned to Tarnow. This

Israel and Carolyn hiking the Grand Canyon, February 2010. (Carolyn Gammon photo)

time he wanted to unveil a *matzevah* for his father's family. When we visited the Jewish cemetery it had recently been All Saints Day, when Poles visit graveyards. The Jewish graveyard memorials were surrounded by candles with crosses and Christian symbols. The children entering crossed themselves. Israel found the Christian candles on the Holocaust memorial offensive and removed one that had been placed on his mother's family's *matzevah*—just one example of how nothing is easy in Poland for returning Jewish survivors.

We returned to the empty lot where the Dagnan factory once stood. We grabbed a taxi and simply said: "Lwowska Street—the Dagnan mill." The factory had been demolished almost a decade earlier, but the driver knew exactly where to take us. By 2009 we knew much more. This time we had drawings and photos of the hideout with us.

Suddenly, looking up at the building on the adjacent lot we realized that the blank wall was a remaining wall from the hideout! In fact, you could still

The extant wall of the hideout on the building adjacent to the demolished Dagnan factory, 2009. (Carolyn Gammon photo)

see the chimney, which ran up through the hideout imprinted on the wall. We stood there transfixed. The hideout had a physical presence, a wall, a chimney. It felt very close and real. I took copious photos and back in Adam Bartosz's office he realized too that this was indeed one wall of the hideout still extant.

Archival work takes imagination and patience. At the State Archives we could not find evidence of the Unger bakery we were looking for. Israel wanted to leave after fifteen minutes. Without the archivist Jan Chumura's generous participation, we might have left. Not even stopping to re-file the documents we had just inspected, he brought the next and the next. There,

Israel's father's signature on a document in the State Archives of Cracow—Tarnow. (Carolyn Gammon photo)

before our eyes, appeared the layout of the house that Aleksander Dagnan said Israel's father had given his father as a thank-you for the years of hiding. We also found a document of another house owned by Israel's father stating his father was from Ryglice— the only proof we have of this on paper. Then, one of those archival moments when time and breath stops—we found his father's signature. Israel recognized the handwriting. It was like a presence.

By the time we left the State Archives packages of documents and files lay unwrapped on every desktop. And we had gifts—a father's signature, a house he had owned, an address of where Israel was born.

The day we headed for Ryglice the weather was cold and clear, though nothing about the history was clear. In Ryglice the Jewish cemetery was not just overgrown but full of winding thorny bushes that tore at our clothes and threatened to trip us up. Israel joked, "I could use my tractor here!" I was breathless with worry that one of us, Israel especially, might fall into a hole and break a leg. I'm sure he was equally concerned about me. The conditions were extreme. There were stones in Hebrew but few last names. If we found a stone with any last name at all it felt like a victory. It felt like some sort of test. I took many photos, as if trying to replace the missing identities with images. We did not find any Ungers.

Back in Ryglice I convinced our shy assistant (provided by Adam Bartosz's office) to ask at the city hall for a town historian. Adam Szczech greeted us in English. Like Jan Chmura at the State Archive, he seemed to sense the uniqueness and importance of the moment. He showed us a copy of a document about property and monies owed. One of the parties involved was a Chana Unger and the date, 1929. When Israel said that Chana was probably his grandmother, the historian immediately made a copy for Israel. Adam Szczech came out onto the street with us. He gestured at the houses around the town square, "The Jews of Ryglice lived here, around the square." He gave us his email for future correspondence and in fact did research for Israel later. We went for a bite to eat at the one restaurant on the square. It had an antiquated feel to it, the dark wooden walls heavy with photos of historic Ryglice. We ate perogies. Israel's father, his grandparents, his aunts and uncles had no doubt walked across the town square we could see from the restaurant windows.

Thus far we had met good people who immediately sensed how difficult, sensitive, and urgent this roots search was for Israel or for survivors in general. The treatment we then received at the Tarnow Registry Office was, in comparison, abominable. Israel's goal was to find at last the names of some of his father's siblings. First we asked to see Israel's birth certificate. Israel had obtained a printout on his previous trip, but now we were thrilled to see all the extra information the original contained: the name of the circumciser, of witnesses, the midwife. The document peopled a past moment in time when Israel was eight days old. At last Israel had the name of a person he assumed was one of his uncles: Lazar Unger had been a witness at the circumcision.

When we asked to take a photo of Israel's birth certificate we were told we could only have a printout—even though the printout contained not even half the information. Israel was categorically denied the right to take a photo of his own birth certificate. He was told he had to write in advance, in Polish, to an office in Cracow for such permission. That we were in Tarnow only for one more day did not stir their hearts. That Israel Unger might not be able to write fluent Polish and for what reason was of no interest to these administrators. The feeling in that small bureaucratic room was: How dare these Jews ask for proof of their birth!

There is no way to describe the atmosphere in that office with a word other than hostile. We were not wanted, we were disturbing the normal flow of business. The request to see a document for Lazar Unger, to prove whether he really was an uncle or not, died on Israel's lips. Israel may never get to know the names of his father's family because of that failed visit to the registry office. We left that office prematurely—sad, furious, and with a reality check. This is also Poland today.

Across the ocean in New York city at the Yeshiva University Archives—home of the Rescue Children, Inc. collection. Israel had previously obtained a copy of a picture of himself and an index card with information documenting that he and Kalman had been part of the Rescue Children program. We were there to look at photos, to see if he appeared among the many children and to pique his memory. Many of the extensive files were not labelled, and so for a couple of hours we searched through envelopes and envelopes of photos without knowing which of the many Rescue Children orphanages all over Europe were being depicted. Marlene, Israel, and I turned over hundreds of photos hoping for a reference to Hôtel Beau Site, Aix-les-Bains. We were about to give up when Israel said, "That tablecloth looks familiar"—the photo showed children sitting at a long table with a checkered tablecloth. We began looking intently at the children. Now all the photos seemed familiar to Israel, but we still had no proof that these were photos of his group. We were hungry and eyesore when I flipped a photo and there it was: "Hotel Beau Site, Aix-les-Bains." All the photos Israel had declared "looked familiar" were indeed photos of his orphanage! We were ecstatic! The entire trip to New York had paid off with the discovery of that one labelled photo. If we had gone for lunch just a few moments earlier, we would have missed it and never actually found the proof.

The proof of the checkered tablecloth became symbolic for me for the accuracy of Israel's memory. Every tiny detail. Every word of that one page was verified over and over as our research progressed.

Meeting Kalman Goldberg on the New York trip was like meeting history itself. The conversation took place in English, Polish, German, and Yiddish.

The checkered tablecloth in the dining hall of Hôtel Beau Site, Aix-les-Bain, recognized by Israel during our archival research. (Yeshiva University Archives)

It took place with tears and staccato bursts of memory. Kalman was the witness outside the hideout. His father had even tried the hideout and could not stand it. The interview was odd in that, being one of the "Schindler Jews," Kalman was clearly more used to talking about his time at the Plaszow concentration camp with Schindler. We wanted to know about his time at the Dagnan mill in Tarnow before he was deported and so the interview seemed like a tug-of-war.

In the middle of it all came the gem of information we had been searching for:

> **Kalman:** I knew about this hiding place.... There was a fellow named Weksler. He had a wife and two daughters. He knew Dagnan. He was there hidden. Then came the liquidation of the ghetto. People went to different places in the deportation. Some went to Auschwitz, some went to Gdynia.
>
> **Carolyn:** What about Weksler?
>
> **Kalman:** Weksler disappeared in Plaszow.
>
> **Carolyn:** The Weksler daughters?
>
> **Kalman:** They survived the war and they went to Palestine.

There was the name at long last: Weksler. Without Kalman Goldberg, Israel would never have found the Weksler sisters in Israel.

Israel and Carolyn, 2009. (Katharina Oguntoye photo)

In November 2011 I travelled to Israel and in Tel Aviv I met Shoshi, daughter of Anna Weksler, and Shamai, son of Czesia. Shoshi said Israel's visit the previous year had been very important to her mother. Anna expressed it this way: "Look what our little boy has achieved!"

A tablecloth, a friendly archivist, a modern Righteous Gentile, an elderly survivor living in New Jersey, a blank wall with the trace of a chimney, a girl from Fredericton who lives in Berlin, a boy from Poland who made Fredericton his home. These were the threads, the clues, the concrete blocks that turned *The Unwritten Diary* into a written one.

The story is now told. Shalom.

Carolyn Gammon

Postscript

Dagnan's List

Even as *The Unwritten Diary of Israel Unger* went to print, the search for the names of my paternal family continued. Carolyn and I continued our research. Several people who read the book contacted us, seeking and offering information. We kept in touch with individuals who were researching Tarnow, and we kept an eye out for relevant information.

Then, in July 2013, Adam Bartosz at the Regional Museum in Tarnow sent us a key document—Dagnan's list. We knew that lists of Jewish slave labourers existed throughout Germany and the occupied countries, as witnessed by Schindler's list, which was made famous by the Steven Spielberg film. Most factory owners would have profited shamelessly from the free slave labour of the Jewish workers and kept lists simply as part of the business. But when the Jewish workers were deported, there was no further need for the lists. Most of them were destroyed, but some survived.

A few factory owners, like Schindler, tried to help their workers by extending their work duties as long as possible. One trick was to have the factory designated as "important to the war effort." To be on the workers' list of such a factory was invaluable to staying alive. I knew that my father had gained this important status as an "essential worker" to Dagnan. As a child I remember talk about such designations and how important they were. We had searched for and asked eyewitnesses about a Dagnan's list during our main years of research (see pages 165–66 of this book). Now the document had surfaced in the Tarnow Regional Museum.

I was very excited to see this list. My story is based to a great extent on my own memories and those of eyewitnesses. Now, with this list, I had concrete evidence, proof on paper of much of our story in Tarnow. Throughout our research I was gratified to have my memories corroborated by our findings. Dagnan's list is an important addition.

The document consists of two pages. One is a letter on Dagnan factory letterhead, signed by Augustyn Dagnan. The other is the list itself. The page

Nowoczesna ryflarnia walcy młyńskich
A. DAGNAN
MŁYN PAROWY. ✦✦✦ WARSZTATY MECHANICZNE
TARNÓW, ul. LWOWSKA 199. 517
TELEFON Nr. XXX   SKRYTKA POCZT. Nr. 86   TELEFON Nr. XXX
Fabr.   Pryw

Konto P. K. O, Kraków Nr. 400.582.
Rach. bieżący w Banku Gospod. Kraj.
w Tarnowie.
Rach. bieżący w Towarzystwie Eskon-
towem w Tarnowie.
Adres telegraf.: DAGNAN TARNÓW.

DOSTARCZAJĄ:

MLEWNIKI
DWU I CZTEROWAŁCOWE.
PRODUKCJA MASOWA.
WALCE ZAPASOWE.

ODSIEWACZE PŁASKIE
(PLANSYCHTRY)
2-3-4-5 I 6 DZIAŁOWE

KAMIENIE FRANCUSKIE
Z KRZEMIENIA LA FERTÉ
WYRÓB WŁASNY.

**INSTALACJA
KOMPLETNYCH MŁYNÓW.**

RYFLOWANIE WALCY
PRECYZYJNIE.

TURBINY FRANCIS'A.

SPECJALNOŚĆ
WYLEWANIE ŁUSZCZAREK
I KASPRÓW MASĄ
SZMENGLOWĄ

WYSOKO-WARTOŚCIOWE
ODLEWY METALOWE.

PORADY TECHNICZNE
Z DZIEDZINY MŁYNARSTWA.

L. O/A.P.

Dotyczy: Passierscheine.   *Tarnów, dnia* 17.August 1942.

Der Stadtkommissar den
TARNOW
Eingegangen
17. Aug. 1942
Tgb. Nr.

Herrn Stadtkommissar
der Stadt Tarnow
in T a r n o w

Laut beigefügter Aufstellungs-Liste unserer Arbeiter
bitten wir hiermit um gefl.Ausstellung der nötigen Einzel-
passierscheine zum Verlassen des Judenwohnviertels.
Unsere Bitte begründen wir wie folgt:
Unser Werk ist in Abteilungen eingeteilt - jede von diesen
Abteilungen arbeitet unabhängig von den anderen und zwar:
1/ Die mechanische Abteilung:
Hier werden alle mechanische Arbeiten und auch Ausbesse-
rungen an Mühlenmaschinen ausgeführt. Falls Walzen für
die Kunden geriffelt werden, arbeiten die Leute auch
Ueberstunden, da die Fuhrwerke mit Pferden bis zum fer-
tigstellen der Arbeit warten.
2/ Transport und Bauabteilung nebst Magazine:
Diese Abteilung ist eng verbunden mit den Autorepara-
turwerkstätten. Auch hier werden ausser den festgesetz-
ten Stunden noch Ueberstunden gearbeitet, ausserdem
sind die Leute die für jeglichen Transport beschäftigt
werden gänzlich abhängig von unserem Behelfslieferwagen
und den Magazinen.
3/ M ü h l e :
sind die Arbeiter beschäftigt zur angegebener Zeit
d.i. von 6⁴⁵ bis 4 Uhr nachmittags durchgehend.
Arbeiter beschäftigt in Poręba:
Als Mühlenbesitzer in Poręba beschäftigen wir 6 Personen
in Poręba beim entwässern des Mühlengrundstückes zum
anlegen der Wasserkanäle und zwar auf Grund der Be-
willigung und Erlaubnis des Arbeitsamtes vom 15.Juli
1942.
Aus oben aufgeführten bitten wir daher um Ausstellung
der nötigen Einzel-Passierscheine, da ein Sammel-Passier-
schein für unseren Betrieb völlig unzweckmässig wäre.

Hochachtungsvoll

Fabr. Maszyn Młyńskich
B-cia A. DAGNAN
T A R N Ó W
AUTOREPARATUWERKSTÄTTE

Letter from the Dagnan factory to the German authorities in Tarnow requesting for the workers
"individual passes for leaving the Jewish quarter." Note that the letter was written two months after
the first *Aktion* in Tarnow.

Aufstellung der beschäftigten Arbeiter.

Mechanische Abteilung - beschäftigt von 7 - 12 und 1/2 - 5 Uhr.

	Vor-u.Zuname	wohnhaft	Arbeitskarten-Nr:	geboren am:
1/	Unger Markus /Leiter/	St.Dąbrowska 47	4907	17.XI.1902
2/	Gärtner Nachem	Krupnicza 9	864	29.III.1900
3/	Bressman Jakób	Krawiecka 6	2915	16.12.1900
4/	Glotzner Samson	Lwowska 24	226	20.III.1901
5/	Eisenberg Jakub	Polna 19	3350	14.4.1903
6/	Bober Stefan	Wehrmachtstr.5	4787	30.I.1906

Transport u. Bauabteilung samt Magazine.
beschäftigt von 1/2 8 b.12.45 und 2 bis 6 Uhr.

1/	Weksler Lazar /Leiter/	Krawiecka 22	5203	3. 6. 1900
2/	Wachtel Józef	Szpitalna 13	5860	3. X. 1911
3/	Frank Liebe	Nowa 12	1	28.II.1914
4/	Birner Ignacy	Magdeburger Pl.4	3603	3.III.1900

M ü h l e - beschäftigt von 6.45 bis 4 Uhr.

1/	Salpeter Szyja/Leiter/	St.Dąbrowska 47	428	6.III.1913
2/	Glückmann Fischel	Polna 19	2624	23.5.1911
3/	Süss Salomon	Ochronek 16	5752	17.4.1913
4/	Friedman Izak	Lwowska 56	1	2. X. 1890

Arbeiter beschäftigt in unserer Mühle in Poręba.

1/	Bochner Chaim /Leiter/	Krawiecka 2c	3488	8.I.1915
2/	Piech Eliasz	St.Dąbrowska 47	3067	14.4.1903
3/	Meszel Tobiasz	Krawiecka 8	3425	18.8.1919
4/	Veiser Chaim	Krawiecka 8		2.3.1916
5/	Wasserberg Maurycy	Widok 18	3494	30.7.1894
6/	Insler Helena	Lwowska 56		8.9.1888.

366 — 371

Dagnan's list provides the names of the workers for whom Dagnan requested individual passes, or *Kennkarte*. Among the names here are three connected to this book: Markus Unger, Israel's father; Lazar Weksler, father of the Weksler sisters; and Chaim Bochner, son of Mrs. Bochner. Note that Markus Unger's occupation is given as "mechanic"—clearly a fabrication intended to make him appear vital to the factory.

on letterhead is a request by Dagnan to the German authorities in Tarnow (to the *Stadtkommisar*) to issue individual passes for Dagnan's workers, rather than a collective pass, for leaving and re-entering the Tarnow ghetto. Dagnan justifies his request by saying he has four separate work units that come and go at different times (sometimes to work overtime) and to different places.

"Based on the list of our workers, we hereby request the issuing of the necessary individual passes for leaving the Jewish quarter," the letter states in its first paragraph. It goes on to enumerate and describe the four work units. The last paragraph states: "For the reasons explained above, we request the issuing of the necessary individual passes, as collective passes are fully unsuitable to the functioning of our factory."

Dagnan's list is exciting for many reasons. The first name on the list is that of Markus Unger, born 17 November 1902. This was my father's Polish name, and this was the first time I had seen his correct birthdate. On the single postwar document I had already, from the Bad Arolsen archives, he was making himself some years younger in the hope of improving his emigration chances.

He is listed as *Leiter*, or head of his working unit for mechanical work within the factory. Augustyn Dagnan's son, Aleksander Dagnan, told us when we interviewed him that many of the Jews had "no real set jobs." "[They] were pretending they were doing something, but really it was an opportunity to escape" (page 166). Listing my father—by trade a flour merchant—as a mechanics worker would have been part of this pretense.

The list says he lives at Starodabrowska 47, which gave me for the first time my family's address in the ghetto and fits with Aleksander Dagnan's assertion that we lived "on the other side of Lwowska" near the mill (page 167). Two others on the list lived at the same address—clearly a house in the ghetto where many families had been forced to live. Of interest to my own family is that an Eliasz Fisch also appears at this address. Given that my mother's maiden name was Fisch and that Eliasz is another name for Eliayu, who was one of my maternal uncles, it could be that we were living with this uncle in the ghetto.

Lazar Weksler, father of the Weksler sisters, is listed as head of the next work unit—transport and construction. When I sent the list to Lazar's grandson Shamai, he too said it was the first time he had seen his grandfather's birthdate and the address where he once lived. Also on the list, as head of the fourth unit of workers in the mill in Poreba, is Chaim Bochner, whose mother hid with us in the attic.

The list poses as many questions as it answers. Carolyn and I wonder why Filip Aleksandrowic, who hid in the attic, is not on the list. We can only conjecture that Mr. Aleksandrowic was highly motivated to make the hideout a reality—truly a hideout—because he was absent from this list of essential workers. The Weksler sisters said they were in the hideout "and other Jews without documents joined them" (page 194). Perhaps the Aleksandrowics had already gone into permanent hiding by the time the list was drawn up. We surmise too that Kalman Goldberg is not on the list because, although he worked in Dagnan's machine shop, he also worked as a chauffeur for the Germans and so perhaps was not listed as one of Dagnan's workers.

In the timeline of the Holocaust in Tarnow, this list was drawn up during the *wysiedlenia*, or *Aktions*. Forty thousand Jews had been forced into the Tarnow ghetto. On 9 June 1942, the first *Aktion* began. More *Aktions* took place in July and September 1942. The ghetto was shrinking. By this time everyone knew that Jews deemed "non-essential" to the Germans were going to be deported and murdered. Dagnan's list was drawn up on 17 August 1942. For his workers, the list was clearly a matter of continued life in the ghetto versus deportation and death.

Being on the list did not guarantee that one stayed alive. Both Lazar Weksler and Chaim Bochner, despite being on the list, were caught in the *Aktions* and murdered. Perhaps the large "X" through this list was made after the liquidation of the ghetto, when the list became obsolete. We wonder too if anyone else on Dagnan's list survived. We would welcome any information.

As is known from *Schindler's List*, such lists could make the difference between life and death. In the case of Schindler, he managed for the duration of the war to keep his workers from being deported. But many factory owners did not or could not do the same. The list did, however, buy time for the Jewish workers. As long as their names were on the list, they were alive and could try to think of other options.

When Amon Göth, the infamous killer from Plaszow concentration camp who was depicted in *Schindler's List* as taking potshots at Jews in Plasow from his balcony, was brought in by the Germans to liquidate the Tarnow ghetto on 3 September 1943, we were no longer in the ghetto. We were in our hideout above the Dagnan factory. For my father and my family, being on Dagnan's list gave us the time we needed to create a hideout and to survive.

Acknowledgements

The Unwritten Diary of Israel Unger was in many ways a collaborative effort, not only between the two authors but also on the part of many dedicated friends, family, and colleagues. We would like to thank the following people and institutions for their assistance in making this book possible.

A personal thanks and much gratitude goes to the Weksler sisters. Upon finally finding Anna and Czesia Weksler (now Anna Sarid and Czesia Opfer) in Israel along with Anna's daughter, Shoshi Macam, and Czesia's son, Shamai Opfer, it was as if the book had gained a new family. This family opened their hearts to the project and helped make it possible in any way they could. We cannot express enough our thanks to all of you.

Another great deal of appreciation goes to Adam Bartosz. Without Adam Bartosz' tireless assistance, this book might not have been written. His contributions took the form of sending Israel the photos and documents of the hideout, meeting us many times for interviews and research assistance, providing us with onsite translators and helpers in Tarnow, and providing us with vital eyewitness reports, helping us with online research assistance from afar. Most importantly, Adam Bartosz gave us the feeling that we had a friend in Tarnow, someone we could trust. It made all the difference.

Thank you to Jan Chmura of the State Archive of Cracow–Tarnow Branch, who provided expert and friendly assistance both in person and by email. Thanks also to Adam Szczęch at the Ryglice City Hall for spontaneously helping us when we arrived in Ryglice and for research assistance later. Many thanks too to Deena Schwimmer, archivist at Yeshiva University Archives, who was very helpful many times.

A very special thanks goes to Dorota Glowacka, Professor of Humanities at the University of King's College and a scholar of Polish Jewish Holocaust studies. Dorota was always there for us when we needed her, taking on translations, confirming Polish translations and points of research. Your heart is also part of this book.

Two eyewitness interviews helped enormously to put together the story. Thank you to Aleksander Dagnan for meeting with us, for speaking candidly and for daring to open that difficult chapter in your family's life in order to help us understand it. Thank you also to Kalman Goldberg for your witnessing and for use of the photos of the Dagnan factory. Without your help we might never have found the Weksler sisters. Thank you too to Kalman's daughter Sandra Goldberg for facilitating communication.

Thank you to Rose Dubinsky (originally from Tarnow) for the telephone interview as well as Felicia Graber for sending us excerpts of her father's story at the Dagnan factory.

Thank you to Janusz Koziol of the Tarnow Regional Museum for translation, historical information, and onsite support. Thanks to Howard Fink (Massachusetts) for access to the unpublished database of Tarnow Jews. Thanks to Petr Zidek in Prague for research assistance. And thanks to Amelie Doge (Berlin), who, through your ongoing email correspondence, provided an excellent platform for Israel's thoughts.

Writing *The Unwritten Diary* meant working with quite a few languages: English, French, Polish, Yiddish, Hebrew, and German. The following people helped with translation: thank you to Yelena Shmulenson (New York) for research in Yiddish-language sources and to Noa Tuvia (Berlin) for translation from Hebrew. Thanks to Katharina Oguntoye and Jobila e.V./Association (Berlin) for providing us with workers for transcription and translation free of charge. In this context, thanks to Uğur Kargin for transcribing the Anne Frank Centre talk tapes and to Dorota Sowinski and Martyna Bec for Polish translation.

The following readers looked at early versions of the manuscript and made helpful comments. David Besner, Eldon Thompson, Hélène Jean, Jon and Bev Randall, Sydelle Grobe, Beth Taylor, Sharon Unger, and Lee Heinrich, Sheila Unger and Andrea Superti Furga, Nancy Richards, Karin Meissenburg, Gerry McAlister, Lori Gallagher, and Tristis Ward. Thanks so much to all of you for your invaluable encouragement. And special thanks to those readers who went the extra mile in giving constructive criticism/editing suggestions: Sandra Ireland and Cathie Dunsford.

For photos, thanks to Joy Cummings and Deby Nash, Andrea Superti Furga, Marlene Unger, and Katharina Oguntoye.

For organizing Israel's first talk in Germany in 2007, thank you to Blindes Vertraunen e.V./Association and the Anne Frank Centre in Berlin. For organizing Israel's second talk in Germany in 2008, thank you to Joliba—Interkulturelles Netzwerk in Berlin e.V./Association.

A big thank-you to the Canada Council of the Arts for a grant that made the writing of the book possible by giving Carolyn the opportunity to work full-time on the first draft. Also thanks to everyone involved at Wilfrid Laurier University Press who recognized the merit of this book immediately and saw it through to publication with respect and efficiency.

We would like to end these acknowledgements by thanking Marlene Unger, who supported the making of *The Unwritten Diary* in too many ways to list. Thank you, Marlene, for the interviews, for transcribing interviews, for reading various versions of the manuscript, for proofreading, and for the loving moral support.

The Unwritten Diary of Israel Unger was five years in the making. There have been friends we have consulted with and family who have supported us. Even if you are not listed individually, please consider yourselves thought of and thanked.

Carolyn Gammon
Israel Unger

Bibliography

I. Archives and Offices

Bad Arolsen
ITS – International Tracing Service
Internationaler Suchdienst
Große Allee 5–9
34454 Bad Arolsen, Germany

German Federal Archives
Bundesarchiv
Potsdamer Straße 1
56075 Koblenz, Germany

Jagiellonian University Archives
Uniwersytet Jagielloński w Krakowie-Archiwum
Al. Mickiewicza 22
30–059 Kraków, Poland

Query Response Centre
Citizenship and Immigration Canada
Ottawa, Ontario K1A 1L1, Canada

Ryglice City Hall
Urząd Miejski w Ryglicach
ul. Rynek 9
33–160 Ryglice, Poland

State Archive of Cracow – Tarnow Branch
Archiwum Państwowe w Krakowie Oddział w Tarnowie
ul. Chemiczna 16
33–101 Tarnów, Poland

Tarnow Regional Museum
Muzeum Okręgowe w Tarnowie.
Rynek 20–21
33–100 Tarnów, Poland

Tarnow Registry Office
Urząd Stanu Cywilnego
ul. Gumniska 30
33–100 Tarnów, Poland

Yad Vashem Archives
Yad Vashem
The Holocaust Martyrs' and Heroes' Remembrance Authority
P.O.B. 3477 Jerusalem
91034 Israel

Yeshiva University Archives
Mendel Gottesman Library – Special Collections
Yeshiva University
2520 Amsterdam Avenue
New York 10033, USA

II. Published Works

All Generations. All generations: For Holocaust Survivors and Generations After. http://www.allgenerations.org.

ARC Group. Aktion Reinhard camps. http://www.deathcamps.org/.

Bartosz, Adam., ed. 2008. *Memories Saved from Fire*. Tarnow: Tarnow Regional Museum.

Chomet, Avraham, ed. 1954–1968. *Tarnow Yizkor: The Life and Decline of a Jewish City.* Tel Aviv: Association of Former Residents of Tarnow.

Museum of the History of Polish Jews. The Virtual Shtetl Project. http://www.sztetl.org.pl.

"The Secret of Dagnan's Mill in Tarnow" by Adam Bartosz. *Memories Saved from Fire*. http://www.msff.eu/ aktualnosci_en.php.

Skoraszewski, Władysław., ed. 2007. *Tarnów: wielki przewodnik. Grabówka*, Band 15. Tarnow: Tarnow Regional Museum.

Unger, Israel. 1994. "A Child's Memories of the Holocaust." In *And It Was My War Too*, ed. Ian Maxwell. Tancook Island, NS: Little Daisy Press.

Books in the Life Writing Series
Published by Wilfrid Laurier University Press

Haven't Any News: Ruby's Letters from the Fifties edited by Edna Staebler with an Afterword by Marlene Kadar • 1995 / x + 165 pp. / ISBN 0-88920-248-6

"I Want to Join Your Club": Letters from Rural Children, 1900–1920 edited by Norah L. Lewis with a Preface by Neil Sutherland • 1996 / xii + 250 pp. (30 b&w photos) / ISBN 0-88920-260-5

And Peace Never Came by Elisabeth M. Raab with Historical Notes by Marlene Kadar • 1996 / x + 196 pp. (12 b&w photos, map) / ISBN 0-88920-281-8

Dear Editor and Friends: Letters from Rural Women of the North-West, 1900–1920 edited by Norah L. Lewis • 1998 / xvi + 166 pp. (20 b&w photos) / ISBN 0-88920-287-7

The Surprise of My Life: An Autobiography by Claire Drainie Taylor with a Foreword by Marlene Kadar • 1998 / xii + 268 pp. (8 colour photos and 92 b&w photos) / ISBN 0-88920-302-4

Memoirs from Away: A New Found Land Girlhood by Helen M. Buss / Margaret Clarke • 1998 / xvi + 153 pp. / ISBN 0-88920-350-4

The Life and Letters of Annie Leake Tuttle: Working for the Best by Marilyn Färdig Whiteley • 1999 / xviii + 150 pp. / ISBN 0-88920-330-x

Marian Engel's Notebooks: "Ah, mon cahier, écoute" edited by Christl Verduyn • 1999 / viii + 576 pp. / ISBN 0-88920-333-4 cloth / ISBN 0-88920-349-0 paper

Be Good Sweet Maid: The Trials of Dorothy Joudrie by Audrey Andrews • 1999 / vi + 276 pp. / ISBN 0-88920-334-2

Working in Women's Archives: Researching Women's Private Literature and Archival Documents edited by Helen M. Buss and Marlene Kadar • 2001 / vi + 120 pp. / ISBN 0-88920-341-5

Repossessing the World: Reading Memoirs by Contemporary Women by Helen M. Buss • 2002 / xxvi + 206 pp. / ISBN 0-88920-408-x cloth / ISBN 0-88920-410-1 paper

Chasing the Comet: A Scottish-Canadian Life by Patricia Koretchuk • 2002 / xx + 244 pp. / ISBN 0-88920-407-1

The Queen of Peace Room by Magie Dominic • 2002 / xii + 115 pp. / ISBN 0-88920-417-9

China Diary: The Life of Mary Austin Endicott by Shirley Jane Endicott • 2002 / xvi + 251 pp. / ISBN 0-88920-412-8

The Curtain: Witness and Memory in Wartime Holland by Henry G. Schogt • 2003 / xii + 132 pp. / ISBN 0-88920-396-2

Teaching Places by Audrey J. Whitson • 2003 / xiii + 178 pp. / ISBN 0-88920-425-x

Through the Hitler Line by Laurence F. Wilmot, M.C. • 2003 / xvi + 152 pp. / ISBN 0-88920-448-9

Where I Come From by Vijay Agnew • 2003 / xiv + 298 pp. / ISBN 0-88920-414-4

The Water Lily Pond by Han Z. Li • 2004 / x + 254 pp. / ISBN 0-88920-431-4

The Life Writings of Mary Baker McQuesten: Victorian Matriarch edited by Mary J. Anderson • 2004 / xxii + 338 pp. / ISBN 0-88920-437-3

Seven Eggs Today: The Diaries of Mary Armstrong, 1859 and 1869 edited by Jackson W. Armstrong • 2004 / xvi + 228 pp. / ISBN 0-88920-440-3

Love and War in London: A Woman's Diary 1939–1942 by Olivia Cockett; edited by Robert W. Malcolmson • 2005 / xvi + 208 pp. / ISBN 0-88920-458-6

Incorrigible by Velma Demerson • 2004 / vi + 178 pp. / ISBN 0-88920-444-6

Auto/biography in Canada: Critical Directions edited by Julie Rak • 2005 / viii + 264 pp. / ISBN 0-88920-478-0

Tracing the Autobiographical edited by Marlene Kadar, Linda Warley, Jeanne Perreault, and Susanna Egan • 2005 / viii + 280 pp. / ISBN 0-88920-476-4

Must Write: Edna Staebler's Diaries edited by Christl Verduyn • 2005 / viii + 304 pp. / ISBN 0-88920-481-0

Pursuing Giraffe: A 1950s Adventure by Anne Innis Dagg • 2006 / xvi + 284 pp. (photos, 2 maps) / 978-0-88920-463-8

Food That Really Schmecks by Edna Staebler • 2007 / xxiv + 334 pp. / ISBN 978-0-88920-521-5

163256: A Memoir of Resistance by Michael Englishman • 2007 / xvi + 112 pp. (14 b&w photos) / ISBN 978-1-55458-009-5

The Wartime Letters of Leslie and Cecil Frost, 1915–1919 edited by R.B. Fleming • 2007 / xxxvi + 384 pp. (49 b&w photos, 5 maps) / ISBN 978-1-55458-000-2

Johanna Krause Twice Persecuted: Surviving in Nazi Germany and Communist East Germany by Carolyn Gammon and Christiane Hemker • 2007 / x + 170 pp. (58 b&w photos, 2 maps) / ISBN 978-1-55458-006-4

Watermelon Syrup: A Novel by Annie Jacobsen with Jane Finlay-Young and Di Brandt • 2007 / x + 268 pp. / ISBN 978-1-55458-005-7

Broad Is the Way: Stories from Mayerthorpe by Margaret Norquay • 2008 / x + 106 pp. (6 b&w photos) / ISBN 978-1-55458-020-0

Becoming My Mother's Daughter: A Story of Survival and Renewal by Erika Gottlieb • 2008 / x + 178 pp. (36 b&w illus., 17 colour) / ISBN 978-1-55458-030-9

Leaving Fundamentalism: Personal Stories edited by G. Elijah Dann • 2008 / xii + 234 pp. / ISBN 978-1-55458-026-2

Bearing Witness: Living with Ovarian Cancer edited by Kathryn Carter and Lauri Elit • 2009 / viii + 94 pp. / ISBN 978-1-55458-055-2

Dead Woman Pickney: A Memoir of Childhood in Jamaica by Yvonne Shorter Brown • 2010 / viii + 202 pp. / ISBN 978-1-55458-189-4

I Have a Story to Tell You by Seemah C. Berson • 2010 / xx + 288 pp. (24 b&w photos) / ISBN 978-1-55458-219-8

We All Giggled: A Bourgeois Family Memoir by Thomas O. Hueglin • 2010 / xiv + 232 pp. (20 b&w photos) / ISBN 978-1-55458-262-4

Just a Larger Family: Letters of Marie Williamson from the Canadian Home Front, 1940–1944 edited by Mary F. Williamson and Tom Sharp • 2011 / xxiv + 378 pp. (16 b&w photos) / ISBN 978-1-55458-323-2

Burdens of Proof: Faith, Doubt, and Identity in Autobiography by Susanna Egan • 2011 / x + 200 pp. / ISBN 978-1-55458-333-1

Accident of Fate: A Personal Account 1938–1945 by Imre Rochlitz with Joseph Rochlitz • 2011 / xiv + 226 pp. (50 b&w photos, 5 maps) / ISBN 978-1-55458-267-9

The Green Sofa by Natascha Würzbach, translated by Raleigh Whitinger • 2012 / xiv + 240 pp. (5 b&w photos) / ISBN 978-1-55458-334-8

Unheard Of: Memoirs of a Canadian Composer by John Beckwith • 2012 / x + 393 pp. (74 illus., 8 musical examples) / ISBN 978-1-55458-358-4

Borrowed Tongues: Life Writing, Migration, and Translation by Eva C. Karpinski • 2012 / viii + 274 pp. / ISBN 978-1-55458-357-7

Basements and Attics, Closets and Cyberspace: Explorations in Canadian Women's Archives edited by Linda M. Morra and Jessica Schagerl • 2012 / x + 338 pp. / ISBN 978-1-55458-632-5

The Memory of Water by Allen Smutylo • 2013 / x + 262 pp. (65 colour illus.) / ISBN 978-1-55458-842-8

The Unwritten Diary of Israel Unger, Revised Edition by Carolyn Gammon and Israel Unger • 2013 / x + 230 pp. (b&w illus.) / ISBN 978-1-77112-011-1

Boom! Manufacturing Memoir for the Popular Public by Julie Rak • forthcoming 2013 / ISBN 978-1-55458-939-5

Not the Whole Story: Challenging the Single Mother Narrative edited by Lea Caragata and Judit Alcalde • forthcoming 2013 / ISBN 978-1-55458-624-0